BEING FAT

Women, Weight, and Feminist Activism in Canada

BEING FAT

WOMEN, WEIGHT, AND FEMINIST ACTIVISM IN CANADA

JENNY ELLISON

UNIVERSITY OF TORONTO PRESS
Toronto Buffalo London

© University of Toronto Press 2020
Toronto Buffalo London
utorontopress.com

ISBN 978-1-4875-0475-5 (cloth)   ISBN 978-1-4875-3082-2 (PDF)
ISBN 978-1-4875-2347-3 (paper)   ISBN 978-1-4875-3083-9 (EPUB)

___

Library and Archives Canada Cataloguing in Publication

Title: Being fat : women, weight, and feminist activism in Canada / Jenny
    Ellison.
Names: Ellison, Jenny, 1977– author.
Description: Includes bibliographical references and index.
Identifiers: Canadiana (print) 20190236604 | Canadiana (ebook) 20190236736 |
    ISBN 9781487523473 (paper) | ISBN 9781487504755 (cloth) | ISBN
    9781487530822 (PDF) | ISBN 9781487530839 (EPUB)
Subjects: LCSH: Obesity in women – Social aspects – Canada. | LCSH:
    Overweight women – Canada – Social conditions. | LCSH: Overweight
    women – Health and hygiene – Canada. | LCSH: Body weight – Social
    aspects – Canada. | LCSH: Fat-acceptance movement – Canada. | LCSH:
    Feminism – Canada.
Classification: LCC RC552.O25 .E45 2020 | DDC 362.1963/980082 – dc23

___

This book has been published with the help of a grant from the Federation
for the Humanities and Social Sciences, through the Awards to Scholarly
Publications Program, using funds provided by the Social Sciences and
Humanities Research Council of Canada.

University of Toronto Press acknowledges the financial assistance to its
publishing program of the Canada Council for the Arts and the Ontario Arts
Council, an agency of the Government of Ontario.

Canada Council   Conseil des Arts
for the Arts   du Canada

ONTARIO ARTS COUNCIL
CONSEIL DES ARTS DE L'ONTARIO
an Ontario government agency
un organisme du gouvernement de l'Ontario

Funded by the   Financé par le
Government   gouvernement
of Canada   du Canada

Canadä

Dies Irae

On that day
Ripples will spread,
Fat will undulate,
Swell, sprawl,
Rampant,
Surging, insurgent.

No recanting then,
No mealy-mouthed forgiveness.
Our vengeance is curved,
Compact and keen.

Fat women
Are not few.
When we rise,
The earth will shake.

C.M. Donald, *The Fat Woman Measures Up*, 1986

Contents

Figures and Tables

Figures

Tables

Acknowledgments

Acknowledgments are the first place I turn when I pick up a new academic book. These passages are where we learn a little bit about the intellectual and personal relationships that shape historical scholarship. A wide circle of colleagues and friends shaped this project, directly and indirectly, and it is a pleasure to (at last) be writing acknowledgements of my own.

Joyful and challenging stories were shared with me by fat activists during oral history interviews that took place between 2005 and 2012. I dedicate the book to these women, who, as I spent hours poring over interview transcripts, became close companions. Many also shared documents and contacts that greatly enriched this work. Thank you to Suzanne Bell, Carla Rice, Allyson Mitchell, Cindy Proskow, Kaca Henley, Doris Maranda, Lynda Raino, and Pauline Rankin for your collaboration. Sadly, some of the women interviewed for this project passed away before the book's completion. Kate Partridge died in March 2018. She was a complex and fascinating woman. Our conversations about being fat continued long after this research was complete and they stay with me today. Ingrid Laue, Ellen Tallman, Janet Walker, Helena Spring, and Margaret Burka shared stories and primary source documents that enriched this work, and I am glad to have known them.

Financial support from the Canadian Institutes for Health Research, Mount Allison University, the Social Sciences and Humanities Research Council, the Ontario Graduate Scholarship Program, the Ramsay Cook Fellowship, and York University sustained this project (and me) throughout my graduate and postgraduate career. This book has been published with the help of a grant from the Federation for the Humanities and Social Sciences, through the Awards to Scholarly Publications Program, using funds provided by the Social Sciences and Humanities Research Council of Canada.

At York University, I drew from a deep well of feminist scholars. Kate McPherson has the unique ability to hear an idea and then repeat it back to you in a more coherent form. She's unimaginably sharp, selfless, and kind, and I have been so lucky to call her a mentor and friend. Molly Ladd-Taylor acted as first reader and mentor at York. Her historiographical insights shaped the book and continue to shape my work. Bettina Bradbury was the first person to sit down with me and talk about sources. How was I going to write about fat people? Lorraine Code, Carolyn Podruchny, Jennifer Stephen, Anne Rubenstein, Michele Johnson, Stephen Brooke, Miriam Smith, the late Myra Rutherdale, and the late Gina Feldberg also provided guidance during these years.

Many good conversations were had, and problems solved, with graduate student colleagues at York, including Funke Aladejebe, Cynthia Belaskie, Tarah Brookfield, Jodi Burkett, Francesca D'Amico, Angela Durante, Jason Ellis, Sarah Glassford, Laura Godsoe, Mandy Hadenko, Jarett Henderson, Dan Horner, Nadine Hunt, Morgan Huseby, Sean Kheraj, Colin McCullough, Ian Mosby, Lee Slinger, Shannon Stettner, and Heather Steel. I would comment to each of you individually, but I have said too much to you already.

Several other scholars have had an important role in this research. Susan Cahn's insightful analysis of my work substantially improved the manuscript. Paul Rutherford gave me my first opportunity to do independent research and taught my most memorable undergraduate courses. Charlene Elliott has always offered practical, no-nonsense, kind advice. Karine Levasseur has been a tireless cheerleader and fantastic listener. Wendy Mitchinson reached out to me to do a shared publishing project not long after I finished my PhD. She didn't need to do so, but she did, and in the process taught me much about grace, attention to detail, and commitment. Deborah McPhail has been a thoughtful collaborator, and her work an inspiration, since we first met in a gender history seminar many years ago. During my post-PhD life, Mount Allison University and Trent University were my academic communities. Thank you to Christl Verduyn, Andrew Nurse, Leslie Kern, Bart Vautour, Morgan Poteet, Susie Andrews, Julia Harrison, and Jeannine Crowe for your support. The cover art of this book was produced by P.J. Cowan, whom I met at Mount A. I love her work and am honoured that she agreed to share it here.

Len Husband along with Robin Studniberg, Dilia Narduzzi, Naomi Pauls, and Breanna Muir have shepherded this book through the publication process. The University of Toronto Press has led the publication of works in fat studies and history in Canada, and I'm honoured to be working with their team. Thank you Len and UTP for providing a platform for this scholarship and giving it a place in the Canadian academic landscape.

In 2015, I joined the Canadian Museum of History as Curator of Sport and Leisure. Though this project was substantially done by that time, CMH provided a home as I completed this book. It is a creative and exciting place to work. Much of the credit for this positive environment goes to Dean Oliver, who has built an intellectually diverse, rigorous, and supportive research division. I am fortunate to be part of this group. I'm also lucky to have Bianca Gendreau as a manager, mentor, and sounding board who consistently pushes me in the right direction. Dominique Savard, Laura Sanchini, and Andrew Burtch and numerous other colleagues have pushed my work in new and exciting directions.

Wonderful friends and family have listened (and listened) to stories about this project: Hayley Snell, Colleen McKay, Lindsay McKay, Heather Davies, Jenny Acton, Ros Hegan, Rose Bagot, John Shiga, Tiani Jimenez, Jamie Liew, Jaclyn Ray, and Stephanie Pearson among them.

During my numerous research trips to Vancouver, my sisters Marcie and Michelle Ellison provided places to stay, loaned their cars, printed documents, and even hosted a Large as Life reunion. More than this, they've been my role models and friends. Howie Outerbridge and Eric Stanger have been generous, offering rides to and from the airport, food, and patience with the sister-in-law/researcher sleeping in the spare room. Beckett, Sasha, and Avery grew up and became cool people during the research and publication of this book. If I taught you guys nothing else, at least you learned that *Bill and Ted's Excellent Adventure* is the greatest historical film of all time.

Mary Burton and Doug Ellison taught me to seek happiness and satisfaction in life and provided me with the emotional and financial support to do so. In many ways, my research has been inspired by them. My mom's stories about the Barbara Ann Scott doll led to my first paper on femininity, while my dad's lessons about sport and health pushed me to think critically about physical fitness. Thanks also to bonus parents Scott Burton, Cathy Ellison, Terrence Clark, and Lynda Gardiner.

This book has come to fruition after many years of teaching, marriage, a postdoctoral fellowship that took me to New Brunswick, a move to Ottawa-Gatineau for work, and numerous other travels. In that time, I've encountered many people who have made my life and work better – but no one more so than Duncan Clark. He's my husband, best friend, closest advisor, and a true partner in life. I laugh every day thanks to Duncan and the two best decisions we made together: Piper and Sebastian Ellison-Clark.

BEING FAT

Women, Weight, and Feminist Activism in Canada

Introduction: Fat Women Are Not Few

It is okay to be fat. This is the basic premise of fat activism, a social movement that has existed in Canada since the early 1970s. Fat activism exists because people need it. In Canada, and most Western nations, being fat is considered a bad thing. Fatness has been seen as a size of laziness, weak will, and personal failure.[1] Inspired by the feminist, civil rights, and gay rights movements, and self-identifying as fat, many Canadian women decided to challenge these unfair and erroneous stereotypes. They formed groups and organized social events, clothing swaps, and opened clothing stores. Fat activists wanted access to the same activities and respect they felt other women received. The movement is not well known. This book aims to change that and to show how it helps us to understand Canadian history at the end of the twentieth century.

Several generations of women have taken up fat activism. This book focuses on the earliest strands of the movement in Canada, which emerged around 1977 and ends around 1997 with the emergence of burlesque performance group Pretty Porky and Pissed Off (PPPO). This twenty-year window loosely correlates with the rise of "second-wave" feminist organizing and thinking in Canada. Fat activists were wrestling with issues other feminists of the era were debating – concerns such as femininity, sexuality, and work. Drawing on A. Finn Enke's idea of the "long reach" of social movements, the book traces the links between fat activism and feminist ideas about body liberation, personal rights, and femininity.[2]

While united by the idea that it is okay to be fat, the movement has taken many different forms, and fat "activism" and the "movement" encompassed a variety of activities. It included groups that had regular meetings and published newsletters, organized events, and elected an executive. I also use these terms to describe other activities like fashion design, self-help groups, plus-size modelling, and dance that were undertaken in the name of empowering fat women. Together, these activities show how women took up feminist ideas of liberation and applied them in their everyday lives.

Researching this book, the subject of fat activism sometimes raised eyebrows. Among other things, I was told that fat activism was not an important social movement or a human rights issue, that studying the 1980s in Canada was "journalism," not history, and that fat people were to blame for their "problems." None of these things are true. Body size is a complex issue. Attitudes towards weight are shaped by historical circumstances. Government, commercial, family, and medical messages about weight inspired fat activism, and the movement is a multifaceted response to these forces. Personal experiences with these messages became the basis of a movement to challenge beauty and bodily norms that still exists today.

Being Fat Has a History

In the twentieth century the body and the "self" became the focus of medical, government, and commercial interest. Becoming healthier, more productive, happier citizens became an important aspect of schooling, public health programs, and commercial services offered to middle-class Canadians. Fat activism was not just a response to health discourses; rather, it was equally a response to social experiences, cultural norms, and media messages about the body.

Physical fitness, not obesity, was the target of public health interventions for most of the twentieth century. It wasn't fatness per se that caused social concern but rather diminishing physical fitness among Canadians. Offered in Canadian schools from the late nineteenth century, physical education classes were originally aimed at building sturdier, more "prepared" citizens.[3] Canadian government nutrition programs and Canada's food guide developed prior to the Second World War were inspired by high rates of malnutrition and infant mortality among the Canadian population at this time, as well as the low body weight, short stature, and weak physical constitution of military recruits for the First World War and Second World War.[4] Following the wars there was renewed interest in nutrition. Initiatives like the Department of National Defence's XBX and 5BX calisthenics programs allowed individuals to test and then gradually measure improvements in their physical fitness through a series of exercises. Fifteen million copies of 5BX and XBX booklets were sold.[5] Deborah McPhail argues that programs like 5BX were a response to a crisis of masculinity. Newspaper debates about Canada's "tubby," out-of-shape men reflected fears about the strength of Canada during the Cold War.[6] Programs in the 1970s like ParticipACTION and the Canada Fitness test further emphasized the need for physical fitness to combat weakness and keep weight low.[7]

It is not a coincidence that the earliest examples of fat activism date to this time period. Alongside increased government promotion of physical fitness and commercial diet programs, the fashion and cosmetics industries grew dramatically after the 1960s.[8] Whether a state-supported health improvement scheme or a commercial product to enhance one's appearance, women have been the primary targets of these messages. Men also experienced pressure to look attractive, but consumer culture and public conversation about body size and beauty was most often directed towards women.

The ideal woman of the post-war era possessed Dior's "new look" silhouette: a "small waist" and "narrow shoulders."[9] Canadian department stores showcased this look in advertisements and fashion shows.[10] For middle and upper class women, the ideal was to work in the home – and sometimes as a volunteer – to reinforce the economic and social status of her family.[11] Most of the women interviewed for this book were born between the 1940s and 1970s. They were the white, middle-income women to whom such messages were targeted.

Canadian fat activism began in the 1970s, but it was part of a transnational critique of fat oppression. Fat oppression is a term that activists adopted, and I use here, to describe forms of stigmatization, marginalization, and discrimination they experienced as part of their everyday lives. It isn't possible to name an exact moment when the movement began, but subsequent events suggest Canadians were likely influenced by ideas that had been circulating in the United States and England since the 1950s. In 1953 Vinne Young, an American fashion designer and self-described "plumps consultant," published *It's Fun to Be Fat!* Young decried the "great American obsession" with weight loss that had intensified in the post-war era.[12] She argued that the "real problem[s]" facing the plump person were negative "social attitudes" and a lack of "social integration" of fat people. Her book outlined a self-improvement program for women to use the "miracle" of their "own personality" in order to get all that they wanted out of life.[13] In 1966 the *Globe and Mail* published an article about the "Big Girls Club" – a group with similar concerns to Young. Englishwoman June Webb told the Associated Press that "fat women want to look pretty too." Webb received hundreds of phone calls after her profile was published in her local paper. Her club grew to two hundred members.[14] Both Young and

Webb were interested in helping fat people improve themselves and develop a more socially acceptable physical appearance. Discrimination or the health consequences of obesity were not discussed because they weren't on the radar.

Time and place resulted in different ideas about being fat. Only a year after Webb formed the Big Girls Club, five hundred people attended a "fat-in" held in New York's Central Park. Organizer Steve Post, a radio DJ, told reporters he was proud of his size and was tired of being told to lose weight. Diet books and a photograph of iconic model Twiggy were burned at this event, which featured posters reading "Fat Power" and "Think Fat." People wore buttons that said "HELP CURE EMACIATION, TAKE A FAT GIRL TO DINNER."[15] Fat activism in the United States snowballed after this event. First, Llewellyn Louderback published "More People Should be Fat" in the *Saturday Evening Post*, arguing that fat people needed to stop being "browbeaten into slimming down toward an arbitrary image."[16] After reading the article, William J. Fabrey wrote Louderback to ask if he would be interested in founding an association "dedicated to the removal of the prejudices" cited in his article.[17] The National Association to Aid Fat Americans (NAAFA) formed in 1969. Half of the members who first joined NAAFA were "normal" weight people who supported the organization's goals. Recruitment literature described NAAFA members as a group of "determined men and women seeking to increase the happiness and well-being of overweight Americans."[18]

NAAFA was inspired by the National Association for the Advancement of Colored People (NAACP). Like the NAACP, NAAFA emphasized equal rights for fat people, solidarity, and public education.[19] NAAFA's refusal to take a radical stance against medical doctors or talk about fat as a women's issue prompted some female members to break off from the group in 1972. They formed the Fat Women's Problem Solving Group, which eventually became the Fat Underground or FU, an acronym meant to communicate group members' feelings about fat oppression. FU members wrote the "Fat Liberation Manifesto," a rallying cry against fat prejudice at work, in public spaces, and in clothing stores, ending with the rallying cry: "FAT PEOPLE OF THE WORLD, UNITE! YOU HAVE NOTHING TO LOSE."[20] This manifesto was included in the collection *Shadow on a Tightrope: Writings by Women on Fat Oppression* (1982), which was cited as a reference in several Canadian women's health publications of the 1980s. Activists in Quebec translated passages from the book into French in 1992.[21]

Based on the differences between NAAFA and the FU, fat activism has been described as ideologically divided along the lines of "fat liberation"

Table 1. Fat activism in Canada, 1977–present

Years	Name	Location
1977–94	Aide aux personnes obèses handicapées du Québec (APOHQ)	Montreal, QC
1979–81	Forgotten Woman Workshop	Cortes Island, BC
1980–?	Fat Is a Feminist Issue Consciousness-Raising Group	Calgary, AB
1981–5	Large as Life Vancouver	Vancouver, BC
1982–3	Manitoba Action Committee on the Status of Women Fat Is a Feminist Issue Consciousness-Raising Group	Winnipeg, MB
1983–5	Large as Life Calgary	Calgary, AB
1984–92	Lesbiennes grosses cinq (LG5)	Montreal, QC
1984–9	Models Rubenesque	Vancouver, BC
1984–2012	Suzanne Bell's Fitness and Fashion	Vancouver, BC
1985–present	Mrs O's Swimming Group	Burnaby, BC
1987–92	Hersize	Toronto, ON
1989–95	NAAFA/CASA Canada	National
c. 1990	Above Average	Prince Albert, SK
1992–c. 2015	Big Dance	Victoria, BC
1996–2005	Pretty Porky and Pissed Off (PPPO)	Toronto, ON
1997–9	Large as Life London	London, ON

and "fat pride."[22] Fat pride groups like NAAFA sought acceptance and equal rights for fat people, whereas fat liberationists like FU made the more radical claim that fat people experienced hate-based oppression and that dieting was a form of social control.[23] The assimilationist/radical divide may characterize the earliest years of the movement in the United States, but these lines were blurred by the 1980s, as Amy Erdman Farrell has argued.[24] Likewise, Canadian fat activism does not fit easily into assimilationist/liberationist frameworks.[25]

Fat Activism in Canada

Thousands of women participated in and were touched by fat activism in the 1980s and 1990s, but the degree to which they identified with earlier American activism, feminism, or other fat activisms varied. There was a lot of diversity within the movement, in terms of issues addressed and the types of activities organized. Many groups were not aware that there were other Canadian women working on the same issues because of linguistic differences or geography (see table 1).

Why did women become fat activists? And what does this tell us about Canadian history? To begin to answer these questions, I reviewed newsletters produced by Large as Life Vancouver (1981–5) and Hersize Toronto (1987–92). To follow the story, I contacted former activists whose names were published in these sources. From there, the research snowballed. I conducted forty-seven interviews with self-identified fat women, many of whom provided more documents and leads on the movement. Between these sources, about seven hundred different individual women are named, and we know that thousands of others accessed the movement through pamphlets, newsletters, events, workshops, and news stories about fat activism. Together, documentary research and oral history interviews provided a rich source of information on the personal experiences of activists and their opinions about Canadian society in the 1980s and 1990s. Details about my interview methods, questions, and experiences can be found in Appendix A.

Two Canadian groups had direct connections with foundational fat activists from NAAFA and FU. Lesbiennes grosses cinq (LG5, 1984 to 1992) was a collective of five fat lesbians inspired, in part, by the Fat Underground. LG5 translated the "Fat Liberation Manifesto" and other FU pamphlets into French and also held events to confront other lesbians about fat oppression. Former FU members and other American fat activists met the future founders of LG5 at the Michigan Womyn's Music Festival in 1979. LG5 members had no knowledge of the existence of Helena Spring of Toronto, Ontario, and Ruth Wylie-Gillingham of Prince Albert, Saskatchewan, both of whom were attempting to start Canadian chapters of NAAFA around the same time. Both women had seen NAAFA featured on American television talk shows.[26] Like NAAFA in the United States, NAAFA-Canada was intended for men and women. The group may have had some male members, but they were not active in the organization of NAAFA-Canada or mentioned in its publications. NAAFA-Canada was formally recognized by the American organization and sometimes used their pamphlets; members sometimes connected at NAAFA conventions in the US.[27]

Canada's first fat activist group had already formed by the time LG5 and NAAFA-Canada launched. Large as Life (LAL) began when members met at a 1979 Gestalt therapy workshop titled "The Forgotten Woman: For Fat Women Only." Numerically and in the scope of its activities, LAL Vancouver (1981–5) was the most significant example of fat activism in Canada in the period under review. LAL also had the greatest geographical reach. Sister groups formed in Calgary (1982–5) and later London, Ontario (1997–9). Following the demise of the Vancouver chapter in 1985, LAL members continued to organize activities for fat women only. These included a Saturday morning swim, a plus-size modelling school and agency, an aerobics studio, a clothing line available nationally at T. Eaton Company (Eaton's), and a plus-size clothing store.

Aside from LAL, most English Canadian fat activism was explicitly feminist. In Calgary, a Fat Is a Feminist Issue–inspired consciousness-raising (CR) group was advertised in 1980. In 1982, the Manitoba Action Committee on the Status of Women also started a "Fat Is a Feminist Issue" group.[28] By the late 1980s, Toronto's Hersize (1987–92) took aim at beauty and bodily norms, media representations of women, and plastic surgery. The group was part a movement among feminist health professionals working to develop public health programs to combat weight preoccupation and "chronic dieting" among all women. Dieting had become a public health concern and programs designed to encourage health at every size were organized in local health units and women's health centres across Canada.[29]

Big Dance (1992–2007) and Pretty Porky and Pissed Off (1996–2005), chronologically the last groups discussed in the book, adopted a different tone than activists of the previous decade. Laura Kipnis argues that in the 1990s fat activists embraced "a more mutinous tone than the earlier generations' lamentations about social prejudice."[30] PPPO's and Big Dance's approaches to beauty, artistry, and sexuality reflect this more critical approach to gender. These groups mark a transition between the historical movement and the contemporary movement. Such boundaries are fluid, but I end here for two reasons: First, there was a discernible break between groups from 1977 to 1997 that grappled with second-wave, liberal, and radical feminist debates about women and PPPO, which was influenced by postmodern, "third-wave" feminist thinking. Second, there was a significant temporal break between PPPO and what followed around 2015.[31]

Contemporary Fat Activism

Body positivity – the idea that all bodies are good bodies – was the focus of *Now* magazine's 1 January 2015 issue. Toronto's alternative weekly newspaper featured two naked, laughing fat women on its cover (see figure 1). Amanda Scriver and Yuli Scheidt were the founders of Fat Girl Food Squad (FGFS), a web community that also occasionally hosted events in Toronto. A photographer, Scheidt had observed that it was rare to see images of fat women eating and looking happy about it. Other activists seemed to avoid talking about food, which is what inspired Scriver in the first place. In a 2015 interview she told me that "fat folks and activists can feel pressure to eat clean or healthy in public but for me it's much more political for an activist to say, 'fuck that, I like food' and stand up against others who police others' bodies and what they eat."[32]

Figure 1. Fat Girl Food Squad founders Amanda Scriver and Yuli Scheidt, as seen in *Now Magazine*, 2015. Photo by Tanja-Tiziana, *Now Magazine*.

For Scheidt and Scriver, loving food and body positivity felt like radical acts. They came of age during the "obesity epidemic" of the early 2000s. Around that time, Statistics Canada data indicated that the number of citizens with a BMI between 25 and 29, "overweight," and over 30, "obese," was steadily increasing.[33] Government and public health programs emerged to combat this apparent crisis, which was said to be costing the health-care system millions of dollars and shortening the lifespan of the nation's children. Several scientists and social scientists have since criticized this approach.[34] They argue that actual increases in the weight of Canadians may be overestimated because of a lack of standardized measurement for weight data.[35] Researchers critical of the concept of an obesity epidemic have shown that factors like waist circumference, cardiovascular capacity, blood pressure, physical activity, and income security are more likely to determine a person's health status than weight.[36]

In contrast to the rhetoric of harm and disease that characterized post-2000 public discussions of food, FGFS encouraged women to enjoy eating. The group organized regular brunches for women to eat in public and be fat together. On the blog, they shared recipes and restaurant reviews. As Scriver observed, food was a taboo topic for earlier generations of activists. But the distinction isn't just that earlier activists wanted to emphasize their healthy habits. Obesity and food consumption were not scrutinized as closely in the 1980s and 1990s as they have been in recent decades. Activists of the 1980s were responding, in part, to Canada's physical activity crisis. Before 2000, overconsumption of food was not a source of significant government intervention.

FGFS's reach and impact was dramatically larger than earlier Canadian fat activist groups because of social media. In only three years, FGFS gained four thousand followers on Twitter, posted hundreds of blog entries, and inspired squads in seven other cities. Blogs and social media helped fat activist ideas travel faster and further than ever before. Ideas circulated more slowly in the 1980s and 1990s. Concepts first elaborated in Los Angeles in the 1970s made their way across the US and into Canada over a period of five to ten years. It took twenty years for "fat oppression," which describes discrimination and marginalization of women based on their weight, to become "fat acceptance," the notion that fat people should focus on enjoying life, and later "weight preoccupation," where women suffer to try to live up to beauty ideals. By comparison, FGFS probably reached as many women in two years as the entire Canadian movement that came before it.

While technology and attitudes towards being fat have shifted the movement, there are important continuities between contemporary and historical fat activism. FGFS took on the same issues as earlier generations of activists that will be discussed in this book: body acceptance; beauty norms; representations of fat people in popular culture; the relationship between exercise, health, and body size; and fashion. Feminism is a common thread of all fat activism, but the degree to which it is named varies. Both Scheidt and Scriver are feminist but noted they were not trained – that is, they did not take women's studies at university. Rather, they came to feminism because of their personal experiences. They believed their lack of training made them different from other activists, but, in fact, experience is an important driver of all fat activism. The movement exists because activists did not see their embodied experiences reflected in the women's movement or in the broader culture.

The Evidence of Experience (and Its Limitations)

Experience is an important concept in this book. Fat activism was and is based on a claim to shared experience – that is, that women who shared a common body type experienced the world in similar ways. Experiential evidence provides insight into women's attitudes towards femininity and feminism that are otherwise not available in historical records.[37] Experiential accounts also provide insight into women's agency – why did people do what they did and how did they feel about it?[38] In this book, experiential perspectives from my 2005–15 interviews show that activists of the 1970s to the 1990s were grappling with what it meant to be feminine or feminist, physically fit, and attractive in an era where "thin was in."

Fat activism also shows us some of the limitations of experience as a lens for understanding history. All of the individuals and groups discussed in this book universalized the category "fat woman." "Fat women" needed better clothes or felt pressure to diet or needed to reject feminine norms. Experiential differences between women were not considered. For example, until recently most fat activism in Canada has been undertaken by and for cisgender women. Women were more likely to form fat activist groups, and those who did defined fat as a woman's issue. Some groups made it clear that they were for women only; others did not have a rule about men. Scriver said that men were welcome because "there can be a fat girl living inside of everyone" but "90 percent" of her readers were female.[39] Whether or not they had a presence, men were and are not central to the fat activist movement in Canada. They were involved in some groups and welcome at others, but they were not major players.[40]

Another reason experience cannot be treated as the only truth is that it obscures ethnic and class differences. In 2015 FGFS were "called out" on social media for their white privilege. Critics felt FGFS did not consider that non-white women might not be able to celebrate food and body positivity in the same way. A few non-white women worked with the group but overall the contributors were, in Scheidt's words, "a wall of white."[41] This detail troubled FGFS because they were trying to be inclusive on their site, but they admitted they had overlooked their own privilege. Going forward, the group worked to be more inclusive.

FGFS was not unique in their struggle to incorporate different perspectives. Part of this was because "fat" was the exciting new identity category activists wanted to explore. But even in the early 1990s some activists were questioning which women experienced fat oppression and how? Since the 1990s studies have shown that black, Latina, and Indigenous women are more likely to be obese.[42] In the contemporary movement, Jill Andrew has addressed race in fat activism more explicitly than any other Canadian activist. Andrew is the co-founder of "Fat in the City," another Toronto-based blog, and founder of the "Body Confidence Canada Awards," which recognize individuals and initiatives that promote size diversity. In 2016 she started an online petition to get size discrimination added to the Ontario Human Rights Code.

Andrew argues that "fat shaming and size discrimination" is often "intertwined with sexism, racism and ableism." Her petition asked to make verbal shaming and employment and housing discrimination of people based on their size illegal. Andrew is the first Canadian activist to ask for fat to be a protected category in a human rights code. Her petition obtained 9,120 signatures.[43] In 2018 she was elected as a Member of Provincial Parliament for Ontario, where she continues to speak out about diverse forms of discrimination.

In 2015 Scriver and Scheidt put their blog on hiatus so they could pursue writing and photography professionally. By then other "squads" had popped up across Canada, the United States, and Australia.[44] Along with Jill Andrew, FGFS has raised public awareness about fat activism and body stigma to new heights. At the same time, being fat remains stigmatized. Efforts to fight "obesity," like the 2016 Canadian Senate report *Obesity in Canada: A Whole-of-Society Approach for a Healthier Canada*, show that weight is still perceived as a crisis rooted in lack of self-control.[45] Fascination with bodies is ongoing, as even a cursory glimpse at Canadian popular culture illustrates. Fat activism remains relevant because of ongoing stigmatization of fat people.

Canada's Fat History

Fat activism shows that public discourse on weight has never been just about health. In the late twentieth century, weight, like dress, demeanour, race, and class, has influenced ideas about a person's character. Slenderness has been seen as evidence of refinement and self-care. Perceptions of the body have shaped immigration and public health policies in the recent past, as the literature on twentieth century moral reform projects and eugenics in Canada has amply demonstrated.[46]

Fat activism offers fresh insight into how Canadians came to know themselves in relation to familial, government, and commercial messages about the body. Government messages on physical fitness and diet can be conflated with commercial messages – and the reverse. Women learned they were fat and that this was unacceptable, unattractive, and unhealthy through a variety of different changes. They didn't necessarily see a difference between things like ParticipACTION's "fat is NOT where it's at" campaign, a doctor shaming them for failing to follow a diet, and a parent telling them to lose weight. The movement illuminates the extent to which negative attitudes toward fat people are embedded in Canadian culture. There are no dividing lines between home, work, and the social world. Fat oppression was everywhere, and activism was a response to cultural discourses rather than a single problem.

Fat activism also offers insight into women's experience of social norms. Historians know that representations of the body don't tell us everything about the past, but rarely do sources actually let us hear women's responses. Within the pages of fat activist newsletters, we see women engaging in a debate about popular culture, medicine, exercise trends, and feminism. We don't have to read against the grain to understand what most fat activists were thinking because they shared their thoughts in newsletters and in research interviews conducted between 2005 and 2015. A complex picture of the impact of feminism and women's experience of femininity emerges from these sources. As Kathy Peiss has shown, women's voices must be included in histories of femininity. Beauty culture is a "web of image rituals, social relationships, and female institutions" whose impact can't be reduced to questions of conformity or nonconformity.[47] Fat activists, like the beauty saleswomen in Peiss's study, show how women actively engage in popular culture. This is why I include fashion and beauty work by self-identified fat women under the umbrella of activism. For women who felt ignored or excluded from fashion, aerobics, and beauty rituals, engaging with these institutions was a form of self-empowerment. Like Peiss, my goal is to take women's concerns seriously.

Lastly, this book contributes to our understanding of Canada after 1980. Historians are just beginning to unpack the meaning of a decade that saw the birth of the Charter of Rights and Freedoms and the rise of neo-liberalism. Politics and culture collided in the 1980s in Canada. Cultural issues – about language, economic, and cultural sovereignty and even hockey – were the subject of political debate and public conversation. Social relationships and culture were politicized as the government waded into debates about human rights, employment equity, and multiculturalism. The 1980s marked the beginning of the end of the post-war liberal consensus on social programs and the beginning of the period of "neo-liberalization" that has reshaped the economy and social programs. At the same time, the inclusion of the Charter of Rights and Freedoms in the 1982 constitution, and subsequent "Charter challenge" cases, contributed to the sense that "rights" should fundamentally organize Canadian society.[48] The Charter inspired new approaches to activism in the decade that followed.[49]

These themes – the politicization of Canadian culture, neo-liberalization, and the rise of "rights" talk – are evident in fat activism. Activists explicitly critiqued fat oppression in Canadian culture, which they encountered in public health campaigns like ParticipACTION, health messaging in schools, and interactions with strangers. Activities like aerobics classes, fashion shows, and clothing swaps were also a critical engagement with Canadian society, which did not offer adequate services or spaces for fat people. In Canada, progressively neo-liberal policies resulted in decreased funding for recreation and health services. Increased responsibility for health was placed on individuals. Commercial services like gyms and Weight Watchers promoted self-control as the antidote to obesity, ignoring more complex factors shaping weight and health in Canada. Finally, "rights" talk in fat activism was influenced both by feminism and the rise of the Charter of Rights and Freedoms. Most fat activists of the 1980s and 1990s didn't claim legal rights, but they did claim an ethical right to be fat. They talked about fat stigma as a form of oppression, even if they saw the solution as social rather than legal.

About This Book

The book is organized thematically around issues addressed by fat women's organizations. Chapter 1 examines fat feminist organizing in Canada. Feminists interested in fat issues believed there was a link between women's oppression and fat oppression. Because they did not find many sympathizers within other feminist organizations of the 1980s and 1990s, they formed groups for fat women only. Chapter 2 examines another community within fat activism: women dedicated to acceptance. Fat acceptance activists believed practical solutions to fat oppression could be found through self-reflection and personal development. These groups focused on sociality and mutual support through the development of workshops, exercise classes, and fashion seminars for fat women only. While there are many variations of fat activism, these chapters will show that all organizations owed an intellectual debt to feminist ideas of the 1960s and 1970s.

In chapters 3 and 4, fat activist approaches to health, femininity, and sexuality are explored. These chapters reveal the central importance of the notion of personal experience in exchanges between self-identified fat women. Questions of femininity and sexuality lay at the heart of a person's decision to join a fat women's organization. Self-identified fat women knew themselves to be, physically, far from the ideal woman. The dramatic impact of ideals of femininity on women's understanding of their bodies is discussed in chapter 3. Activists' sense that they were outsiders led them to think critically about their lives. Members of fat women's organizations developed searing critiques of society and their peers' understanding of physical attractiveness, even as they continued to struggle to accept that they were fat and this fact was unlikely to change.

Chapter 4 explores the ways that fat activists responded to the idea that fat was unhealthy. In participants' life stories, doctors and diet programs were critiqued because both claimed to have "solutions" to the "problem" of fatness, yet both failed to deliver. Evidence of their own failed experiences with dieting came to be the basis for fat women's challenges to the claim that being overweight was unhealthy. Collectively, experiential knowledge helped group members to know that what they were experiencing was not just personal; rather, it was a "truth" common to all fat women. In the process, fat activists came to see their bodies as potentially healthy and physically fit.

Activists were critical of activities that were promoted for weight loss. In opposition to these kinds of programs, they trained as fitness leaders and organized their own spaces to exercise, swim, and dance. Chapter 5 looks at physical activity for fat women. The convergence of aerobics and fat acceptance invites a re-examination of the claim that aerobics reinforced conventional gender norms. Here, aerobics classes emerge as a critical, woman-centred practice that was developed, initiated, and driven by participants. Fat women's aerobics classes were feminized spaces, but participants saw the practice as liberating and empowering.

Chapter 6 follows fat women through the process of finding and purchasing clothing. Their difficulty finding clothing meant that fat women were well versed in matters of cut, fabric, and fit and took special care to preserve even the most mundane purchases. The struggle to find clothing inspired many fat women to open their own stores. At their best, stores created by fat women, for fat women became a valued resource for women longing to be fashionable. The ways that proprietors understood the "problems" facing fat women were not entirely positive. The stock, price point, and sizes available in each store represented a feminized, white, and middle-class understanding of "the fat woman." Despite this limitation, plus-size retailing offered many women the opportunity to bring their visible identity in line with their "true" selves. For this reason, independent plus-size retailing can be seen as an extension of fat women's organizing in the 1980s. Fashion "activism" serves as a reminder that women were not necessarily seeking structural change; instead, they were looking for changes in consumer culture and in attitudes towards fat women.

This book provides critical insight into the way that groups of women understood and experienced their weight in the late twentieth century.

The project confirms Joan Jacobs Brumberg's claim that women came to see the body as the "ultimate expression of the self" in the late twentieth century, but it also shows how "body projects" could be the basis for meaningful experiences.[50] Thousands of women were inspired to join the movement because of their frustrations with Canadian society. While the obesity epidemic has dominated public discussion of weight since 2000, fat activism has a complex history that shows weight has long been a topic of concern to Canadians. Between 1977 and 1997 fat activism took many different forms in Canada. In the process of organizing activities with other women, individuals were able to rethink and redefine the meaning of being fat.

1 *FIFI*: Feminist Approaches to Being Fat

In her 1978 bestseller *Fat Is a Feminist Issue: A Self-Help Guide for Compulsive Eaters* (*FIFI*), Susie Orbach argued that being fat was a form of rebellion. Overeating was a coping mechanism for women dealing with sexism and pressure to look and act feminine.[1] Examining the reasons one ate would help women to stop using food as comfort, according to Orbach.[2] *FIFI* walked readers through a series of consciousness-raising (CR) exercises designed to help them examine their beliefs about food, men, and femininity. Contrary to how many have used the slogan "fat is a feminist issue" as a rallying cry against weight bias, Orbach's book was intended to help women lose weight through CR.[3] *FIFI* is part of the history of fat activism, however. It was the most popular feminist text to illustrate the links between weight and women's oppression. *FIFI* was also an important part of the feminist debate about femininity from which fat activism emerged. The book helped inspire critical analysis of weight, even though it did not actually call for fat liberation.

Weight was not part of the Canadian feminist debate about femininity until the late 1970s, around the time *FIFI* appeared.[4] Before that time, media images of superficial and sexualized women were the focus of feminist concern. In their presentation to the Royal Commission on National Development in the Arts, Letters, and Sciences (Massey Commission, 1949–51), the National Council of Women critiqued one-dimensional representations of women in media.[5] Later, at the Royal Commission on the Status of Women (1968–70), Regina schoolteacher Wilma Brown complained that "images of women ... depicted them as 'senseless idiots.'"[6] Organizational efforts to reform images of women in the media followed this foundational feminist activism. In 1973 Women for Political Action intervened at a Canadian Radio-Television and Telecommunications Commision (CRTC) licensing

Table 2. Feminist fat activism in Canada, 1982–2005

Years	Name	Location
1982–3	Fat Is a Feminist Issue Consciousnes-Raising Group	Winnipeg, MB
c. 1982–9	Maranda-Friedman "Facing Your Fat" Workshops	Vancouver, BC
1984–92	Lesbiennes grosses cinq (LG5)	Montreal, QC
1987–92	Hersize	Toronto, ON
1996–2005	Pretty Porky and Pissed Off	Toronto, ON

hearing against a television station they claimed aired sexist shows and advertisements and had a poor record of employing women.[7] This intervention was followed by a groundswell of local and national feminist activism around media reform.[8] Pressure to be feminine prevented women from achieving equality. Groups like MediaWatch believed that reforming the media would help to change attitudes towards women. Fat-specific feminist groups emerged because this debate about femininity and sexualization failed to address body size. Fat activists felt alienated by feminists who continued to diet or rejected partners based on their weight.

Feminist fat activists have articulated four approaches to weight, which are outlined in this chapter. They used the related concepts of "fat oppression," "weight obsession," "weight preoccupation," and "performativity" to challenge assumptions about weight and gender. Activists who saw body norms as a form of "oppression" directed their critique of feminine norms outward, towards the social structures that reproduced sexism. Those who saw weight as a dangerous "obsession" or "preoccupation" believed that social change would occur when women resolved their negative feelings about fatness. By the mid-1990s fat activists took up Judith Butler's idea of gender "performance" as a way to think about being fat.[9]

Despite meaningful epistemological differences between the groups discussed in this chapter, all feminist fat activists believed there was a relationship between gender and fat oppression. The goal was to liberate fat women from the constraints of femininity. This chapter shows that some fat activism was a trajectory of other feminist organizing of the 1970s, 1980s, and 1990s in Canada. When they could not find resources or sympathy within existing women's organizations, fat activists established new groups to explore being fat and female. These groups rearticulated earlier visions of women's liberation by revealing an axis of oppression, gender, and body size, which other feminists of the period had failed to address.

Fat Oppression

A questionnaire circulated at lesbian-only events in Montreal in 1984 asked "regular sized women" for their opinions of fat lesbians. Among the questions were:

> What first comes to mind when you see a fat lesbian?
> Are you afraid of becoming fat?
> Have you ever had or do you have any fat lovers?
> Have you ever felt attracted to a fat lesbian without knowing her?[10]

Members of LG5 circulated the questionnaire to determine whether fat oppression and "looksism," terms borrowed from the Fat Underground (1973–9), existed within Montreal's lesbian community. LG5 member Louise Turcotte said in a 2006 interview that the group wanted to make sure that fat oppression was not "just in" their "heads."[11] She was shocked by the hostility of responses. Respondents to the questionnaire expressed uncertainty about fat partners – and worse. Fat lesbians were described as fleshy masses and greasy women who were unable to move their bodies naturally.[12] In 2006 LG5 member Michèle Charland said the questionnaire was a wake-up call. It helped her to lose her "naivety" and accept the extent to which fat phobia had permeated the lesbian community.[13]

Shadow on a Tightrope, the American fat liberationist text, was the starting point for LG5's discussions. Prior to the group's formation, there had been a lobbying group for obese people in Quebec. Aide aux personnes obèses handicapées du Québec (APOHQ) (1979–c. 1989) worked on helping people who were disabled by their obesity access social services. English-Canadian fat acceptance groups also formed prior to 1984, but LG5 were not aware of or interested in these approaches.[14] Instead, LG5 began by translating excerpts from *Shadow*, starting with "La grosse illusion" / "The Fat Illusion."[15] The article by Vivian Mayer (a.k.a. Aldebaran) argues fat oppression was a form of social control. Women, even feminists, were operating under the illusion that being fat or thin was a matter of self-control. Medical evidence suggested that weight was genetically determined and permanent weight loss nearly impossible. But the fat illusion kept women in a cycle of dieting and self-surveillance.[16] Fat liberation would be the next step in the process of women's liberation.[17]

LG5's translations of *Shadow on a Tightrope* reveal that feminist ideas travelled across borders. Turcotte and other Quebecois feminists encountered American fat activism through personal relationships and feminist activism, which I will discuss in greater detail in chapter 3. For the purposes of this chapter, the translations offer insight into how feminist ideas were transformed as they are introduced in new times, places, and translated into different languages. LG5 reinterpreted fat activist texts to reflect their understanding of women's oppression. Each translation from *Shadow* included a preface where LG5 outlined what they hoped readers would take away from the text. For "The Fat Illusion," LG5 wrote that lesbians who refused to acknowledge fat oppression were fostering the development of a class of thin women (*les minces*), who believed themselves to be superior to another class, fat women (*les grosses*).[18] Fat oppression was not only the product of the stereotyping, rejection, and humiliation of fat people but also of a heterosexual class regime.

For LG5, class was about income *and* maintaining a "heterosociety" that made money from women's disempowerment. Like the Fat Underground, LG5 rejected the idea that fat was a psychological problem.[19] They encouraged readers to see fat oppression as something that shaped their everyday lives. Issues like accessibility to public transit and employment discrimination were raised by LG5, ones that were not focused upon by other groups.[20] As much as LG5 put a Marxist spin on "The Fat Illusion," their critique of public space also echoed the growing disability rights movement (DRM) in Canada.[21]

Kathy Davis argued that the book *Our Bodies, Ourselves* was relevant in different contexts because it gave "authority to women's embodied experiences "and treated them as "active knowers."[22] Fat activist texts did much the same by validating women's experiences and providing a platform for their critiques. In texts like "The Fat Illusion" women learned that being fat was not their fault and that it didn't – or shouldn't – matter. Readers were encouraged to take control of their bodies, while LG5 emphasized that society must adapt to different bodily needs. LG5 paired these ideas with their critique of capitalism and heterosexuality. LG5's introduction to "The Fat Illusion" shows that fat activism had fluid boundaries. Successive generations have interpreted classic texts differently and infused new meaning into the work of earlier activists.

When they met in 1983, LG5 co-founders Louise Turcotte and Michèle Charland were active in Montreal's lesbian feminist community. Charland helped organize the annual "Take Back the Night" march and Turcotte was a "radical lesbian" who had participated in France's student movement in the late 1960s. She was also a founding member of the feminist collective Amazones d'hier, lesbiennes d'aujourd'hui (AHLA). In their journal AHLA described "radical lesbianism" as:

> une solution pour contrer le système patriarcal. C'est un rejet des patterns hétéros ... Les lesbiennes ne vivant pas avec un homme ne sont donc pas des femmes ... Les lesbiennes radicales remettent en question le terme "femme" en voulant l'abolition de la class "femme," par laquelle les

hommes s'approprient les femmes. **Le lesbianisme radicale, c'est vouloir la destruction du système social de l'hétérosexualité.**

a solution for countering the patriarchal system. It is a rejection of heterosexual patterns ... lesbians that don't live with men are not women, they throw into question the very category of "woman" and try to abolish the class "woman," wherein women are the property of men. **Radical lesbianism seeks the destruction of the heterosexual social system.**[23]

AHLA was inspired by Monique Wittig's assertion that "lesbians are not women" because they contributed to the destruction of the "heterosociety." Wittig, a French feminist theorist, was a friend and mentor to AHLA / LG5's Louise Turcotte. For Wittig, the contemporary "heterosociety" was built on an ideology of sexual difference: Western economic and political systems relied on women's unpaid labour to function. The idea that women were an exploited class resonated with Turcotte. Lesbianism offered women the "possibility of escaping patriarchal control on both the material and the ideological level."[24] As LG5's introduction to "The Fat Illusion" shows, Wittig's theories shaped LG5's fat activism.

LG5 also reflects debates within lesbian feminism of the 1970s and 1980s. Charland and Turcotte were part of a generation of lesbian feminism that consciously rejected "heterosexual" feminine beauty norms in terms of hairstyles, make-up, and clothing. Many lesbian feminists of the era "sought to invent their own distinguishing forms of cultural currency" by wearing short hair and loose clothing.[25] Both women were disappointed to realize that this ethos did not include body size. For LG5 members body size, like sexuality, was a personal issue. Fatness was a taboo topic for feminists just as lesbianism had been a decade earlier. In the 1970s liberal feminists in Canada and the United States tried to downplay lesbian rights issues because they believed it damaged their popularity.[26] Lesbianism was a "lavender menace" and a "bedroom issue" that was not fundamental to women's equality.[27] This divide led to the development of autonomous lesbian feminist organizing in both countries.

Lesbian feminism was for "woman-identified-women" who committed themselves to "other women for political, emotional, physical, and economic support."[28] Lesbian feminists parted company on questions of action: Should lesbians work with gay men or establish separate communities? What relationship should lesbian feminists have with other feminists? Unity did not follow from these debates. Instead, the 1980s saw the further "subdivision of activist lesbians into specialized groupings,"[29] including lesbians of colour, lesbians with disabilities, and fat lesbians.[30] Since then, queer theory has challenged the categories of gender and sexuality altogether.

Turcotte first realized that fatness was a taboo topic when she brought it up with other feminists. Charland approached Turcotte to join a CR group to talk about being fat for the same reason. In a 2006 interview, Turcotte and Charland described this meeting as transformative. Together, the group realized that they had felt the same reluctance about using the term fat (*grosse*) as they initially had about the word lesbian (*lesbienne*). Women at the meeting shared their frustration that fat was "never addressed in the lesbian world." Some had been laughed at by their lovers and ostracized at lesbian dances and this made them "very, very angry."[31] Encountering other women who felt the same way about being fat was a "click" moment: "a moment of truth ... recognition" that the way they were treated as fat women was "oppressive and wrong."[32] They began to call themselves LG5, a literal description of the five self-identified fat lesbians that made up the membership.

Through the 1980s, LG5 staged a series of public interventions aimed at confronting lesbian feminists about fat oppression.[33] One such event took place at a November 1984 event, "*Si la chicane vous intéresse*" / "If you are interested in the fight," where 180 women met to discuss uniting Montreal's fractured feminist movement.[34] At 11:10 a.m., to the surprise of the event organizers, LG5 members rang a small bell. Over the protestations of conference organizers and some attendees, LG5 members stood collectively and read out the responses to their questionnaire on fat lesbians.[35]

Perhaps deliberately, LG5's action paralleled the Lavender Menace protest organized by Rita Mae Brown at the Second Congress to Unite Women in New York City in 1970. To protest the exclusion of lesbian issues from the mainstream feminist agenda, women spread out in the audience and stood to display Lavender Menace T-shirts. Brown wanted feminists to acknowledge that lesbianism was not just a personal issue.[36] Fourteen years later, LG5's intent was to persuade lesbians that fat was not a personal issue. While many women spontaneously joined Brown's protest in 1970, no one joined LG5 in theirs.[37] The most supportive comment was from a woman who argued body weight was not a political issue, but it was important to discuss the matter because all women have "*un rapport 'fucké' avec la nourriture*"/"a fucked up relationship with food."[38] This gesture of support notwithstanding, the audience at "*Si la chicane*" was unenthusiastic about fat liberation. More than twenty years later Turcotte recalled with satisfaction that the discussion of feminist unity had gone "kaput, kaboom" that day. LG5 had "got even" by forcing women to hear "out loud" the horrible things they had anonymously written on LG5's questionnaire.[39]

LG5's last public action was a special issue of *Amazones d'hier* titled "La grosseur: Obsession? OPPRESSION!" / "Size: Obsession? Oppression!" (see figure 2). Translations of articles from *Shadow on a*

Figure 2. "La Grosseur: Obsession? Oppression!" / "Size: Obsession? Oppression!" special edition of *AHLA*, edited by LG5, December 1992. Courtesy of Louise Turcotte.

Tightrope were included in this issue, along with two specially commissioned pieces by American activists. The issue is evidence of a network of fat lesbian activism that developed in North America in the 1980s that I will discuss in detail in chapter 3. In terms of feminist fat activism, the journal reflected a shift in approach to fat oppression. Turcotte took aim at the increasingly popular view that fat oppression resulted in women's obsession with weight. Turcotte may have been referencing Kim Chernin's popular book *The Obsession: Reflections on the Tyranny of Slenderness* (1981). Echoing Orbach, Chernin argued that Western culture taught women not to grow too large or too powerful.[40] It was no coincidence that social pressure to diet had increased at the same time as women's political strength was growing. Pressure to be slim was intended to "cut women down to size" and diminish their power.[41] For Chernin, as it was for Orbach, a woman's relationship to food and hunger was a metaphor for her dissatisfaction with sexist and patriarchal culture. She wrote: "Obsession is, in fact, a drama, in which that inner being one has hoped to dominate and control keeps struggling to return. The obsession expresses both the will to destroy this self, by mortifying the body and starving the flesh, and the longing to be reunited with it, through the eating up of food."[42]

Turcotte's editorial argued that the notion of "weight obsession" depoliticized fat by focusing on women's emotional struggles.[43] She argued that fat people were oppressed by prescriptive heterosexual ideals. Obsession was beside the point. Like other activists working on gay and lesbian rights in this time period, LG5 believed that politics were never just personal. All aspects of sexuality and weight needed to be aired publicly so as to set in motion a "process of discovery and revelation, of transparency and honesty," through which fat oppression would be understood and then eradicated.[44] LG5 members did not think that individual struggles with weight were as oppressive as the broader social structures that oppressed fat women.

Weight Obsession

LG5's understanding of fat oppression echoed radical and lesbian feminist ideologies. Social change could only be achieved through a transformation of the fundamental power structures of Canadian society. LG5 believed change would follow from acknowledging and eradicating the "class" differences between men and women, fat and thin, rich and poor, and so on. By contrast, fat activism modelled after the obsession model saw fat oppression in psychological terms. Feminists employing the term obsession believed that "personal transformation" was "the key to a 'consciousness revolution' that would liberate the individual" and, in doing so, "radically transform society."[45] This inward-directed approach to fat activism reflects a liberal feminist ideology. Power differences would gradually disappear once women had equal opportunities to men. Working to improve women's self-esteem would help to eradicate weight preoccupation.

Inspired by Orbach's *FIFI* and Chernin's *Obsession*, CR groups and workshops for fat women formed across Canada in the 1980s.[46] Women came together to talk about being fat. Some met through local feminist groups, while others paid to join workshops led by feminist therapists. Susan White of Winnipeg had no feminist resources to help her think through being fat when she saw an advertisement for a "Fat Is a Feminist Issue" CR group in the December 1981 newsletter for the Manitoba Action Committee on the Status of Women (MACSW).[47] The opportunity appealed to White because *FIFI* asked what she believed was a fundamental question: "If women so hate being fat and so wish they weren't fat, then why do they keep doing things that keep them fat?"[48] White felt that *FIFI* offered useful "societal explanations" for fat oppression.[49] Through MACSW White met four women with whom she connected for about two years. While scholars have rightfully criticized *FIFI*'s generalization of fat women's experiences, for White the book was meaningful.[50] The links Orbach made between weight, gender, and power were a catalyst for self-reflection. White agreed with Orbach's point that "women actually keep themselves fat as a self defense mechanism in a sexist society." She felt her weight was a self-defence mechanism that ensured men would relate to her intellectually and not sexually.[51]

FIFI was also the inspiration for workshops developed by counsellors Doris Maranda and Sandy Friedman in Vancouver, BC. Friedman had been an intern at The Forgotten Woman workshop on Cortes Island in 1979, described in the introduction, and her own practice was influenced by *FIFI*. She and Maranda had talked about the book as MA students in psychology.[52] Their workshops promised to help women think about what food meant to them and develop strategies to "get in control of ... bingeing ... and life."[53] Compulsive eating was part of an "addictive process" that "comes from looking outside of you for your own sense of self." Maranda and Friedman wanted to help women to know themselves "from the inside out rather than the outside." The goal of their workshops was to encourage participants to develop "an inner reference to decide how they felt about themselves."[54]

Maranda and Friedman wanted to help women become aware of how gender and weight shaped their everyday lives. One Maranda-Friedman exercise borrowed from Orbach asked attendees to reflect on how they would "take up space" if they were a man. Asking women to sit, stand, and walk as men was a way for the counsellors to illustrate their assertion that women had a "submissive role" in society.[55] Susan White's consciousness-raising group also performed visualization exercises from Orbach's *Fat Is a Feminist Issue II: A Program to Conquer Compulsive Eating* (1982). One exercise asked women to picture themselves at a cocktail party – first at their current weight, and second as they would ideally like their body to look.[56] This exercise was an eye-opener for White:

> I was shocked at myself. Because when I visualized the party at my current, my then weight ... I couldn't believe it, the image that came up. I was sitting in a corner, against the wall, in a chair by myself. I was off at the side and other people were partying and having a great time and I'm on the sidelines. Then I visualized the other scene, I'm now thinner. I swear to god the image that came up was, I'm right in the middle of the party, I'm wearing a sexy cocktail dress, I'm dancing up a storm. I was shocked ... It was such a revealing moment.[57]

As a feminist, White was shocked to realize that being fat had shaped how she interacted with people, and the activity helped her see how deeply her self-image impacted her way of interacting with other people.

Like Orbach, Maranda-Friedman operated on the assumption that all fat women had a conflicted relationship with food. Eventually they came to believe that food was not just a fat women's issue and changed the name of their workshops to "Learning to Love Yourself." Maranda-Friedman changed their approach because so many women who "felt fat," but were not fat, came to their workshops.[58] Maranda-Friedman decided to organize their workshops around a problem – weight obsession – rather than a shared body type. Later they applied their approach to other constituencies, including a workshop "for gay men only," which was held at Vancouver's Gay and Lesbian Community Centre in 1987.[59]

By comparison to Maranda-Friedman and Susan White's *FIFI* group, the 1979 Forgotten Woman workshop was not intended to be feminist. In 2005 The Forgotten Woman organizer Ellen Tallman explained that her goal was to get women to learn "how to care for themselves as they were and not be their own enemy." She recalled that many women who came to her experienced "shame and despair over what they hadn't been able to shift and change in relation to their body size." Tallman felt the solution was to help women to restore the "various parts of" themselves "that were not connected."[60] Tallman was a Gestalt therapist.

Gestalt encouraged patients to examine their behaviour and to use this analysis as a catalyst for self-improvement.[61] Despite the similarities to the other therapeutic approaches discussed here, Tallman rejected the notion that fat was a feminist issue. Puzzlingly, she felt attaching weight to gender implied women were victims.[62] According to Gestalt therapy, people needed to take personal responsibility for their problems in order to move forward and restore their whole selves.[63]

While there are differences in approach and nomenclature, CR groups and therapeutic workshops by MACSW, Maranda-Friedman, and Tallman had a common goal: to liberate women from weight obsession. Charlotte Cooper has been critical of weight obsession activism that is for women of all sizes. In her view such "mainstream projects" rely on "generic body politics" and lead to "assimilation" of fat perspectives.[64] Cooper is correct that weight obsession programs have not been fat specific, but it is not accurate to call them apolitical. Self-help movements are one way that women have empowered themselves by developing new ways of knowing. Simply rejecting body norms was not possible for all women. Casting hegemonic norms aside required, as Lorraine Code has argued, "working collectively to reshape the stereotype-informed structures" that diminish women's sense of authority.[65]

FIFI workshops and CR groups may have been liberal feminist, in that they emphasized personal change more so than they challenged structural inequalities. Nonetheless, both the obsession and oppression approaches had a meaningful impact on participants. Both are based on the idea that feminine ideals – that women are or should be emotional, soft, maternal, passive, small, and physically weak – were at the root of women's problems with weight. Most importantly, the obsession model shows that many women believed the psychological and social dimensions of fat oppression were related: a better personal understanding of fatness was a part of a larger and longer process of social change.

Weight Preoccupation

In 1985 a "political group" aimed at the "prevention and treatment of eating disorders" was spearheaded by Dr David Garner of Toronto General Hospital. Garner, an eating disorder specialist, approached women with whom he had had a prior clinical and professional association to start Freedom from Eating Disorders (FED). FED planning meetings were held throughout 1985–6, and in 1987 the group began public outreach as Hersize. Hersize was created to be a "political force." The group built on earlier feminist and fat activism about weight.[66] Members wanted to raise awareness about the dangers posed by "weight preoccupation." Weight preoccupation affected women of all sizes who were "over concerned" about their weight and/or chronic dieters.[67] Weight preoccupation resulted from negative images of women in popular culture and contemporary body norms. Building on earlier definitions of fat oppression and weight obsession, Hersize acknowledged that "the cycle [of weight preoccupation]" was "exacerbated ... for women who actually are fat. They must deal not only with any internal messages of dissatisfaction, but also with the extreme weight prejudice that exists in the culture at large."[68]

Hersize's work bridged fat activism and professional women's health work. Dieticians and physicians alike had observed increasing pressure to be thin in the early 1980s. For clinicians like Garner, popular culture was the root of the problem. Garner was well known in the field of eating disorders for his groundbreaking analysis of the body weight and height of *Playboy* centrefolds and Miss America contestants between 1955 and 1979. His study revealed a growing discrepancy between women's average weights and ideal (that is, popularly represented) weights. *Playboy* centrefolds and Miss America contestants had become significantly taller *and* thinner than average women.[69] Garner's work was influential because it provided data to support feminist critiques of media images. By 1988 the group disassociated with Garner, however. That year the Ontario Board of Examiners in Psychology suspended him for professional misconduct with a patient.[70]

At least two of Hersize's founding group members worked professionally in eating disorder research and support at the time. Carla Rice was then employed at the National Eating Disorder Information Centre and Karin Jasper was a feminist psychotherapist who went on to publish the children's book *Are You Too Fat, Ginny?* (1988) and, later, was co-editor of *Consuming Passions: Feminist Approaches to Weight Preoccupation and Eating Disorders* (1993).[71] This overlap between professional health work and activism has been a common feature of members of Canadian women's movements, which have tended to work cooperatively with the state and public institutions to achieve social change.[72] It suggests that Canadian fat activists had stronger links to feminist women's health activism than the American movement.[73] Hersize drew on the existing "cultural feminist infrastructure" to raise awareness about fat oppression at newsletters, events, and workshops, a method also used by LG5, MACSW, and the Fat Underground.[74]

By 1988 Hersize activism focused on three areas: a newsletter, lobbying Canadian media organizations, and media literacy for high school and university students. Available mailing lists show that about one hundred individuals and organizations subscribed to

Hersize newsletters.[75] Most went out to health centres like University of British Columbia Hospital Eating Disorder Clinic and the Oshawa Department of Health. Dieticians and mental health clinicians also appear on these lists, including Sandy Friedman of Maranda-Friedman.[76] Hersize's newsletters were similar to Fat Underground pamphlets. Research-based critiques of dieting were included alongside analysis of contemporary culture and policy. For example, in 1990 Carla Rice authored a piece on bariatric surgery. Citing research showing the surgeries had high mortality rates and limited effectiveness, Rice argues the surgeries remained popular because of "fat hatred": "Virtually all women in our culture are socialized to associate self-worth with appearance. We learn to shave, pain, pluck, camouflage, colour, curl, trim, tuck, diet and exercise before we begin to seek answers to other questions, like who we are and what we hope to do with our lives." Rice linked people's willingness to risk bariatric surgery with weight preoccupation.[77] In another article, Rice argued "fat phobia" in media representations instilled in women "deeply-rooted pictures about the nature of women," glamour, desire, and success.[78] Hersize brought new life to fat activism by linking weight preoccupation with feminist critiques of the health and the media.

Lobbying Canadian media organizations was another Hersize project. Like MediaWatch and other feminist groups, Hersize monitored magazines for demeaning images of women. Members brought objectionable ads to Hersize meetings. If everyone agreed a letter was drafted. A guide called "This Ad Offends Me! How to Write Letters of Complaint with Regard to the Objectionable Portrayal of Women in Advertising" was in Hersize's meeting minutes. The guide suggested groups write letters in a four-paragraph format: first, introducing the offending ad; second, stating the nature of the complaint; third, scolding the corporation or media organization for the sexist nature of the ad; and fourth, suggesting what kind of action needed to be taken.[79] A letter from Hersize to CBC Television critiqued a "Special K" cereal advertisement that aired on the network:

> The advertisement displays a very thin, scantily clad woman who eats "Special K" so that she "can't pinch an inch." The message implies that becoming thin is the sole reason for eating "Special K" cereal. This reinforces the popular belief that women must achieve thinness in order to be considered attractive and worthy. Furthermore, such advertising is psychologically and psychically damaging to women because it pressures them to diet and struggle to attain unhealthy and unnatural body sizes.

We believe that as manufacturers of a breakfast cereal product you could concentrate your efforts on boosting "Special K's" nutritional value and display some creative flair in your advertising. You may even capture a "large" and invisible market by promoting "Special K" as a good nutritious meal for people of various body sizes and shapes. Breakfast cereal is not considered a "diet" food, advertising it as such is only alienating potential non-dieting buyers and encouraging women to diet (and not eat your breakfast cereal).[80]

Hersize demanded body diversity long before "body positivity" became the focus of fat activism. Women, they argued, come in various body sizes and shapes, all of which should be considered attractive. Representing fantasy figures was potentially dangerous to women who tried to emulate these "unnatural" bodies. Hersize wanted advertisements to represent "real" women.

What might a real woman look like? Hersize members developed a slide show about "changing standards of beauty" to explain the concept to high school and university students. Paintings by Peter Paul Rubens (1577–1640) and images of voluptuous women like Marilyn Monroe were compared to contemporary advertising images of submissive and emaciated women.[81] Jean Kilbourne popularized this strategy – the technique of using advertisements to illustrate changing images of women. Her 1979 film *Killing Us Softly* (1979) showed that media images of women were becoming increasingly violent and pornographic.[82] Hersize showed Kilbourne's *Still Killing Us Softly* (1987) at their Exploding Media Myths workshop in 1989, along with their slide show (see figure 3).[83] Some scholars and activists have since revised their position on weight preoccupation because women have a variety of approaches to media images, and eating disorders have multiple causes.[84] In the late 1980s, however, the idea that media images were harmful resonated with many women. As an example, Naomi Wolf's *The Beauty Myth* (1990) was on Canadian bestseller lists for two years. Wolf argues that as many as 60 per cent of college-age American women were suffering or had suffered from eating disorders.[85] Ideals of slenderness were resulting in the "mass self-immolation by hunger" of a generation of American women.[86] Though their activities predated Wolf's book by three years, Hersize member Mary Francis Ellison (no relation to the author) recalled that the release of *The Beauty Myth* gave Hersize "more credibility" and resulted in "more requests for speaking engagements and more requests for media commentary."[87] Hersize tapped into a desire by their generation of women for a feminist analysis of popular culture and gave their audience a framework for understanding weight preoccupation.

Hersize: Weight Prejudice Action Group presents:

Exploding Media Myths:
women reclaiming the mirror

An exploration of how the media presents unrealistic images of women which do not reflect our diverse body sizes or individual identities. The media's definition of a healthy and desirable woman will be revealed and analysed through the presentation of the film "Still Killing Us Softly" as well as a brief slide show of advertisements compiled by the Hersize group. The presentation will be followed by a discussion and, for those who wish to participate, a workshop on personal and political action for reclaiming the diversity of our identities and redefining beauty.

October 24, 1989
• 7:00 pm -10:00 pm • Jewish Community Centre • 750 Spadina Road (Spadina & Bloor) • Free Admission • Phone: (416) 535-4653 • An Eating Disorder Awareness Week Event

Figure 3. Poster for Hersize's "Exploding Media Myths" event, 1989.

Further insight into the excitement Hersize generated is found in a letter written to the group following the Exploding Media Myths workshop. In a breathless outpouring, the author wrote,

It is one o'clock in the morning and I am too excited to sleep after attending the presentation by Hersize tonight ... It was incredible to be a part of the audience last night and to see with new eyes the shocking contempt our society has for the feminine aspect of human nature as well as the female body. What frightens me the most is that I have been "psychically numbed" to the insidious and poisonous pedagogy about women especially accepting these images without batting an eye. Just a few months ago I sneered at the "radical-feminists-without-a-sense-of-humour" who had stuck a sticker on a subway poster declaring that "this advertisement promotes hatred toward women." But after seeing "Still Killing us Softly" and your slide presentation I was overwhelmed with horror and grief ... what you are doing is so important there aren't words to describe it. I had such a feeling of (that well-worn word) empowerment tonight.[88]

The author had a change of heart about the "radical feminist" position on women. Hersize helped her to see that she had a personal stake in the issue of media images and it gave her a language to describe how she previously felt: "psychically numbed." The writer joked about the stereotype of feminists "without-a-sense-of-humour" and saw her own sense of "empowerment" as "well-worn." Her wariness about feminism was assuaged thanks to the workshop. Feminist activism can give "meaning" to the "lived experiences of women" by helping them to "negotiate the tensions between these experiences and the cultural and institutionalized discourses in which they are embedded," as Kathy Davis has noted.[89] Hersize helped this woman to see feminism differently and showed her that she was "psychically numbed" by social messages about body size. The media was an ideological force that had paralyzed women and negatively shaped her perception of her body.

Hersize took the concept of fat oppression in a different direction from their predecessors in the United States and Canada. Based on a continuum model, the group believed that all women experience some form of weight-based preoccupation. While fat women were more likely to experience stigma, all women suffered from the burden of trying to live up to feminine ideals. At the same time, Hersize's focus on beauty and bodily norms was an intellectual link between itself and other feminist iterations of fat activism, like LG5 and the feminist workshops discussed earlier in this chapter. The link was that femininity and body size shaped how women come to know and live in the world. These critiques of fat oppression and weight obsession/preoccupation were particularly timely, since they coincided with growing government and media interest in eating disorders, binge dieting, and plastic surgery, as well as the publication of *The Beauty Myth*. Hersize's activism, therefore, was emblematic of a moment when critiques of fat oppression met a more general concern about the impact of media images of women, and when public health officials began to take action on these issues. Public health responses to weight preoccupation will be discussed in chapter 4.

Silences

Canadian fat activism of 1977–97 tended to be premised on a universal understanding of women. "Women" were paralyzed by media images. "Women" felt the need to be slimmer. "Women" were oppressed by fat stigma. The media represented "women" negatively. After a few years of working on these issues, Hersize members began to ask themselves: Which women? Some members were troubled by the lack of ethnic diversity within the group.[90] A plan for a special issue of the newsletter about women of colour was shelved because members did not feel that they could adequately address the topic.[91] They tried to reach out to women of colour through an ad in their newsletter:

> **ATTENTION: WOMEN OF COLOUR**
> **HERSIZE** is interested in hearing about the experiences of weight and shape issues of women of colour. For some time the **HERSIZE** steering committee has been struggling to better understand the impact that fat prejudice might have on various groups of women. We would greatly value input from our readers on this subject. Please call or write to **HERSIZE**.[92]

Placed around 1990, this ad had no impact on the composition of Hersize. The possibility that media images were primarily a "white women's" issue left members of the group feeling uncertain. Some members felt they had been racist in failing to address the concerns of women of colour.

Around the same time, other activists and academics were engaged in a debate about universal definitions of woman.[93] Black feminists challenged the "racist and ethnocentric assumptions of white feminists" about families, work, and gender roles. It was not possible to understand gender oppression without also considering race, ethnicity, and class.[94] This debate within Hersize was never resolved and led to the eventual disbandment of the group after 1992.[95] Founding members Carla Rice and Karin Jasper continued to grapple with body image and weight obsession through their ongoing work in women's health programs and in the academy.

Almost all Canadian fat activists discussed in this book were silent on matters of race, and most also failed to consider the role that social class, language, or ability might play in a person's experience of fatness. Part of this was because of the focus of these groups on fatness itself. Activists did not consider the complex ways being fat could intersect with other experiences. Of this period of activism in the United States, activist Judith Stein admitted that people were "not talking about class a whole lot" because fat liberation was the focus of their discussions.[96] The tendency to universalize and essentialize the "experience" was also seen in the women's movement in Canada and the US at this time. By the 1980s, black women, Latinas, and other women of non-white ancestry condemned feminists for speaking "only about middle-class white women's experience."[97] The women's movement, critics charged, had failed to acknowledge that "major systems of oppression are interlocking."[98]

Lack of diversity has continued to be a concern for fat activism. Charlotte Cooper argues the contemporary movement appeals mostly to white women because of its focus on consumption and challenging the obesity epidemic. Access to clothing and promoting "health at every size" are white women's issues and do not challenge power inequalities. Fat activism must align itself with other marginalized groups to regain its true momentum.[99] Consumption and obesity stigma are more complex than Cooper renders them here, but her analysis is otherwise relevant to Canada. Historically, fat activism in Canada has lacked diversity and has not considered the ethnic, regional, and class dimensions of being fat.

In Canada, Indigenous people have had the highest rates of obesity and diabetes, but they were not addressed in fat activism of the 1980s or 1990s.[100] Indigenous issues continue to be marginalized within fat activism even though a searing scholarly critique about obesity and racism has emerged in the ensuing decades. Jennifer Poudrier has shown that this problem is often attributed to a so-called "thrifty gene" that allowed hunter-gatherer people to store body fat and survive through periods of famine. The theory, which has never been proven, is that Indigenous people have a *genetic* predisposition to obesity because their bodies evolved to store fat.[101] Poudrier found that Indigenous people are seen as the "embodiment of deleterious genes."[102] Indigenous people were and are seen as "primitive" in the medical literature. The focus on genetic aspects of obesity "diverts attention from other basic health requirements like food security, employment and safe environments."[103] Dr Barry Lavallee also argues that socio-economic status and trauma are at the root of Indigenous obesity and diabetes rates. Lavallee suggests that Canada's "universal healthcare system" assumes patients have the money to pay for dieticians or gym memberships, which is not realistic for many Indigenous people.[104] Though focusing on medical care, Lavallee's example is a reminder that race and class are factors in whether and how people can "fight" fat stigma.

Many of the women interviewed for this book understood where my questions were leading when I asked about the demographics of their organizations. In response some noted that there was one (or two) non-white woman in the group.[105] Yet only two of my research participants identified as Indigenous and one as African Canadian. These women, Jessica Carter, Pat Donaldson, and Julie Levasseur, all suggested that fatness had different meanings in different communities. Such differences were not articulated in any of my documentary research, but each of these women identified their experiences as somewhat distinct from those of other Canadian fat activists.

Carter, who is African Canadian, felt that she had had more positive fat role models than other women she met. Carter felt that in black families "fullness is ... a sign of beauty." She also saw herself "in what Black men consider to be attractive." Carter felt this difference was reflected in and perpetuated by media images of women. Television shows of the 1980s and 1990s directed at white women featured "really, really, really skinny women," whereas shows featuring black people "like the Cosby Show and New York Undercover" frequently featured "fuller figured women." Carter did not deny the existence of oppressive beauty standards, rather she noted that "the size issue is not oppressive" for black women.[106] Carter's experience reflects a broader debate about black women and body size. While some scholars maintain that black women in the US and Canada do not experience fat oppression in the same way as white women, others argue that it is an oversimplification to claim that fat black women are less oppressed than their white counterparts. In "Fat Is a Black Woman's Issue," Retha Powers argues that black women are subject to the same cultural messages about slenderness as other women.[107] Tamara Beaubeouf-Lafontant further suggests that the image of the happy, fat, black woman is a continuation of the stereotype of maternal, de-sexualized "mammy" figures in US history.[108]

The question of parallel beauty standards also came up in interviews with Indigenous women. Julie Levasseur echoed Carter's point that white women were subject to a different kind of pressure than other social groups. She believed that "more commercial pressure comes down" on white women rather than "Aboriginal women who tend to be poorer," but Levasseur noted that Indigenous women were not exempt from pressure to be thin. She observed that among her mother's generation there were differences between women who claimed an Indigenous identity and those who moved towards a European identity. Where her aunts who married white men "tended to be focused on how they looked and their makeup and their fashion," her mother had "married an Indian" and was not expected to be interested in beauty culture.[109] Pat Donaldson similarly noted a difference between her childhood growing up in the bush and her later experiences with beauty culture: "Out in the bush you're not thinking about whether or not you're beautiful," whereas once she was in a high school with non-Indigenous students she started to think more about her physical appearance.[110]

Research suggests that Indigenous girls and women have felt pressure to look more conventionally feminine when living in urban centres, as Donaldson described.[111] Scholars have also identified the stereotypical ways in which Indigenous and white women have been represented by and to white people.[112] There is still more to learn from Indigenous and non-white women about their histories of beauty and body cultures. Carter, Donaldson, and Levasseur cannot speak for all non-white women. Their observations do, however, reveal gaps and silences within fat activism.[113] Silences in the historical record also serve as a reminder that experiential knowledge must be understood as one truth among larger social and cultural currents about fatness. As Lorraine Code has argued, "knowledge, truth, or even 'reality' can be understood only in relation to particular sets of cultural or social circumstances."[114]

Performing Fatness: Pretty Porky and Pissed Off

Ideological differences between fat activists echoed shifts in feminist theory and practice. Activists wove feminist critiques together with the idea that it was okay to be fat, developing the concepts of fat oppression, weight obsession, and weight preoccupation to describe their experiences. The concepts were not interchangeable, but they did share epistemological and material origins in American fat activism of the 1970s. Differences that in the contemporary context might seem minor mattered very much in early conversations about fatness, lesbianism, media images, and self-esteem among activists of earlier decades.

In the 1990s fat activist critiques continued to evolve. Fat activism took on "a more mutinous tone than the earlier generation's lamentations about social prejudice," as Laura Kipnis has observed.[115] Influenced by Judith Butler's notion of "performativity," fat activism of the 1990s challenged the idea that people have a fixed identity (as woman, man, gay, straight). Fatness, like gender, was a construct – it was "something made up."[116]

Toronto's Pretty Porky and Pissed Off (PPPO, c. 1996–2005) reclaimed and redeployed stereotypes to challenge the idea that being fat was and is grotesque and undesirable.[117] The group's first demonstration took place in June 1996 on Toronto's Queen Street West. PPPO members "wore tight-fitting crazy outfits, rock-star-diva wear, loud prints, hot pink polyester dresses, and feather boas."[118] They handed out leaflets (see figure 4) to passers-by that read:

> **We're tired of bursting at the seams.** Binding waists, bursting buttons and slim pickins are getting us down ... the average north american woman is size 14 and UP. Most stores don't carry these sizes. Us plumped-up ladies are fed up with clothes that don't fit and feel bad. Being fat doesn't have to mean feeling gross.[119]

PPPO's goal was to link fat oppression to capitalism and patriarchal standards of beauty, but their tone was different than activists of earlier generations.[120] They did not seek acknowledgment of fat oppression but took for granted that it existed. They did not try to create networks of support and safety for fat women; instead, they focused their critique on society. Both playful and combative, PPPO challenged the marginalization of fat women in the fashion industry. The group reclaimed put-downs and stereotypes about fat women like "porky" and "plump" and used them to challenge stereotypes. A memorable action detailed by PPPO member Allyson Mitchell was termed "fat drag": four members walked on stage and placed a cake on a chair. Each performed a solo dance on stage that emphasized their most prominently fat body feature (thighs, bums, stomachs). At the end of the performance the group "slowly and teasingly lowered" themselves "on the cakes and smushed them with" their "big fat butts," after which they "all stood up, swiped a fingerful of cake from ... soiled leotards, and coyly offered a taste to the audience."[121] PPPO challenged expectations about the ways in which fat women moved, using their physicality to confront, entertain, and provoke audiences.

PPPO refocused attention on fat oppression and named fatness as a feminist issue after a decade of feminist activism focused on eating disorders and weight preoccupation/obsession.[122] The group's fat focus was prescient, however, because they emerged just prior to the World Health Organization's 1997 declaration of a "global obesity epidemic." PPPO bridged the period between older feminist activism and newer debates about health. Though their activism focused on sexuality and fashion, by 2001 they were being asked to answer questions about health. A 2001 *Globe and Mail* op-ed lambasted PPPO's approach. Leah McLaren scoffed at Allyson Mitchell's critique of health, citing alarming

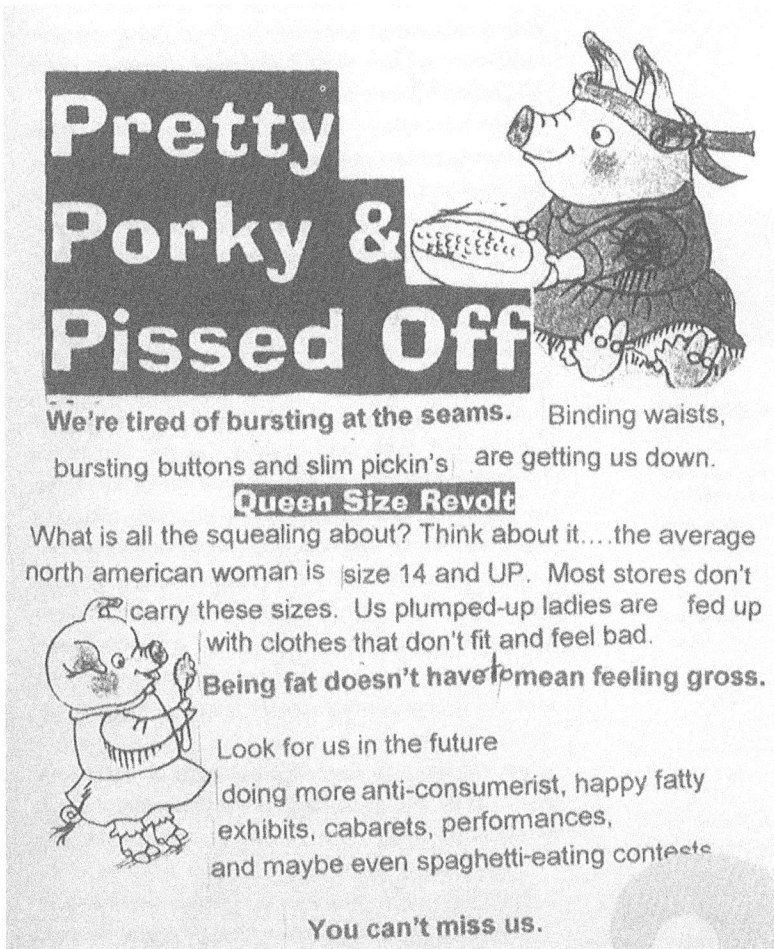

Figure 4. Flyer for "Queen Sized Revolt" by Pretty Porky and Pissed Off, c. 1996. Courtesy of Allyson Mitchell.

data about health consequences of obesity. McLaren conceded that eating disorders are a problem but said they were less dangerous than promoting obesity. It is absurd to suggest PPPO or any fat activist group were encouraging people to gain weight. They were not. McLaren nonetheless concluded that "the women in Pretty, Porky, and Pissed Off could be just as pretty, and a lot less pissed off" if they just "tended to their problem."[123] "Health" trumped feminist concerns about body image in McLaren's piece, which demonstrated how the discourse on weight was shifting in the 2000s.[124] At the same time, McLaren's story displayed cultural continuity – her reviews reflected long-standing cultural assumptions about being fat.

Conclusions

Feminist fat activism was both a response to and part of the feminist movement. Feminist debates of the 1970s and 1990s were woven through the fabric of fat activism during this time. Each group had a different take on, and way of, being fat. But all groups were building on feminist critiques of femininity and weight. This was true of LG5, who engaged with both American fat activism and Monique Wittig's work that argued fat oppression was a form of class warfare against women. Workshops inspired by FIFI took up Susie Orbach's idea that women's weight was linked to their marginalization in Western societies, and participants used that knowledge to enact personal change. Weight obsession groups married these concepts to women's health movement concerns about eating disorders and the impact of media images. While farthest from earlier debates about identity, PPPO used performance art to challenge gender and sexual norms.

Whether liberal or radical, looking inward or outward, the women discussed in this chapter wanted to find ways to think and talk about fat as a feminist issue. When they could not find resources or sympathy within existing women's organizations, they chose to establish new groups where they could comfortably explore the personal dimensions of being fat and female. Activists were grappling with the relationship between gender and fatness, and they were also pushing at the boundaries of the women's movement in this time period.

Coming together as fat women was productive. New groups formed and fat activists also expanded awareness of fat oppression in feminist groups. They introduced concepts of fat oppression, weight obsession, and weight preoccupation into the movement. When other women were not responsive to these ideas, they formed new groups. Fat activism likewise expanded over time. Ideas discovered in early texts of the movement – like FIFI and Shadow on a Tightrope – were rearticulated by Canadian women. Canadian fat activists never just appropriated earlier fat epistemologies. Ideas "travelled," as Kathy Davis has described the evolution of feminist ideas across time and space.[125] Canadian fat activists took from earlier texts the ideas that were most useful to them. Activists also changed or added information to adapt feminist and fat epistemologies to their circumstances. "Fat is a feminist issue" describes not just a book but also a variety of activisms and ways of thinking about being fat.

2 Between Women: Fat Acceptance Organizations

Kate Partridge, Joan Dal Santo, and Janet Walker were among twenty women who attended The Forgotten Woman: For Fat Women Only workshop in 1979. Cold Mountain Institute, where the workshop took place, offered weekend therapy groups. It was located on Cortes Island, which was two ferry rides and a long car drive north from their homes in Vancouver, British Columbia. The event was advertised as:

> An intense experiential exploration of our relationship to our body size and shape. In an effort to get at *forgotten*, unknown or unexplored material in relation to our weight, we will be on a juice fast, use journals and dream material and appropriate therapeutic techniques.
>
> This program is suitable for anyone who considers herself overweight, but may be of most use to those who are considered by others to be overweight. Medical permission required. Fee: $250.[1]

Dal Santo and Walker admitted in 2005 interviews that prior to their meeting they had avoided friendships with other fat women. The idea for The Forgotten Woman came out of a conversation between Dal Santo and her therapist, an instructor at Cold Mountain. Having reached a plateau in her therapy, the recently divorced Dal Santo told her therapist that she felt it was time to work on the fact that she was fat and "seemed to be stuck with it."[2] Partridge, at the time a PhD candidate in psychology at Simon Fraser University, felt it was time to deal with "the whole self-image thing."[3] Janet Walker was also recently divorced and a mother of two. Her therapists paid Walker's workshop fees because they so strongly believed she should attend. Walker was uncertain about leaving her children with a babysitter but felt that she "had to go. It was sort of like life and death, it was really important."[4] All three women described themselves as having been fat their entire lives.

Participants in The Forgotten Woman were encouraged to explore their feelings about fatness in general, as well as about their bodies, in the five-day workshop. One visualization exercise began with each woman lying on the floor, fully clothed. They were instructed to "feel and care" about each part of their bodies and encouraged to "pay extra attention" to parts of their body they did not like. Another activity asked participants to "get into their bodies" and dance freely around the room.[5] This exercise was described in a 1980 *Chatelaine* article about the retreat. Dal Santo recalled this experience positively in a 2005 interview, noting "I just remember us dancing freely and enjoying the movement in our bodies, which is something that I think a lot of us, me for sure, and I think others too, didn't do often."[6] Dal Santo also felt validated by her interactions with other women. Each woman went to the workshop intending to think about herself as an individual: Why was she fat and what should she do about it? But they came out of the event believing the answers to these questions could be found in conversation with other fat women.

Kate Partridge enjoyed the workshop but starting feeling discouraged about her weight a few weeks after she returned to Vancouver. The workshop did not fix the problems she had finding clothes and exercise opportunities in Vancouver. Partridge wanted to see if other fat women were interested in tackling these issues together. In spring 1981, she contacted the fashion editor of the *Vancouver Sun* to do a story on the dearth of fashion choices for plus-size women. Readers were encouraged to contact Partridge if they were interested in doing something about it. So much interest was generated from the story that Partridge called a public meeting at a local community centre. Fifty women attended the gathering.[7]

Partridge outlined her understanding of the problems facing large women at this meeting. She talked about feeling stigmatized, the lack of fashionable clothing over size 14, feeling self-conscious about exercise, job discrimination, and low self-esteem.[8] In a 2005 interview Partridge remembered feeling that "just to stand up there and say, I'm Kate, I'm fat, I'm okay and so are you" was very powerful.[9] Many women in attendance agreed. They formed Large as Life (LAL), an "action group" for fat women. The group's mandate was outlined in their first newsletter:

> Our bodies need and deserve a moderate food intake and regular exercise. In order to do these things, we must learn to accept, respect and value our bodies because of their size. And we must remember that even though we are large, we can be healthy and we can be beautiful.

We can no longer allow ourselves to feel like, or be treated as, second-class citizens just because we come in large sizes. Each one of us is a valuable person who deserves the freedom to express and be herself. It is the goal of Large as Life to help create this freedom, and we can only do it by working together.[10]

LAL was for women who wanted to work together to improve their self-esteem and opportunities. LAL's focus on femininity and fashion was not explicitly feminist, but their approach to empowerment was based on models from the women's movement.

Parallel to the fat feminist activism discussed in chapter 1, LAL and other groups began meeting in living rooms and community centres to talk about being fat. Participants in these groups directed their analyses toward everyday life. Perhaps they would be happier if they could find ways to accept that they were fat, and this fact was unlikely to change? New forms of fat activism developed out of these conversations. These "fat acceptance" groups believed that fat women would be happier if they had places to exercise, dance, shop, and socialize. Fat acceptance groups were different from fat feminist activisms. Challenging gender and social norms was not the sole focus. Instead, pleasure, sociality, and comfort were the goals. Members of these groups applied fat activism to everyday problems like finding clothing that fit and identifying safe spaces to talk and exercise. In the process, they extended the breadth and scope of fat activism.

Numerically, and in terms of its scope and impact, LAL was the most popular fat activist group of any kind in the 1980s. Active for four years, Large as Life inspired a number of other social and commercial ventures centred on swimming, exercise, and fashion. Not all acceptance activism in Canada can be traced to Large as Life, however. This chapter also documents the work of co-ed fat acceptance groups and Big Dance, a dance class and company for fat women.

Fat acceptance groups shared the same general principle as feminist fat activist groups, which was that it was okay to be fat. The difference between fat feminist activism and fat acceptance lay in the ways that groups put their knowledge into practice. Women working towards fat acceptance did not think they needed theory or ideology to explain what they experienced to be true: women faced greater marginalization and social exclusion for being fat. Fat acceptance organizations were not a repudiation of the idea that fat was a feminist issue. For most groups this detail was a given because members had experienced sexism and social exclusion based of their body size. Nor did all members of these groups identify as activists. But fat acceptance groups were feminist,

Table 3. Fat acceptance activism in Canada, 1981–present

Years	Name	Location
1981–5	Large as Life Vancouver	Vancouver, BC
1983–5	Large as Life Calgary	Calgary, AB
1984–2012	Suzanne Bell's Fitness and Fashion	Vancouver, BC
1985–present	Mrs O's Swimming Group	Burnaby, BC
1989–95	NAAFA/CASA Canada	National
1992–c. 2006	Big Dance	Victoria, BC
1997–9	Large as Life London	London, ON

activist, and political: they formed communities, they made fatness more visible and acceptable (for members and the public), and they challenged feminist norms.

Like fat feminist activism, fat acceptance groups were a trajectory of feminist movements of the 1970s, 1980s, and 1990s. Gender mattered very much to fat acceptance groups, even if they did not explicitly define themselves as feminist. The groups examined in this chapter fit well with Kathy Davis's description of the women's groups that translated *Our Bodies, Ourselves*: they were "deliberately and strategically interpreting" their shared experiences and "actively pursuing potentially empowering courses of action" based on their subjective experiences.[11] Fat acceptance groups reveal that many women used feminist concepts to help understand the "cultural and institutionalized discourses in which they" were "embedded."[12]

Large as Life: Start Living Now!

During its four-year lifespan, Large as Life Vancouver had about one hundred active members and a newsletter that reached five hundred people. Branches of the group later launched in Calgary, Alberta (1983–5), and London, Ontario (1997–9). LAL also spawned Suzanne Bell's fitness studio and clothing store and "Mrs O's," a group that still meets weekly to swim. Former members preserved most of the existing documentary resources of this period, including the group's newsletter, the *Bolster*, as well as pamphlets and photographs. Meetings, open to members and potential members, were held monthly (except in July and August) between September 1981 and April 1985. Newsletters and interviews with former participants indicate that about fifteen women attended each meeting.[13]

Joan Dal Santo and Janet Walker joined Kate Partridge in LAL. When asked if there was anything distinctive about the women in attendance at the first LAL meeting, Dal Santo remembered: "It wasn't just a bunch of educated middle-class women, it wasn't a bunch of intellectuals, it wasn't anything. It was a whole cross-section of people, housewives, and business people, women feeling, I think they all felt that they were forgotten, that they were put down, that they were not cared for in society in any way, not valued."[14] Although virtually all of the women who joined LAL had at some point felt stigmatized by their weight, they saw in each other intelligence, style, and potential. Walker remembered that there was "an aliveness that you didn't associate with fat at the time" at the first LAL meeting.[15] Evelyn Booth, who read the newspaper article about fashion and called Partridge, said that she had never been in a roomful of large women prior to the June 1981 meeting. She recalled being "impressed" by the number of women in attendance: "I was pleased that there were so many women who were rebellious. That in itself powered me up. It was like da da da daaaaa, Joan of Arc."[16] Booth used the metaphor "coming out of the closet" to describe what it was like to join a group of fat women talking about being large.[17] (See figure 5.)

Booth's commentary echoes the work of Eve Kosofsky Sedgwick, a feminist scholar who has drawn parallels between fatness and homosexuality. Though "coming out" has different connotations for homosexuality, which is invisible, than fatness, which is highly visible, Sedgwick maintains there are similarities.[18] She argues that the metaphor of "coming out" resonates with fat women because their identities are "still so ... coarse and demeaning as to challenge recognition" by other people.[19] Sedgwick argues that fat women were likely to be rejected or subject to humiliation because of their choice to identify as, and accept, their fatness. What Booth described went beyond Sedgwick's understanding of "coming out" as a revelation to friends or family members, however. In this case "coming out" was also an acknowledgment to oneself: I am fat. What now?

Studies of contemporary activists have examined the impact of "coming out" as fat. Activist and scholar Samantha Murray "came out" after discovering the existence of the movement. She saw her declaration of fat pride as a way to challenge "the assumptions made about fatness are that the fat person is slothful, lazy, weak-willed, unreliable, unclean, unhealthy, deviant, and defiant."[20] The aftermath was, for Murray, disappointing. She found the focus on fat pride very limiting.[21] Even though Murray had decided to think differently about her body, she felt that her body was still seen negatively by others.[22] Charlotte Cooper echoes Murray's critique, suggesting that body positivity is easily appropriated by commercial forces and lacks a political edge.[23]

THE REAL THING - snapped by Suzanne Bell.

Members of the
1982/83 Board:

(from left to
right)
Jacquie Kernick
Joan Dal Santo
Joanne Rosenbaum
Heather Morgan
Ingrid Laue

(in front)
Evelyn Booth

Missing:
Suzanne Bell
Laura Thaw

**LARGE
AT
LARGE**

President*

Treasurer*

Membership Secretary*

Recording Secretary*

Corresp. Secretary

*running again for a position on the LAL Board.

26 BOLSTER

It all began with the Non-Profit Organization Large-as-Life

Figure 5. Large as Life executive team, 1982–3. Suzanne Bell mounted this page in a photo album to document her time with the group. Courtesy of Suzanne Bell.

Women interviewed for this book felt differently. Decades later, they remembered their participation in fat-centred groups positively. It was an important first step in their life-long efforts to accept being fat.

LAL was active thirty years prior to the approaches Murray and Cooper describe, but it stands as a counterpoint to critics who see acceptance as a superficial model of activism. LAL was productive. Fat women educated themselves about fitness, fashion, business, and health. Members organized social events and developed services for fat women, providing safe spaces for personal empowerment. Even if participants did not call themselves feminist or critique larger social structures, they politicized their everyday lives. In the early 1980s, in the earliest years of the movement, groups like LAL forged a new path for women. Contextualizing these decisions historically allows us to see them differently, as part of a variety of activisms that allowed women to challenge gender norms.

LAL's mandate emphasized activities and action, which was a different approach to fat oppression than fat feminist organizations. Their mission statement, honed for the second issue of their newsletter, read that LAL is "seeking to help large women increase self-acceptance, personal strength, and skills. In practical terms, this means improving the availability to large women of needed goods and services, and specialized fitness classes ... LARGE AS LIFE is an action group; members are encouraged to become actively involved in the group's projects which are designed to promote our aims."[24] Members had different feelings about whether the group was feminist. In interviews conducted between 2005 and 2008, some described LAL as a feminist organization,[25] while others refused to identify it as feminist.[26] Still others referred to it as an organization that promoted "gentle enlightenment" but not the "boot stomping stuff,"[27] because they believed that feminism had a negative connotation for the general membership of LAL.

A June 1982 letter to the editor in their newsletter, the *Bolster*, helps to illuminate the group's approach to feminism. LAL member J. Rowntree wrote a letter to the editor asking the incoming LAL Board to stay away from politically oriented activism: "I'm glad to be a member of LAL which I think has the great potential of inspiring positive thinking, greater self-esteem, and an interest in fitness. I feel that by each individual gaining in these areas, others around us will most definitely notice the change over. I do draw the line at our becoming a strident, self-interested political pressure group or dabbling into changes in the human rights code ... Please keep things simple – no politics."[28] Rowntree wrote in response to a newsletter profile where two board members, Laura Thaw and Suzanne Bell, expressed support for fat rights.[29] Thaw responded to Rowntree in a follow-up article. She argued that whatever fat women did was political because "the mere fact of" their "size is a political statement ... as members of what I consider to be an oppressed minority, circumstances have made that choice for us." Political activism, Thaw continued, begins "with ourselves. We must create greater self-esteem and self-acceptance within ourselves ... the next level would be to 'share ourselves' with other large women, those as yet unable or unwilling to join LAL."[30]

"Politics" were explicitly and inexplicitly equated with feminism. Rowntree's use of the term "strident" and her plea for LAL to "keep it simple" echo media discourse on feminism from the 1970s. In the 1970s the Canadian and American press negatively compared "strident" and "militant" women to their more "feminine" counterparts.[31] This dichotomization may be one of the reasons some LAL members made a distinction between "practical" and "politics." The fact that fat women needed and wanted an action group was in itself political, as Rowntree noted. Looking at their message in the context of 1980s women's movements shows that the group was trying to negotiate around feminism and develop an approach that appealed to a cross section of women.

Where LAL faltered was not in their choice of activities but in a lack of discussion about different ways to be fat. Like fat feminist organizations and most social movement organizations, group members seemed to assume that all fat women were concerned with the same issues: self-esteem, fashion, and fitness. Early on, a reader wrote to the *Bolster* about sexuality: "Some of our members may be homosexual: will they be accepted here no matter what sexual preference the rest of us may have?" The group responded *"LARGE AS LIFE* is an organization without religious, racial or sexual bias."[32] Ingrid Laue, editor of the *Bolster* at this time, noted that lesbians "wouldn't have a sign on their chest saying I'm a lesbian, but we knew, we knew ... It wasn't anything we objected to or found in any way odd ... this [British Columbia] is lotus land."[33] Partridge said she wanted to appeal to "ordinary, middle of the road women," reflecting her personal concerns.[34] Other feminist organizations of the 1980s also tried to ignore or limit discussion of sexuality and race because of fear of how it might impact the movement. LAL was no different. Their activism was meaningful to the mostly white, heterosexual women they served, and they did not consider that "ordinary" was a privileged category.

LAL's strength was to provide a safe space and platform to women who felt marginalized and had the ability to challenge fat oppression. Early meetings were similar to feminist consciousness-raising groups of the 1960s and 1970s. Members came to "uncover their oppression by speaking their experiences."[35] As in CR groups, LAL members sought each other out and succeeded in turning "what had previously been seen as individual idiosyncrasies into commonalities."[36] At meetings members shared stories about their failed attempts at dieting, negative experiences with doctors, and frustrations about dating, among other things. Discussing the group's mandate in an early edition of the *Bolster*, Joan Dal Santo said that LAL could play a role in "responding to and dealing with put-downs" of large women.[37] Dal Santo believed that members had a responsibility to each other to take action when someone or something "robs us of our dignity."[38]

The *Bolster* was a significant part of LAL's activism. It had a circulation of five hundred in September 1982, extending the impact of the group well beyond in-person meetings.[39] It featured articles by LAL members, editorials, press clippings, solicited advertisements from local retailers, and "clip art." The clip art was actually stock images of women that editor Ingrid Laue enlarged with her own pen (see figure 6).[40] The *Bolster* shows that LAL members were critically engaging with fat oppression. Early on there were a few rights-related topics like "How to Get the Job You Want in Spite of Fat Phobia on the Job Market"[41] and "Do Fat People Have Rights with Jane McBee," a British Columbia Human Rights Officer.[42] Eventually, though, group members focused on politicizing fashion and exercise, providing alternative sources for both to their readers.

LAL's most significant growth happened after Kate Partridge was featured in *Canadian Living* in summer 1982. Partridge modelled clothing by Penningtons, Addition Elle, and LAL member Jan Mindlin in this article (see figure 7). LAL also advertised a contest with the magazine: women who filled out a survey on the fashion needs of large women were eligible for a $500 shopping spree at Addition Elle.[43] Over 3000 women submitted surveys, which, unfortunately, have been destroyed.[44] In response to the article LAL also received about 350 letters from all over Canada.[45] Letters published in the newsletter were from women living in smaller cities. Writers expressed support for LAL and joy that a group was addressing the lack of clothing options for fat women. Anne Leslie of Riverview, New Brunswick, wrote that she was "most interested in the Large as Life Association and whole-heartedly agree with you that many women promise to look after themselves 'after' they have lost weight ... I like myself as a human being ... I wish there was clothing available that would help me reflect those feelings."[46] Nancy Kaizer of Middleton, Nova Scotia, also mused, "perhaps it is time to get on with my life." Kaizer told LALers, "I consider this the first step, actually admitting to a stranger that I am big."[47] Shannon

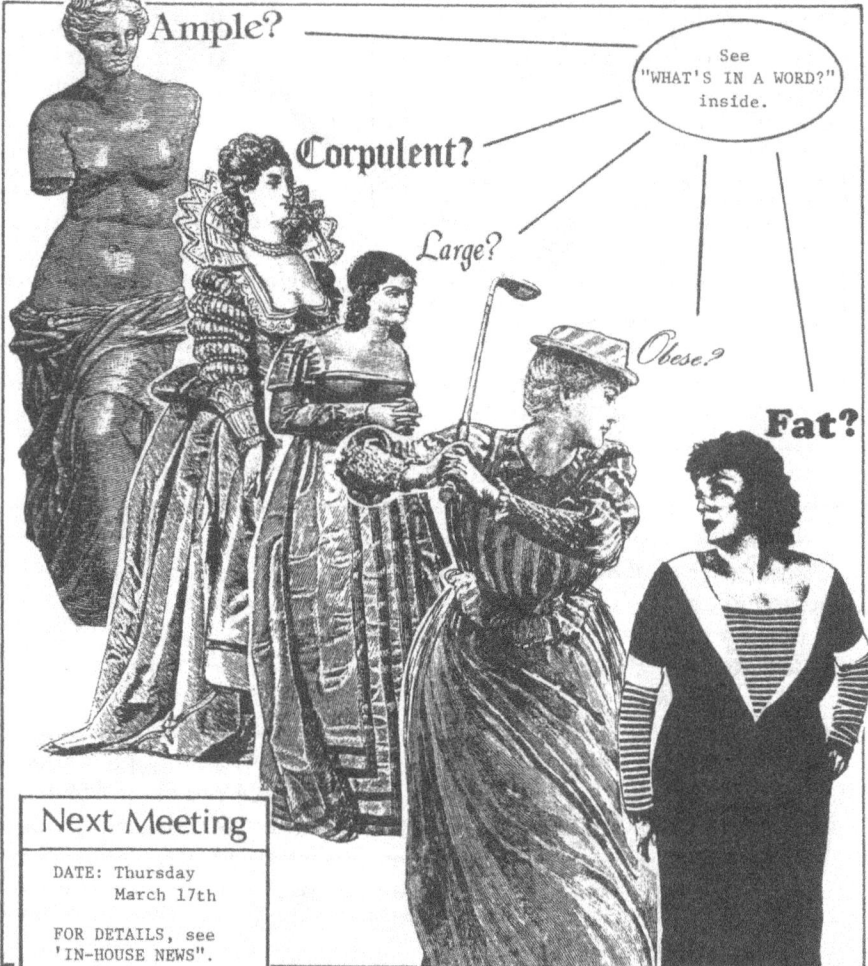

Figure 6. Cover of the March 1983 issue of the *Bolster*. Editor Ingrid Laue cut and pasted these images from other sources, enlarging the figures by hand when she felt they needed to be more curvy. Canadian Women's Movement Archives, HQ 1459 B7 B64. Courtesy of Suzanne Bell.

Figure 7. Kate Partridge wearing Jan Mindlin designs in *Canadian Living*, August 1982. Photo by John Stephens.

Andrew of Grande Prairie, Alberta, similarly wrote that the article was a "heart-warming experience" for her because she realized "others share my most personal yet most obvious problem."[48]

Even this small sampling shows that the *Canadian Living* article struck a chord with women across Canada, providing a glimpse into the dialogue that the idea of fat acceptance inspired. As Valerie Korinek has shown with *Chatelaine* in the 1960s and 1970s, seemingly passive mediums of communication like magazines engage women and inspire action. LAL's public actions spoke to readers who felt marginalized by their body size. Such "click" moments were an important part of the growth of women's movements at the end of the twentieth century.[49]

LAL membership and the *Bolster's* circulation numbers peaked in 1982 in the months after the *Canadian Living* profile. By 1983 the original members began to burn out, a common challenge for social movement organizations.[50] Kate Partridge moved to Calgary and Ingrid Laue resigned her position as editor of the *Bolster* in May 1983. Suzanne Bell and Joan Dal Santo remained until the spring of 1984 and then moved on to other endeavours. Both women felt burdened by the challenges of motivating other women to continue LAL's activism.[51] In May of 1984 Claudia Savage assumed the presidency of LAL and the group shifted direction. Philosophically, Savage did not believe in depending on a group to "direct your life" and saw LAL as more of a social outlet for women to talk about being fat than an activist group that organized public events like fashion shows.[52] Older members, like Janet Walker, left LAL around this time. By the fall of 1984 the *Bolster* folded, and membership was waning.[53] Until early 1985 members continued to meet in each other's apartments.[54]

Two other LAL chapters formed after Vancouver. Kate Partridge established chapters when she moved to Calgary, Alberta, in 1983 and London, Ontario, in 1997. In these cities, Partridge did not change the formula that worked in Vancouver. LAL Calgary offered personal development seminars and fitness classes through the Calgary Board of Education.[55] In London, LAL held regular meetings and launched a successful fitness program.[56] Partridge told me in 2005 that she sometimes felt ambivalent about being the leader of these groups. She didn't like being a "professional fat lady" or using her body size as the lens through which she saw her life. She felt there was much more to her "self" than her fatness.[57] For Partridge it was sometimes difficult to feel empowered in the face of fat oppression.

In spite of these struggles, there is evidence that LAL resonated with women for a long time after the groups disbanded. LAL inspired entrepreneurship and career choices of women during and after the life of the group. Suzanne Bell opened her own fitness centre and clothing store in Vancouver in 1985 and retired in 2010. Evelyn Booth operated Models Rubenesque, a modelling school and agency for fat women, until 1989.[58] Sandra Friedman, co-organizer of "Facing Your Fat" workshops with Doris Maranda, was also a Large as Life member and later a subscriber to the Hersize mailing list. Friedman continues to focus her practice on women's weight and food issues and is the author of *When Girls Feel Fat: Helping Girls Through Adolescence* (1997).[59]

A swimming group that branched off from LAL still meets regularly, evidence of the resilience of fat acceptance. Women who attend the swim refer to the group as Mrs O's. The title invokes the name of Jacqueline Kennedy Onassis; members pay for private pool time and they liken this luxury to the lifestyle of the famous millionaire widow. Attendance was and is completely voluntary and the group's time in the pool is unstructured. Over the years the group advertised in Suzanne Bell's clothing store's newsletter as well as in posters around Burnaby and New Westminster, British Columbia.[60] While Mrs O's began as a LAL activity, members of the group do not see it as a continuation of the group. Former LAL president Claudia Savage became the de facto leader of Mrs O's and was again wary of pushing for social change. The appeal of swimming was "the fact that maybe I have new friends and things to do and places to go and people to go with."[61]

Members of Mrs O's interviewed for this book did not feel that participating in a swimming club for fat women was political or feminist.[62] In a 1998 letter to *Radiance* magazine, Savage described the group as one that had helped her to accept herself so that she "seldom" thinks about her size.[63] The idea that Mrs O's is a neutral space where size does not matter seemed important to members when I attended one of their Saturday morning swims in 2006. Fifteen members were in attendance when I visited. Some women spent the hour swimming laps in one section of the pool. Smaller groups of women floated or treaded water in other parts of the pool. My presence seemed to spark a lot of discussion on size issues that the three long-time members interviewed said was not the norm. In interviews, two long-time members, Lynne Grauer and Lois Smith, said that size did not come up unless someone had had an "incident" involving body size, meaning they had been shamed about their weight.[64] Smith acknowledged that the premise of the group was that it was more welcoming to swim with women with larger bodies, but talking about weight was "not the purpose of the place."[65] Grauer felt that it was not necessary for members to talk about being fat because everyone already knew what that meant.[66]

Mrs O's members claimed that a group of women who met because they were fat but didn't ever talk about being fat was puzzling. Former members told anecdotes about *other* women's experiences of fat oppression but said it was not a problem they often experienced. For example, Smith said that some members of the group "always change in the little cubicles."[67] Savage confirmed that some women prefer to "hide" their bodies from other members.[68] Smith and Savage both said that they had no problem being naked in front of other members. Smith felt safe within the group but admitted that she would find being publicly associated with Mrs O's embarrassing: "Maybe embarrassing, a little embarrassing ... I guess I like the people in Mrs O's and I like to be associated with it, also. I don't particularly want to go into a group where the only reason for being there is because we are all overweight and you want to tell the world that you can't discriminate against it ... I don't feel discriminated against, particularly. So, I don't feel I have to join that fight."[69] The evasive responses of group members may have been a reaction to my questions about whether they saw the group as feminist. Or, they may reflect ambivalence about being fat. Members made it clear in our 2006 interviews that they did not see themselves as fighters or nonconformist.

Grauer, Smith, and Savage said that Mrs O's was about pleasure and friendship. Mrs O's gave Smith "the pleasure of being in the water and being able to do what you like."[70] Savage described swimming as a "delicious activity ... not an exercise ... a joy."[71] Grauer's attachment to the group was tied to the ups and downs of her life and her body. She first joined after giving birth to her second child. Being around people who were large "was good," but what she really enjoyed was an escape from isolation as a stay-at-home mom. Twenty years later Grauer considered herself slim, but leaving the group was unthinkable. She said, "I've gone for so long. I've built all of these relationships, even if I was really skinny there are women that I like ... it's not like a program where you finally graduate." Size fell into the background as members of Mrs O's helped each other along, through family and personal illness. "Of course," Grauer remembered of a friend from Mrs O's who had recently died of cancer, "I know she was big. But, I always just thought of her as, like, a person."[72] Like Kate Partridge, Grauer did not like using fat as the lens to understand personal experiences.

The repudiation of feminism by some members of LAL and Mrs O's was evident in other women's groups of the 1980s. Most notably, Indigenous women formed their own activist organizations starting in the 1970s because their concerns were not part of the mainstream feminist agenda.[73] Enke has shown that American feminist organizations were also oblivious to their exclusivity. In Canada, as in the United States, women formed new alliances because feminism did not look or sound like they did. Like Enke, I argue that these stories of women who sought "solidarity in collectivity" are essential to the history of the movement. We have an incomplete understanding of the history of feminism unless we consider who formed groups in response to the movement.[74] Grauer, Savage, and Smith took great pains to make it clear that they were not feminists or activists, but their decision to spend twenty years meeting and swimming with other fat women suggest a connection. By staking a claim to public space in order to foster pleasure, sociability, and friendship among like-bodied women, Mrs O's members politicized their identity.[75] Mrs O's and LAL were part of the trajectory of women's liberation. "Knowledge and knowledge practices" based on personal experiences were "translated" by these groups of women.[76]

Co-Ed Fat Activism

To almost all of the activists described in this book, fat was a women's issue. Women interviewed believed that being fat did not have the same impact on men's attractiveness or their social or material success. One way several women explained the difference was to point to the social acceptability of men's "beer bellies." When asked why fat was a woman's issue, one woman explained that "a man with a big beer belly" would get very little criticism from friends and family, whereas women with big stomachs were called "baby belugas" among other things.[77] A LAL member told me she resented that fat men "with a big belly with no shirt on" could go "walking down the street" with "nobody paying any attention to him," while fat women were subject to verbal comments regardless of how they dressed.[78] Acknowledging she couldn't characterize all men, another LAL member observed that most men "seem to be very pleased with themselves and not really concerned about their bellies."[79] Another person noted that men lose weight more easily than women. She was "not as impressed when a man says he lost forty pounds in two weeks. Usually they just have to stop drinking beer or something."[80] Other women I interviewed were willing to concede that being fat was "pretty miserable" for everyone, but men probably found it more difficult to admit.[81]

In comparison with men, interview participants felt that women could not "get away" with being fat. In their experience, heterosexual men rejected women because of their body size. The truth about fat and gender was confirmed by comments from men, including fathers, former partners, and strangers who reinforced each woman's sense of themselves as fat and therefore ugly. As teenagers, some women got negative reactions from boyfriends. Jan Mindlin of LAL remembered that her boyfriend was "a freak" about her "thighs" and encouraged her to drop ten pounds.[82] Lynne Grauer of Mrs O's overheard a date exclaim "woah" when she came downstairs to meet him for a date and felt teenage boyfriends were critical of her pear shape.[83] Evelyn Booth felt that that her ability to "pass" with men diminished as she got older and her stomach grew larger.[84] Sue Masterton linked her experiences with men to her overall sense of self:

> I never felt that I was attractive enough to be in a relationship. So I've avoided them. I have what I call breakthrough men. And those are men that don't seem to, I guess that probably see the real me ... And, I can never understand that ... I've bought into the belief that I'm not good enough because of my weight. I know there are women that are large and have relationships and the weight doesn't bother them to the degree that it does for me. But for me it really does ... Plus my dad. I think he was trying to shock me into losing weight or whatever. So, he was actually very cruel to me and said things that were very hurtful. About my weight ... my ... unspoken belief was that all men deep down felt the way that my father did.[85]

Masterton's shame was reinforced by commentary from men in her life. For these women, the truth about being fat women lay, in part, in such experiences with men.

Such truisms about gender differences are complicated by the history of co-ed, men's, and lesbian women's participation in fat activism. Lesbian members of LG5 and poet Christine Donald found that fat was also unacceptable to female partners.[86] Lesbians could also be critical of their fat partners, an issue I discuss in greater detail in chapter 3. The presence of men in the movement also challenged the idea that fat was a women's issue. Canada had no fat men's organizations, but the 1990 National Film Board documentary *Fat Chance* looks at the issue from a man's perspective. Documentarian Jeff McKay followed Rick Zakowich to a NAAFA meeting in the United States where he found community and support that was lacking in Canada.[87]

Two co-ed organizations (i.e. mixed-gender organizations for fat men *and* women) existed in Canada: Aide aux personnes obèses handicapées du Québec (APOHQ, 1978–c.1987) and a Canadian branch of the National Association to Advance Fat Acceptance (NAAFA Canada, c. 1987–1995), which later became the Canadian Association for Size Acceptance (CASA, c. 1995–8).[88] Neither of these organizations attracted as many members as LAL. APOHQ succeeded in bringing some men into the movement, but NAAFA Canada/CASA did not.

In a 1979 *Le Devoir* (Montreal) photograph, Gilles Leblanc, a man with a "460 lb frame" appears sitting on a bench. Beside him is a sign that reads *"Je nai jamais vu le Métro"* / "I have never seen the Metro." Leblanc was protesting the turnstiles that prevented him from entering Montreal's underground transit network. He told reporters that obesity was, in effect, a handicap because it prevented people from taking public transportation, going to the movies, and purchasing clothing at regular prices, among other problems.[89] The sit-in was one of several publicity stunts Leblanc undertook in 1978–9 to draw attention to the social exclusion of the obese. Formed in Montreal in 1977, Leblanc's orgnaization, Aide aux obèses handicaps du Québec (later Aide aux personnes obèses handicapées du Québec), was Canada's first fat activist organization. Leblanc's goal was to get funding for a drop-in centre where people with obesity could meet and also get help from doctors, exercise specialists, and dieticians.[90] Leblanc may have been drawing on the disability rights movement, which around this time was beginning to politicize the issue of access to public space.[91] He was challenging the boundaries of public and private life in Canada, which was a tactic of the DRM as well as feminist and gay and lesbian activists of the era.[92]

Leblanc and APOHQ emphasized fat people's social isolation and their need for assistance and education about nutrition. APOHQ is the only organization discussed in this book that did not challenge the idea that obesity was unhealthy. Perhaps not coincidentally, APOHQ was also the only fat advocacy organization to receive government support to promote and develop services for people who were "handicapped" by their obesity. The province of Quebec offered APOHQ support for research and nutrition education for children identified as obese.[93] Leblanc's dream of a drop-in centre for people with obesity was also realized around 1980. Montreal Mayor Jean Drapeau was photographed cutting the ribbon with Leblanc.[94] And, in the late 1980s Leblanc advocated for more funding for a sister organization, Le centre de distribution d'aides techniques (CDAT), a charity that provided large-sized wheelchairs, hospital beds, and other medical items to hospitals caring for "morbidly" obese patients.[95] Leblanc benefited from the policies of Quebec's first Parti Québécois government (1976–81, 1981–5), which was expanding social services at this time.[96] The "modèle québécois" sought to foster a stronger more unified national identity by improving social services.[97]

Failing to challenge stereotypes about fat people may have limited the impact of APOHQ and CDAT. Lise Bergeron, a self-identified fat woman who worked with APOHQ in the 1980s, told me in a 2006 interview that people were reluctant to join. They wanted the assistance of CDAT to access social services but felt ashamed of being associated with an organization like APOHQ.[98] Where members of woman-only groups expressed excitement and a growing sense of community by joining fat activist organizations, members of APOHQ and recipients of CDAT support expressed gratitude for their help, but they had no interest in joining the group.[99] Leblanc died in 1994 and APOHQ no longer exists. CDAT continues to provide support to obese patients by lending large stretchers, hospital gowns, and patient lifts to hospitals across Canada.[100]

APOHQ's success may have also been limited due to their focus on disability rights for a constituency that did not necessarily think of itself as disabled.[101] As Lennard Davis has observed, "disability disturbs people who think of themselves as nondisabled." People do not like to think of themselves as incapacitated or abnormal.[102] Controversy ensued in 1997 when Linda McKay-Panos filed a complaint against Air Canada for failing to accommodate her "disability" – fatness – which was caused by another health condition. Prior to a flight between Calgary and Ottawa, McKay-Panos contacted Air Canada to ask if she should buy two tickets so as to ensure her comfort. Air Canada told her that she did not need to purchase two seats. Once McKay-Panos boarded her flight, she realized one seat would be inadequate. Air Canada staff refused to move McKay-Panos or the passenger next to her. McKay-Panos took up part of a second seat, and neither she nor the person next to her were able to use their table trays during the flight. In response, the Canadian Transportation Agency ruled that airlines must accommodate obese passengers who have a disability.[103]

Asked to comment on McKay-Panos's situation in 2001, Helena Spring of NAAFA Canada told the *National Post* that labelling a fat person disabled was "insulting and degrading."[104] She further noted that obese people could be "extremely healthy" and so the category of "disabled" was "unfair."[105] Spring's view was that disability was "less than" normal. Spring wanted fat people to be seen as normal and was unable to grasp McKay-Panos's critique of public space. Like APOHQ before her, McKay-Panos saw disability rights as a framework for addressing fat people's accessibility concerns. In a 2006 interview McKay-Panos said that public anger at the decision was probably rooted in the belief that being fat is seen as a personal failing, not a health condition.[106] Activists who dominated the movement in the 1980s and 1990s were focused on proving that fat bodies could be capable and healthy. Disability was viewed negatively, as Spring's comments show. McKay-Panos's case was another example of the exclusivity and lack of acknowledgment of differences among fat activism of the era.

Founded ten years after APOHQ NAAFA Canada emphasized that fat people were just like everyone else. Spring and another Canadian

NAAFA member, Ruth Wylie Gillingham of Prince Albert, Saskatchewan, joined the US organization in the late 1980s after seeing American members on television. During the 1980s NAAFA's public reputation was that of a social networking organization for fat people and fat admirers or "FAs" as they are still called in the movement. By this time the organization was beginning to take a more activist stance on employment and insurance discrimination. Spring and Gillingham, however, saw joining as an opportunity to be part of a community where fat people were considered happy and sexually attractive. Spring thought, "You know, I've got as much going for myself as these women have ... if these women can do it, why can't I?"[107] Similarly, Gillingham was inspired by "seeing other women like me, fat women, standing up, holding their head high and being proud of who they were."[108] Each woman requested a list from the American parent organization of all existing NAAFA Canada members. Together, they set out to develop a Canadian community of fat women, fat men, and FAs who felt the same way.[109]

Both Gillingham and Spring wanted NAAFA Canada to be a social group, but because they lived so far apart, they worked separately to build the organization. Gillingham started a newsletter for the seventy-five existing NAAFA members in Canada. She republished stories from NAAFA newsletters and Canadian newspapers about employment discrimination and health.[110] Gillingham had modest success with the newsletter, but she felt contact with members was important. She spent as much time as she could talking to members by phone, but it was very expensive.

Helena Spring lived in Toronto, a larger and more diverse city than Gillingham, and she, too, struggled to develop an active social network of fat people. Spring's hopes were high after attending a 1987 NAAFA convention in Flint, Michigan, where she felt "enveloped into such warmth and kindness and caring and just sisterhood and brotherhood."[111] On her return to Toronto, Spring quickly became frustrated by the difficulty she experienced getting people to attend NAAFA Canada meetings. She invited members to socialize in her apartment and was disappointed by a lack of interest in these events. She felt limited by NAAFA's refusal to provide money to get a Canadian group going and also by people's unwillingness to pay for a membership.[112] In turn, activists in Canada and the United States reported that Spring was difficult to work with and that she lacked a clear vision for NAAFA.[113]

Eventually Gillingham lost interest in her NAAFA activities, and Spring decided to change direction.[114] Around 1992, Spring started the Canadian Association for Size Acceptance (CASA). She used the term "size acceptance" to try to attract people who had been uncomfortable with the word fat. CASA's newsletter, *Canada WYDE*, was reminiscent of a women's service magazine in that it assumed readers shared "a common experience ... regardless of class, race, sexual orientation, region or age."[115] It featured tips on fashion and articles on body image.[116] *Canada WYDE* also featured a "personals" section in each issue, which will be discussed in chapter 3. Beyond this, it is difficult to assess the success of CASA based on *Canada WYDE* and an interview with Spring. *Canada WYDE* appears to have been produced primarily by Spring. In 1997 *Canada WYDE* folded due to lack of revenue. Spring discontinued active work with CASA and NAAFA at that time.[117] Gillingham went on to form an aerobics group, "Above Average," in Prince Albert, Saskatchewan, which will be discussed in chapter 5.[118]

It is telling that neither Spring nor Gillingham found what she was looking for in NAAFA or CASA, nor were they able to develop a strong network of allies in Canada. Comparing NAAFA and CASA to other more lively and resilient forms of activism that came before and after it suggests that gender very much mattered for many of those interested in joining an organization for fat people. The majority of women interested in fat activism in Canada in the 1980s seemed to prefer working with other women. As feminists and lesbians, some were not interested in men's perspectives. Others simply felt uncomfortable around men. They did not think fat men experienced the same kinds of problems that they did. Failing to acknowledge that gender mattered may have limited APOHQ, NAAFA, and CASA. After all, this was a period when Canadian politicians, public institutions, and popular culture were grappling with questions of equity, bodily autonomy, and representations of women in the media.[119] Likewise, neither disability nor pride seemed to be effective models for organizing a co-ed group in the 1980s. Using a glossy newsletter as a site for social interaction didn't work either. Instead, groups and settings that encouraged material and experiential connections between women, like LAL and Mrs O's, drew the most enthusiasm and consistent support.

Big Dance

Ideological shifts over time are apparent within fat feminist organizing but change over time is less marked among fat acceptance groups. In the 1990s, sociality and fun remained the focus even when the activities changed. In 1992 Big Dance, a class and dance company for fat women, formed in Victoria, British Columbia. In the early 1990s, Big Dance was the most consistently visible fat activism in Canada.

Lynda Raino, a dancer and teacher, formed the class at the suggestion of a friend. Compact and muscular, Raino saw herself as an outsider in the dance world. Raino identified with fat women because they, too, lacked the long and lean – "ideal" – dancer's body. Women who attended Big Dance classes and joined the dance company did it because it was fun and "safe."[120]

Big Dance offers yet another example to demonstrate the similarities and differences between feminist fat activism and fat acceptance. Like the feminist group Pretty Porky and Pissed Off (PPPO), Big Dancers used movement to explore the physicality of fat women. But, where PPPO was intended to challenge perceptions of fat women's sexuality and femininity, Big Dance was focused on celebrating different female forms. PPPO was more overtly confrontational in their approach to the public, while Big Dance aimed to entertain the public. And yet the outcome of each group was similar. Each group empowered women to see and use their bodies differently, and they challenged body norms through dance.

Among the women in attendance at the first Big Dance class, and interviewed for this book, were Terryl Atkins, Trudy Norman, and Runa Fiander. Atkins and Norman were both working in social services at the time and Fiander was a registered massage therapist. Each woman was apprehensive about who might attend the class and what they might be asked to do. Atkins had previously considered joining a "normal" dance class but "didn't have that much nerve." She feared that she could not "hide much" in a roomful of "normal" people: "you're hanging out there ... I wasn't going to embarrass myself."[121] Atkins was the first person Norman spotted when she walked into her first class and was relieved to see that she "was really a large woman." Norman said it helped her to feel like she was "in the right place."[122] Fiander felt that dancing in a class with fat women would be more supportive than a class of "normal" women. Fat women would understand if "you were doing splits and your pants split" or "your boobs flopped" because "everybody else had the same problem."[123] When they walked up the stairs Atkins, Norman, and Fiander saw other women who looked like them. They knew they were in the right place because they could see that this was not a "normal" class (see figure 8).

Raino learned how to work with fat dancers on the job. In a 2006 interview she observed that, initially, fat dancers were timid about making big gestures. They tended to take tiny "pee pee steps" because they were not comfortable with sweeping, gestural movements. She also discovered that large bodies did not necessarily move in the same ways as smaller bodies, because "you can't bend forward, there's boobs

Figure 8. Big Dance Flyer showing dancers Neely Carbone (left) and Terryl Atkins, c. 1993. Courtesy of Lynda Raino.

there."[124] At first, this lack of personal experience of being fat was evident to the dancers.[125] Eventually Raino learned how to work with the physicality of fat bodies. She saw that fat dancers could achieve a "line" that was different but equally beautiful to classical dancers: "Ballerinas will tell you that 'line' is only achieved by the very thinnest bodies where the lines are straight ... But when you take a large body and you make a curving line ... if they stand ... with a curved arm and a curved back and a curved hip, the curves are huge on their bodies and make for a much more delicious curve. So, sweeping gestural moves are lovely on big bodies."[126] The challenge was to get the Big Dancers to move their bodies in ways that would achieve this curvy line. Atkins found learning to jiggle her body and make "all that flesh ... very apparent" was a "huge hurdle."[127] For Trudy Norman, making large gestures ran contrary to a lifetime of attempts to appear smaller. Big Dance classes forced her to "acknowledge" her "body and the way it was and what it did."[128]

When interviewed, Big Dancers recalled that their confidence grew over time. In their first year the class collectively decided to skip the studio's recital. They did not feel comfortable performing in front of strangers. During their second year Big Dance performed a number to the tune of The Band's "I Shall Be Released." The dancers were fearful of the response they would get from Raino's "normal" dancers and the audience, but, in Fiander's words, the crowd "ate up" their performance.[129] Atkins likewise could tell that "everybody felt it."[130] From this time on Big Dance became well known. The class was invited to perform at events like the University of Victoria's International Women's Day concert. In 1997 eight of the original Big Dancers formed a dance company. There was no audition process. Women joined because they were committed to becoming even better dancers. The company was invited to perform at the North and South American World Dance Alliance Conference in Vancouver, British Columbia. Big Dance was also featured in segments on the American television programs *Entertainment Tonight* and *Good Morning America*. A documentary film *The Big Dance* was also made about the group and aired in Canada on the W Network.[131] We cannot know the full impact of this coverage, but certainly this level of media coverage was unprecedented for a fat activist organization until Fat Girl Food Squad in 2015.

A few months into the class, dancers began to meet on Friday nights. After a few weeks Atkins found that she was talking about "everything under the sun" with the other dancers. She liked being with a group of large women "because you go out and it's like, there was no way of ignoring us because we were sort of loud and rowdy and laughing a lot. And, we'd eat what we absolutely wanted. There was none of this salad with the vinaigrette."[132] Body size was the focus of many conversations. Norman recalled that everyone "talked about what it was like to dance and how difficult it was. I can't do this, or I can't do that, or how did you do this or that."[133] The group also began to joke about other ways they could educate the public about being fat. Maybe a booklet of jokes about fat people's experiences, "like, the idea if you go to sit on a chair, you're always checking the chair to see if it can hold your weight."[134] They also joked about getting a pink bus and touring around as "Priscilla, Queen of the Dessert," a play on the popular Australian film from the time, *Priscilla, Queen of the Desert*.[135] Their reasons for meeting were different, but members of Big Dance fell into the same types of conversations as many other fat activists.

Kathy Davis argues that social movements are forged in such informal interactions. Big Dancers developed "oppositional knowledge" about the body through conversation and dance.[136] Dancing was activism. It transformed dancers' opinions of themselves, and it potentially changed other people's attitudes towards fatness. Atkins found that dance made "you very aware of your physicality, your size, and what that meant in terms of moving and stuff. It was right up front and centre because you were feeling it now as opposed to being used to not moving, which many of us were, very used to not moving, not taking up space." Norman cried when I asked her how it felt to "have the right body for right now?" For her, it was "really special ... to take up space in the world and to celebrate who you are. Not think about what might have been, or what if you'd been skinny [laughs]. But about living in the present and really celebrating being in the body that I'm in and using that. Using dance, your body is, the body is the instrument that you use."[137] Terryl Atkins described a sense of transformation in the way she moved in the world: "The ability to feel very confident about yourself. Because, instead of being fat and apologetic for it, almost like apologetic for your existence out there in the world of, you know, people who are unlike you. All of the sudden we had this sense of status. I felt that ... speaking up for myself, being able to express myself in my body and not care. I mean there is always a part of you that cares. But not care in general what people think about you, like out on the street, that kind of thing."[138] For Atkins and Norman, performing in front of an audience was part of a process of personal and social change. Gaining respect for their unique skills and physicality helped them to let go of some of the shame they had previously felt about being fat.

In 2002 Atkins and Norman decided to dance nude, an obvious indicator of the transformative power of their work in the company. They performed a piece inspired by the choreographer's grandmother. The dancers were persuaded when the choreographer explained the piece was a "celebration" of her grandmother's large body.[139] An "audible gasp" was heard when the lights went up during the San Francisco performance.[140] Atkins and Norman could hear audience members whispering "they're naked"[141] and "oh, my."[142] Fortunately for Norman, she had her back to the audience. She stifled a laugh and then "just went from there."[143] In the end, taking off their clothing felt empowering and sensual to the dancers.

Fat was a theme of a number of pieces Big Dance performed. Although the participants embraced their roles as "big" dancers, they were less sure about size being the theme of their work. Members were divided about the mission of Big Dance. Some felt that Big Dance was about fostering a more positive image of fat people, while others felt the group's meaning derived from their contributions to dance. Like the divisions within LAL about feminism, Big Dance members were not sure whether their work was political. Atkins was among those women who did not like the pieces that played with stereotypes about being fat. One in particular, a take on Disney's *Fantasia*, irritated her. She felt the pink tutus the dancers wore for this routine were ridiculous and that the dance made fun of the way fat bodies moved. Atkins saw Big Dance as a political entity and thought the group could more explicitly push a fat activist agenda. She thought that some members of the group were so indebted to Raino for the opportunities she had provided them that they were unwilling to challenge her choice of themes. Atkins said in a 2006 interview: "Inasmuch as we didn't agree sometimes with what she wanted to do with us as bodies, we felt an enormous amount of indebtedness to her because she started it. Because she gave us this opportunity that allowed us to grow in this particular way. Which, I mean, absolutely life changing things for a lot of people. So, a lot of times that indebtedness overweighed some of the embarrassment and stuff."[144] Atkins speculated that Raino did not know what it felt like to be fat and so did not understand that some of her choreography might be embarrassing. She thought that Raino did not always realize of fat that "implicitly it was political."[145] Petra Kuppers makes a similar argument in her analysis of fat dancers in the US. Usually, fat women's bodies speak for them – "their size is already performance prior to any staging of it."[146] For Kuppers and Atkins, Big Dance was always and already a political statement because putting fat women on stage challenged perceptions about the body. There was, therefore, no need to make the dances about body size.

Raino admitted in a 2005 interview that she may have overemphasized body size in the early routines. She said that she was "caught up" in the idea of fighting oppression through dance. As the group developed, she became concerned that the audiences were focusing on the politics of fat – "was the message that big was beautiful? Was it that we should feel sorry for fat people?" – and not on the dances themselves. So Raino herself shifted from thinking the group should comment upon body size through dance to seeing it as an artistic contribution. She did not like that people focused on "how wonderful it was to see them dancing when it's not allowed."[147] Norman agreed with Raino that audiences and the media focused too much on how "courageous" the dancers were. Both women felt this sort of commentary undermined the legitimacy of Big Dance's contribution to the art of movement. Though she was personally invested in fighting fat oppression, Norman wanted to be taken seriously as a dancer. She felt that she had something "special and different" to share as a dancer and that to be "celebrated for that and really make an impact on the dance world because of it ... was a seriously cool thing."[148]

The semi-professional Big Dance company stopped performing in the early 2000s, but the Big Dance class was offered on and off throughout that decade. Presently the course is not offered. Terryl Atkins's decision to move to Kamloops, British Columbia, may have precipitated the group's disbandment. Runa Fiander and Trudy Norman still live in Victoria but felt that their time with Big Dance had run its course. They stressed in their interviews that the time and physical commitment required to dance on a regular basis was challenging.

Within the history of fat activism, the significance of Big Dance lies in their focus on pleasure. The Big Dancers' commentary shows that dance made being fat easier and even satisfying. Dance changed how participants thought about their bodies, most dramatically for Atkins and Norman who were transformed from shy first-time dancers to avant-garde nude dancers in a matter of years. Big Dance also reflects a tension within fat activism in Canada: Do we fight oppression by changing our attitudes about ourselves, or by changing the attitudes of others? It seems the takeaway was different for each member of Big Dance. Some, like Norman, identified themselves first as a dancer and second as a fat woman. Others, including Atkins, felt that Big Dance should extend its activities beyond performing. That there were different outcomes or understandings of fat women's experiences does not take away from the fact that Big Dance classes provided a positive space for fat women to explore their physicality. Dancers were moving their bodies in ways that they had not thought possible and to which the public was not accustomed.

Conclusions

Big Dance is emblematic of the ways that fat acceptance blurred the boundaries between activism, commercialism, and everyday life. Rather than seeking social transformation or challenging gender norms, members of these groups wanted to be "normal." Normal was a word that came up frequently in my interviews with self-identified fat women, though it was not clear if they distinguished between being "average" or "ideal" when they used the term. What was clear was that being fat was experienced as a material deviation from normality that had, up until joining an acceptance group, negatively shaped each woman's life.

Many feminist scholars have seen body norms and ideals as oppressive, and they were and can be. And, the "imperative to be normal" was frustrating for self-identified fat women who understood that being fat was a transgression of socially acceptable femininity in the late twentieth century.[149] Unlike their counterparts in fat feminist organizations, however, fat acceptance activists did not seek to fundamentally transform what was considered normal. Rather, they wanted to extend the boundaries of normality by creating spaces where fat people, literally and figuratively, fit in. To be more like normal women was not problematic; quite the opposite, it was important to their sense of social inclusion and acceptability.

Activists' belief that fat people were treated poorly and their desire for change resulted in several forms of fat acceptance. Discontinuity between groups was a prominent feature of the movement in the 1980s and 1990s. Part of this disjointedness resulted from language differences, geography, and a lack of access to pamphlets and newsletters created in other cities. Additionally, each group had specific ideas about how to respond to fat oppression. Some groups took an explicitly feminist approach, while others focused on fashion. All groups failed to consider difference an important issue and did not incorporate sexual orientation, ability, and ethnicity into their visions for fat liberation.

Discontinuity and differences between groups reflect other patterns in Canadian social movement history. Miriam Smith has observed that gay and lesbian activism in Canada consisted of many local movements and informal networks of individuals who were simultaneously involved in other social movements.[150] This pattern of local identities and informal networks with multiple sites of activism continues to be apparent in the following chapters, which address fat activist approaches to sexuality, health, fitness, and fashion. Sometimes, the ideological divisions between fat feminist and acceptance activists reflected concern about similar issues, as with their critiques of femininity and sexuality. At other times, as was the case with fitness and fashion, fat acceptance groups took empowerment in new directions that did not reflect feminist perspectives on gender and the body of the time.

3 "If Only You'd Lose Weight...": Femininity, Sexuality, and Fat Activism

Sue Masterton's mother took her to her first weight-loss group in the 1960s. A few years earlier Sue's parents had consulted a physician about her weight. The doctor assured them they had nothing to worry about – their daughter would slim down when she hit puberty. But the weight didn't fall off. Instead Sue "really started to gain the weight," and her mother signed her up for Weight Watchers, a commercial weight-loss program.* As an adult, Sue remembered feeling ashamed to join Weight Watchers because "there weren't any other kids in the group." She did not lose much weight on this diet. In her twenties and thirties, Sue went on to try several others: she returned to Weight Watchers a few times, joined other commercial weight-loss programs, and also organized two support groups, one with a friend and the second as part of the non-profit Take Off Pounds Sensibly (TOPS) system.[1] Each diet worked for a while. Sue enjoyed the compliments about her weight loss but sometimes became annoyed if people were too effusive about her success.

Sue attended The Forgotten Woman workshop in 1981 along with the founders of Large as Life (LAL). She went to get "in touch" with her body and to think about why she was fat in the first place. Reflecting upon the workshop, Sue could hardly believe some of the activities she had participated in that weekend. The most surprising activity was designed around naked body awareness. She recalled that it took some "convincing" but after "neatly" piling her clothes where she "could get to them quickly," Sue danced naked around the room in a display of body

---

* Commercial weight-loss programs sell dieting. These offer counselling; food or exercise programs; pills, shakes, or other supplements to help people lose weight. Commercial programs are distinguished from not-for-profit groups like Take Off Pounds Sensibly and informally organized support groups because they market weight loss to female consumers.

liberation. Her excitement was tempered when the course instructor made unwanted sexual advancements after hours. She was not attracted to women and felt uncomfortable. Sue did not describe the unwanted touch as sexual harassment, which it was, only that it made her feel vulnerable at a time when she was trying to gain greater confidence.

Sue returned to Vancouver feeling, on balance, very excited about what she had experienced at The Forgotten Woman. She did not attend LAL meetings, but she joined their aerobics classes and also agreed to model for a plus-size agency founded by a friend. The prospect of modelling was both scary and exhilarating for Sue. Her entire life she had been told that she had a "pretty face," but she did not feel comfortable when people paid attention to her body.

The boost Sue experienced from these pursuits was tempered by put-downs from friends, family, and strangers. She once had to call the police when a group of men taunted her at a drive-in-restaurant parking lot shouting, "look at the fat girl in the car," as they simultaneously threw French fries at Sue, to see if she would go after them. After this experience Sue decided that what she really wanted, and needed, was a body that matched her face: she elected to have intestinal bypass weight-loss surgery. The procedure was covered by provincial health insurance at the time, if the patient passed a medical exam. On 12 July 1985, Sue had the surgery, which she hoped would be a "magic bullet" to a better life, one where she could "wear beautiful clothes," "attract a man," and "be acceptable" in her parents' eyes.[2]

Sue began to experience major complications about five months after her intestinal bypass surgery. She lost eighty-five pounds, but the side effects of the surgery – diarrhoea and loss of appetite – were brutal. Sue started to suffer from malnutrition and eventually went into liver failure because food was passing through her body so quickly.[3] If they did not reverse the procedure, Sue might "run into more difficulty and possibly die," but if they did the reversal she was likely to regain the weight she had lost. Sue was not sure if she wanted to let go of the dream of being thin. She decided to have the procedure reversed, but only after thinking it over for a week. Within a few months Sue recovered and gained back the weight she had lost. Reflecting on this time in her life, Sue admitted "the desire to be thin rather than overweight was so great" that she was willing to "risk her life for it." Twenty years on, she was "tempted" by improved gastric bypass procedures that were gaining popularity in the early 2000s. But, overall, Sue had come to accept that her body was out of fashion for "our time" and that dieting did not work.[4]

Sue's story reflects many late twentieth-century feminist concerns about feminine norms: that women were struggling to live up to unrealistic standards of beauty, that they were preoccupied with their body weight, and that they were, literally, dying to be thin. At the same time, Sue's story resists such a straightforward reading. Embedded within her account are moments of self-satisfaction *and* insecurity. Sue wanted to be considered conventionally attractive, but, when people complimented her on her appearance, she felt annoyed that they only cared about her looks. She strived to find ways to accept herself and her body, and yet she also risked weight-loss surgery because she believed people could not see her "true" self.

For Sue, saying it was okay to be fat not only meant letting go of the dream of being thin but also ignoring a range of familial and cultural messages about beauty. "Aesthetics" were a "terrain of struggle" for women in the 1970s. Women debated the impact of feminine norms, and rejecting beauty was equated with being feminist or a lesbian.[5] Accepting that you were fat was tantamount to rejection of femininity, and this was not what Sue wanted. Instead, she was trying to reconcile her experiences with her desire to be thin and beautiful. Sue and many women interviewed for this project had been taught from a young age that their bodies were a problem. This message was clearly communicated by parents who put their daughters on diets and denied them dessert at the dinner table.

Negative attention was also drawn to the bodies of girls when they had to find clothing or get weighed at school. As teenagers and into their twenties, this message focused particularly on a young woman's femininity and physical attractiveness. In order to "find a man" she needed to lose weight.[6] In their everyday lives and interactions, young women were told that their weight was unattractive and a barrier to their future happiness. Women who went on to become fat activists felt frustrated by these experiences for a variety of reasons: they felt attractive, they could not lose weight, they felt happy, they had a man, and/ or were not interested in men at all.

This chapter examines the ways that fat feminist and fat acceptance activists of the 1980s and 1990s talked about femininity and sexuality. Fat activists grappled with their desire to feel attractive, even as they condemned expectations about women's physical appearance as unfair and sexist. Fat feminist activists saw slenderness as an oppressive heterosexist ideal of passive sexuality and decorous femininity. Women needed to embrace a more natural and "authentic" aesthetic that was not aimed at pleasing men. Fat acceptance groups wanted to expand understandings of femininity and sexual attractiveness to include fat women. In both cases, activists argued, fat women should be able to feel attractive and sexually desirable on their own terms. All groups also critiqued women who failed to understand that slenderness was central to concepts of beauty. Like other aspects of fat activism, body size was the focus. Differences of race, class, and ability in relation to femininity and sexuality were not discussed.

As was also typical of the movement, the perceived problems and the meaning of femininity and sexuality were interpreted differently between fat activist groups, and sometimes within them. For this reason, this chapter is organized around five themes that emerged in interviews with fat activists and in documentary sources: femininity, sexuality, relationships, gender, and "fat admirers." Commentary by activists on these issues shows that feminist critiques of beauty and bodily ideals influenced fat activism. This chapter also shows how public debates about gender roles and expectations were influencing the way activists talked about their bodies. Fat activists thought critically about what it meant to be attractive because they were so often told that they were not, and could not be, so.

Problematizing Femininity

Simone de Beauvoir's observation in *The Second Sex* (1949) that females are not born but rather are "made" women remains a key insight about gender.[7] "Woman" is a social construction and is not innately different or inferior to "man." Numerous feminist activists have used this idea to critique femininity itself, as a distraction and a construction that impedes a woman's expression of her "real" or "authentic" self. For fat feminist activists, feminine norms were at the core of fat oppression and weight obsession. In her foundational analysis on this topic, Mary Russo describes fat women as those who have "refuse to surrender the critical and cultural tools of the dominant class."[8] Citing Russo, other scholars have suggested that fat women represent open defiance of beauty norms, and by doing so they "acquire oppositional power from" their "ambivalence" and ability to transcend their embodiment through skill, personality, or beauty.[9] Fat was and is, in itself, a form of resistance to feminine norms.[10]

The idea that being fat was (and is) a form of defiance helps us to think about the critical possibilities of activism. It doesn't, however, offer a way for understanding the lived experience of being fat. It assumes that fatness was a choice or a conscious rejection of femininity. Women like Sue Masterton struggled to know what to feel about their outsider status. At times she felt empowered and at other times she was overwhelmed by negative cultural messages about fat women. Sue's experiences, and those of the women discussed in this chapter, show that all activists were aware of feminist critiques of femininity.

Members of fat women's organizations either embraced femininity or rejected it, depending on their approach to activism. The variety of approaches to femininity shows that there was a significant gap between proscriptions of female behaviour and women's practices. As historian Andrée Lévesque has shown in her accounts of women who "broke the rules" in twentieth-century Quebec, women have consistently challenged feminine ideals through their clothing, relationships, and career choices. Like the women who were the subject of Lévesque's study, conformance and nonconformance to femininity was a choice. Most of the self-identified fat women interviewed for this book could – and did – explain their experiences in relation to prevailing norms of femininity.[11]

Problematizing Sexuality

To be feminine was not necessarily to be sexually desirable, though the two were never entirely separate, either. Western women have tended to be thought of as sexually passive moral guardians; only the "fallen" express interest in sexuality.[12] In the 1960s "second-wave" feminists began to challenge these rules. Kate Millett's *Sexual Politics* (1970) offered a searing critique, outlining the "misogynistic representations of women and feminine sexuality" of "canonical" psychoanalytic and philosophical texts.[13] Millett argued that Freud, among other thinkers, tended to reinforce the notion that women are naturally sexually passive.[14]

Men's sexual domination of women was further reinforced, according to feminists like Andrea Dworkin and Robin Morgan, through the reduction of women to sexual objects in popular culture and pornography.[15] Representations and expectations of women's sexuality, like femininity, seemed to contribute to power imbalances and women's ongoing oppression. How could women subvert the heterosexual male "gaze" and develop an authentic sexuality? Some feminists came to believe that lesbianism offered a different and essentially female model of sexual desire.

Among fat activists, women who identified as both fat and lesbian articulated the most coherent critique of sexuality. For the purposes of this research, I describe this critique as "fat lesbian." It is important to note, however, that the women who were debating the role of fatness in lesbian sexual politics did not envision "fat lesbianism" as a discrete movement. Rather, they identified as both fat and lesbian and wanted to interrogate the ways that looksism impacted their relationships with other women. Fat lesbians expressed disappointment with lesbians who continued to buy into the "heterosexual," thin, feminine body and described a sense of rejection and isolation from individual partners and more generally at lesbian events.

Writing in the Canadian feminist periodical *Lesbian Fury* in 1986, "Kathy" challenged readers to examine this issue: "Look around at dances, where are the fat women – they are either at home or not danc-ing. When is the last time YOU asked a fat woman to dance?" Fat lesbian activists believed that their sisters in the movement should let go of their desire to be – and to be with – slim women, just as they had let go of the trappings of heterosexual femininity, like make-up and long hair.[16] Fat lesbians believed the link between slenderness and heterosexual feminin-ity was obvious: the preference for a slim body was the product of a desire to cut women down to size and keep them sexually submissive to men. "Kathy" and many other fat lesbians were working from a radical femi-nist position of the 1970s, which saw femininity as trivial and oppressive.

Distinct fat lesbian critiques first emerged within the movement in the late 1970s in the United States.[17] In 1978, Judith Stein and other lesbians formed a "Fat Lesbian Group" at the Cambridge Women's Center in Massachusetts.[18] The following year, the Boston group met other like-minded women at the Michigan Womyn's Music Festival (Michfest). Michfest began in 1975 near Ann Arbor, and it was and is a music festival "for all womyn, and only womyn."[19] In 1979, six thou-sand women attended the festival that boasted vegetarian food, on-site camping, music, and community activities, including workshops and support groups on topics of interest to attendees (for example, sessions on artificial insemination, womyn of colour, dyke hoboes, Overeaters Anonymous [OA], and a compulsive-eating support group).[20]

Fat lesbians at Michfest 1979 felt they were treated poorly. Women frequently went topless at Michfest, and fat attendees felt uncom-fortable about taking off their clothes. Of this experience Judith Stein remembered: "I mean, you're in an environment where women are not wearing all of their clothes. And for fat women taking off your blouse was a big deal, never mind taking off all your clothes. It was huge. And there was unpleasantness. Not in every moment, but lots of it. So there was lots of solidarity, coming together as fat lesbians."[21] Lesbians began to meet informally in a teepee raised on-site. The groundswell of inter-est in fat lesbian issues at Michfest led to further planning. In 1980 Stein helped to organize fat women's support group meetings at the festival, and she coordinated workshops about fat oppression for women of all sizes.[22] Perhaps because of this protest, Overeaters Anonymous and compulsive-eating groups were not listed on the Michfest schedule in 1980, though they did return in subsequent years and have remained there off and on to the present day.[23]

Canadians were a pretty common presence at Michfest. Prior to form-ing LG5, Louise Turcotte and members of another group she belonged to, Amazones d'hier, lesbiennes d'aujourd'hui (AHLA), attended. Canadians reported being hassled by border officials who questioned their attendance at the lesbian-identified festival and some had trouble crossing the border.[24] Women from Quebec were a particularly visible presence at the festival after 1982 when they began to organize a francophone caucus and translation system for French attendees.[25] In 1986, the festival guide even included a statement of support for francophones living in Canada, who were described as a group engaged in a "struggle for ... cultural survival in an 'Anglophone-wide' continent and ... confronted with assimilation ... a form of linguistic and cultural oppression which is akin to racism, ablism, etc."[26]

Just as Quebec-Canadian politics permeated life at Michfest, ideas from the festival made their way back to Canada. Turcotte took home pamphlets and ideas from the fat women's workshops run by Stein and others in 1980. Her introduction to fat activism at Michfest led to some reflection on her relationships with other women. She sensed that her appearance mattered to other lesbians but had had difficulty naming the problem until she met Judith Stein.

For a few years after their first encounter at Michfest in the 1980s, Turcotte kept in touch with fat lesbians in Boston and Oakland.[27] She translated pamphlets by her "American friends" in the Fat Underground (FU) and "Fat Lesbian Group" into French for AHLA's lesbian separatist feminist journal. In 1992 LG5 edited a special collection of the journal called "La Grosseur? Obsession? Oppression!" / "Size: Obsession? Oppression!" It included their translations of American work.

Outside Quebec, Christine Donald was the most visible voice of fat lesbianism in Canada. Donald – or Hilary Clare as she is now known – was a prominent activist on behalf of the Coalition for Lesbian and Gay Rights of Ontario in the 1980s and 1990s.[28] In 1986 she published *The Fat Woman Measures Up* with Ragweed Press (see figure 9). This collection makes more of an emotional appeal to lesbians than LG5. Donald writes intimately about sex, discussing sex itself more openly than other activists. In "The Thin Women Woo Each Other" Donald describes fat women as "fearful to lay claim / to the thin conventions of romance / afraid of bulging out / of the slinky dress of sex-on-fire."[29] Other poems speak about feelings of rejection and humiliation by lovers who have pressured "the Fat Woman" to lose weight. In "The Lovers of Fat People" Donald writes that "the lovers of fat people / often feel hard done by / because loving the obese / is difficult ... The lovers know / they must like the fat / because the confident in body / lose weight better."[30] Donald seems to be referencing *Fat Is a Feminist Issue* here, or perhaps dieting philosophy of the 1970s more generally. She takes aim both at lesbians who hassle fat partners about their weight and the assumption that being fat is a result of low self-esteem or a lack of self-care.

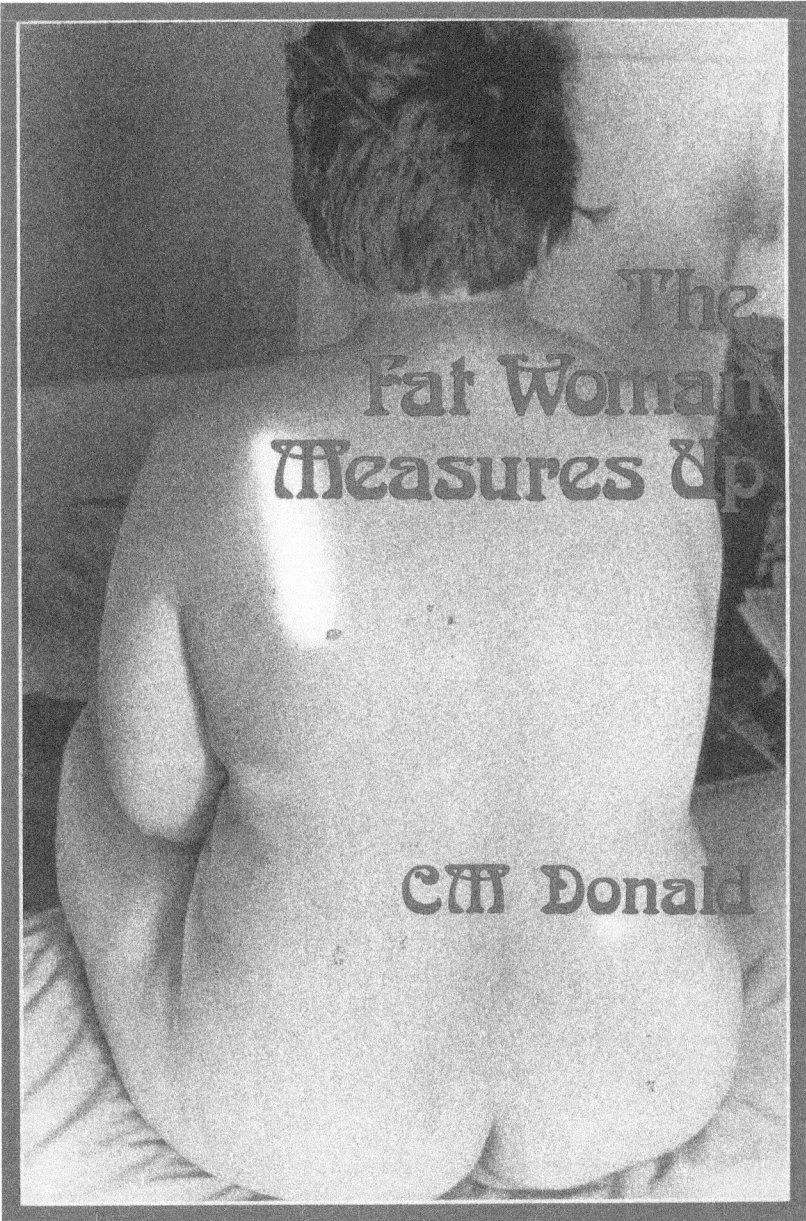

Figure 9. Cover of *The Fat Woman Measures Up* (1986) by C.M. Donald, featuring the photo "I love women and rainbows" by Marty Crowder. Courtesy of Hilary Clare.

In a 1986 interview, Donald explained that her poetry was meant to draw attention to the parallels between being gay and being fat, saying: "Fat people are oppressed in many of the same ways that gay people are, for being the object of jokes to being denied jobs ... One difference would be that you can't hide being fat, even if you want to and the major difference for me is that I don't get a lot of support for being positive about my body."[31] Like members of LG5, Donald had been rejected because of her body size. Her work is different from her predecessors in Canada in that it evokes the more intimate ways in which bodies and self-presentation were implicated in lesbian movements of the 1980s.

Historian Becki L. Ross has shown that during the 1970s lesbians' critiques of gender and femininity extended to self-presentation and clothing choice. Many lesbians embraced the "natural look" so as to "repudiate" the "heterosexual" feminine look. Women who wanted to look conventionally attractive were thought to be invested in "appearing attractive to men and in servicing men."[32] Donald's work suggests that a lesbian's rejection of heterosexual femininity did not always extend to the bedroom. As a consequence, fat women were fearful that other lesbians rejected them based on their size alone. Donald and other fat lesbians thought body size was a political issue and sought to show that preference for slim women was heteronormative.

The Fat Woman Measures Up was unexpectedly successful. The book sold out its first print run – probably five hundred copies – within the first year of publication. A second edition was released in January 1987, for which Donald received a Canada Council grant and travelled in Canada and the UK for a book tour.[33] An idea of how women responded to Donald's book can be gleaned from a handful of letters she received from readers across the country. Helen H. of Toronto thanked Donald for offering a book she could "carry ... in case of emergency," such as "when someone says, 'But you have such a pretty face!' Or when a thin friend says that she **has** to lose some weight."[34] Another woman wrote as a "still closeted lesbian" to say that Donald was "right on the mark" in her description of fat oppression.[35] Through her poetry readings and public appearances, Donald gave voice to a community of fat women who, in turn, wrote to the author to talk about the unexpected problem that size presented in their sexual relationships with other women. The enthusiastic responses of Donald's readers echoed those of *Canadian Living* readers who had written to LAL a few years earlier. Donald helped to illuminate fat oppression in a way that made sense to her readers.

Donald's work also shows that there were intellectual, if not always personal, connections between fat activists in North America. Among Donald's archival papers is a letter from Judith Stein of the Fat Lesbian

Group. Describing herself as a "fat dyke," Stein requested an additional copy of *The Fat Woman Measures Up* to give to her partner.[36] Donald's work also sparked debate in lesbian feminist periodicals of the 1980s. After her appearance in Vancouver in 1987, the lesbian newsletter *Angles* published a review. Donald was described as "nurturing" by the reviewer, who said that she "honestly didn't notice her 250 pounds" because "it was spread over five feet and ten inches ... and she had such a lovely smile."[37] Pauline Rankin, a member of the Vancouver Lesbian Connection, wrote to *Angles* to express her dismay at the reviewer's characterization of Donald. Rankin noted that comments like "she had such a lovely smile" were insulting to fat women.[38]

Donald's poetry helped Rankin to give voice to her experiences of fat oppression. In the 1980s LAL Vancouver was Canada's most popular fat women's organization. Though LAL had openly lesbian members, it did not speak specifically to or about sexual orientation. Rankin was aware of LAL and had also taken part in one of Maranda-Friedman's "Facing Your Fat" workshops.[39] These encounters with fat acceptance did not appeal to Rankin because they offered personal solutions to a problem that she felt was political. After Donald's appearance in Vancouver, Rankin decided that she could and should use her skills as a peer counsellor to raise awareness about fat oppression among gays and lesbians. She decided to offer free workshops on fat oppression at the Vancouver Lesbian Connection in 1989 and did so again in the early 1990s.[40] For Rankin, a workshop would offer the most effective way to name and explore fat oppression within gay and lesbian circles in that city.

Rankin's approach to fat oppression was slightly different from that of other fat lesbians, probably because it emerged in the 1990s and was coincident with other shifts in lesbian and gay activism. Around this time a lot of gay and lesbian activism in Canada was shifting away from a liberation framework towards rights-based claims.[41] At the same time, gay, lesbian, feminist, and other activists were increasingly concerned with questions of difference, as the nature of identity itself was being challenged by queer and anti-racist scholarship.[42] The categories of male and female were thrown into question with the recognition that there were and are multiple ways of identifying and inhabiting one's body.

Rankin modelled her workshops on anti-racism training: her project was to help people "unlearn" basic assumptions about fat people. She wanted to create a safe environment where people could express their ambivalences about fatness, which Rankin then countered with ideas from American fat activist text *Shadow on a Tightrope*, facts on dieting and eating disorders, as well as poetry.[43] Like other activists before her, Rankin was drawing on her personal experiences to educate gays and lesbians about fat oppression. Her story helps to illuminate the unexpected and unintended ways that the concepts of fat oppression and fat liberation "travelled" among lesbians in Canada. Christine Donald's *The Fat Woman Measures Up*, feminist journals like AHLA, and *Angles* helped to spread the word. Approaches to sexual orientation, much like other iterations of fat activism, were transformed in different historical and linguistic contexts.

Relationships

Outside of their public interventions, LG5 members sometimes had difficulty translating their critique of fat oppression into body acceptance. Charland and Turcotte remembered that, at first, they felt uncomfortable with being fat and looking at other fat women in a sexual way. Charland recalled feeling very uneasy when Turcotte arrived at an LG5 meeting with a calendar of images of fat women she had received from her "American friends."[44] Everyone "looked" and "passed along" the erotic pictures, but they "couldn't talk about it" and decided to postpone their discussion of the images until the following meeting. Charland took the calendar home with her and "forced" herself to "look at it every day." She was shocked by her own shock at the images: "I thought within the group we ... we ... are comfortable with our own. But in a naked picture it was different." Turcotte had intended to provoke discussion but admitted that she found the images to be "very raw" because they forced her to confront her own negative "perspectives on fat women."[45]

The calendar incident illustrates that fat feminist activism had some limitations. In defining fat oppression as a product of a heterosociety that imposed exacting standards of beauty on all women, LG5 advanced fat activism. But identifying discrimination did not always help individual women to resolve their feelings of rejection and humiliation. Members of LG5 very rarely discussed their frustration with being fat, nor did they develop strategies for self-acceptance.

Sexuality was a challenging topic for LAL members as well. The *Bolster* was uncharacteristically vague when reporting on sex. For example, on 19 September 1983 LAL held a "Fun Fashion Nite," which included a local fashion designer and a display table from Love Nest Lingerie featuring "sheer nighties, gorgeous teddies and other sexy goodies (that) delighted the viewer."[46] A report on the event in the group's newsletter noted that several members had ordered clothing from the fashion designer, but there was no mention about any sales of lingerie. The goods from Love Nest Lingerie were described, but members' reactions to them were not. Did the women present feel that the lingerie was sexy?

Six months earlier a discussion of "Fat and Sexuality" was described as a "delicate" meeting topic in the newsletter. It described a "lively discussion" that apparently occurred at a talk by Sandy Friedman, but the content of that discussion was not included. Instead, it was reported that members "were encouraged to look at sexuality in connection with our life experiences and conditioning ... The more we own our own feelings and begin to keep fewer secrets from ourselves, the more energy we will have to live more creative and fulfilling lives."[47]

In an April 1984 *Bolster* article called "They'll Take Romance" about the dating experiences of members, the author and members quoted in the article chose to remain anonymous. This decision is significant because most articles in the *Bolster* were signed, suggesting again that sex and relationships were sensitive subjects for members. "They'll Take Romance" argued that being fat need not be a barrier to romantic relationships. It was possible for fat women to be successful with romantic partners as long as they projected an air of self-confidence. Here, the author of the article cited the experience of an anonymous LAL member who "projected an aura of sexuality" that "men read ... and reacted to." It was also important for LAL members to learn to pick up on subtle cues from potential partners. Such was the experience of another LAL member who was followed into an antiques store by a man who engaged her in conversation about cuckoo clocks. This woman "hadn't recognized that her mood was an attractant, and she was blind to the fact he wasn't really interested in clocks." Another member confirmed it was important not to "assume men wouldn't want her because of her fat."[48]

In the *Bolster*, heterosexual romance was seen as one of the potential outcomes of fat acceptance. Anonymous LAL members quoted in the article suggested that all women needed to do to meet men was to project self-confidence. "They'll Take Romance" also took on this issue. Dating services were frowned on because people who used regular dating services tended to have "rather crass assumptions about immediate sexual availability." A dating service that tried to match fat women and men was likewise dismissed by members who felt that size should not be the basis for attraction between men and women.[49] The best place to meet men, the article suggested, was at clubs or at work "where one can get to know people at leisure through shared interests." "They'll Take Romance" concluded with a success story about a widowed LAL member who, at age sixty, married a man she met through friends. The bride's daughter gifted her "a lingerie trousseau in size 46," and the "well-educated outgoing woman" was enjoying "for the first time in her life ... chamgagne [sic] breakfast in bed."[50]

The airy tone of "They'll Take Romance" belied the often difficult struggle members of fat acceptance groups had with their sexuality. In interviews LAL members were reluctant to go into detail about their personal relationships and responded with nervous laughter and long pauses when questioned on this topic. It was clear that the belief that fat bodies were not attractive to men impacted the confidence of heterosexual female participants. Concluding that others saw them as ugly made it harder for some women to see themselves as attractive. Reflecting on the feminist critique of beauty, Kate Partridge of LAL noted that she "never felt like a sexual object, I had always felt asexual because I was fat ... I didn't even get to feel being a sexual object, which was so awful ... I didn't feel like a human being until I was in my early twenties. I didn't feel like a woman until I was in my early thirties, in terms of gaining identity. It's been a hard struggle."[51] Runa Fiander of Big Dance also recalled going through periods where she "wasn't feeling sensual" and believed that fat was "a really easy way to protect yourself and not have to worry about that."[52]

On dates and in social settings, unsolicited comments from heterosexual men added to the sense that being fat was unattractive. Suzanne Bell, LAL member and aerobics instructor, recalled a period of her life when "men ... would say you're so beautiful, if only you'd lose weight you'd be so desirable." Thirty years later Bell succinctly summarized her thinking on this critique: "fuck off."[53] Not all women were able to overcome bad experiences or dismiss such criticism. Following the breakdown of her marriage in the early 1980s, activist Kaca Henley described herself as "self-loathing ... because ... [her husband] said that making love is for young and attractive people and not for fat and ugly people like us." In the twenty years following her divorce, Henley avoided relationships with men. She described her sexuality as "gone" and something was "broken" that she did not feel compelled to "fix."[54] Sarah King, a LAL aerobics class participant, believed men could not be attracted to her sexually "because, I mean, fat is ugly, isn't it?" King believed her fatness had "pushed" her towards marrying a gay man, who was "sort of a safety thing ... because I don't have to take off my clothes and I don't have to have sex."[55] These women felt vulnerable in situations where being physically attractive seemed to matter most.

Having a fat body did not preclude having a conventionally attractive face. "Such a pretty face," the title of Marcia Millman's path-breaking book on fat oppression, was a truism heard repeatedly by self-identified fat women.[56] Although it may have been intended as a compliment, many women found the comment insulting. To its recipient "such a pretty face" implied "it's too bad you are such a fat girl."[57] Or, "you're not acceptable the way you are,"[58] and "if you lost the weight, your life would begin."[59] Focusing on one attractive feature implied that the rest of a person's body was not attractive.[60] As Joan Jacobs Brumberg has documented, in the late twentieth century many women believed that their bodies reflected their character.[61] Fat impeded LAL member Joan Dal Santo's sense of her own attractiveness; she "fell short on the feminine because" she "wasn't petite ... wasn't small."[62] It was not just about body size but also shape. LAL's Evelyn Booth noted that it was "just certain things" that made fat less unattractive, "that certain parts of your body are not as smooth as they used to be."[63]

The notion of a mind/body divide or a split between a women's appearance and their true selves also frequently emerged in my interviews. Kate Partridge expressed this in terms of there being "somebody else underneath whatever the surface is."[64] Partridge struggled to articulate who she should be because she knew that she was more than her "surface." She strived to feel whole but sometimes felt like being fat on the outside made it difficult for others to see her "true" self.

"I've Had Men"

Negative or ambivalent experiences with sex were not the rule among the women I interviewed. Speaking on behalf of LAL in the early 1980s, Jan Mindlin attempted to explain her positive dating experiences to a Vancouver radio audience. "I've had men," she explained to an interviewer in response to a question about relationships. Mindlin laughed remembering this interview in 2006. In retrospect it was "funny" because it "made it sound like" she had "slept around a lot."[65] What Mindlin was trying to get at was her belief that men were attracted to confident women, regardless of their size. Suzanne Bell similarly believed that, once she came to see herself as desirable, men saw her as attractive. For Bell, "attitude" was "powerful."[66] Jody Sandler, a fat women's fitness instructor from Vancouver, likewise did not recall any bad experiences with men, citing good relationships with her brothers and father as important influences. She rejected the idea that men dislike like fat women and implied that it was women that had "an issue with fat." Men "just want you to show up, they just want you to be there ... They just want you to be soft and loving and kind. They just want you to be happy with yourself, because if you're happy they're happy." Sandler believed that some fat women became lesbians because of "bad experiences with men," which made "them angry."[67]

Sandler's oversimplification of lesbian critiques of heterosexuality notwithstanding, we can see that she shared with Bell and Mindlin the belief that it was possible to be fat and attractive. Unlike some other participants in this study, these women did not feel there was necessarily a disjuncture between their minds and bodies. They did not find that it was difficult to be fat and also feminine and sexual. Members did not discuss at the time, nor in their interviews, whether and how their proximity to feminine norms impacted their experiences. Mindlin and Bell were and are both white, beautiful women, with expertly applied make-up and stylish clothing. They had forms of body privilege that did not appeal to or were not available to all fat women.

It is noteworthy how central men were to all fat activist discussions of femininity and sexuality. Including men in debates about fat women's sexuality makes sense in the context of gender relations in the 1980s. Fat activists, like many women, were trying to navigate changing social expectations about gender. It was unclear where men should fit into discussions about fat oppression, because the relationship of men to women was itself in question. Fat lesbians saw men as patriarchal figures who worked to oppress women. Heterosexuality, likewise, was seen as a system that contributed to power imbalances. Reflecting Marxist and radical feminist critiques of the era, fat lesbians saw men as part of a broader socio-economic system that exploited women. It was because feminine norms and slenderness were supposed to be male preferences that fat oppression within lesbian communities was so frustrating. Fat lesbians believed that lesbians and feminists should know better and should be able to let go of their hang-ups about slenderness.

Men were both desired and frustrating figures in the rhetoric of predominantly heterosexual fat acceptance groups like LAL. Members expressed anger that men were able to "get away with" having a fat body when women were not. Other women were angry at men who had demeaned and ignored them because of their size. Like fat feminist and fat lesbian activists, they wanted their partners to get over cultural stereotypes and preoccupations about fat women. Despite these frustrations, documented in interviews and the *Bolster*, fat acceptance groups were not very vocal about relationships. Where women could maintain control over their feelings about their bodies, clothing, and habits, they could not force men to appreciate the beauty of larger bodies. Instead, the onus was on individual women to improve themselves. The message was that success with men might follow from self-acceptance.

Fat Admirers

In the 1980s there was some demand for a social or a dating network for heterosexual fat women, as evidenced by the "personals" section of NAAFA's (later CASA) magazine *Canada WYDE*, which was edited by Toronto activist Helena Spring. Each personals column consisted of ten to fifteen advertisements. In total, fifty personal ads were published between 1996 and 1997, most by women seeking men. But, fat admirers or FAs, thin men who have a sexual preference for fat women, placed ten advertisements. Advertisements placed by the FAs sought a sexual connection with a "big, beautiful woman" (BBW). This could include "cuddling" with "voluptuous women" in order to "explore the higher realms of the soul."[68] Three of these ads were looking for more specific qualities: one man sought a "passive female for a loving caring and sharing friendship,"[69] another was an "attached male" seeking a "first encounter with a BBW who is busty, feminine,"[70] and a third wanted a woman who weighed four hundred pounds "minimum" and promised that he "liked playing Santa Claus all year round."[71] Ads from male readers sought an explicitly sexual connection with fat, feminine, and, often, passive women.

The remaining forty advertisements, placed by women, put less emphasis on body size. Some women's personals were quite direct, a "single, white lady, 40, wishes to meet gentleman. Christian values, good sense of humour, non-smoker, friendship first."[72] Other women described their physical appearance specifically, such as "comfortable, casual & cute woman, 40, 5'8, size 46. Variety of interests ... Looking for my match!"[73] The majority of advertisements were saucy and inviting: "SENSUAL ... STATUESQUE This BBW requires a tall, dark and honest male over 35 and still fertile. Should be beyond sexist issues, solvent, sensitive but not easily intimidated."[74] Only one woman placed an ad looking specifically for a "cuddly large framed gentlemen [sic]" – body size preferences were not usually indicated.[75] Even when women's advertisements contained overtly sexual overtures, they also asked for more: love of the outdoors, travel, financial security, humour, and open-mindedness. Where men's ads sought particular physical attributes, women's advertisements looked for additional personal qualities.

Canada WYDE's personal advertisements reproduced many of the stereotypes about fat women's sexuality and FAs that have been debated by activists and scholars. As Laura Kipnis has shown, preference for fat women has been categorized as a fetish by the adult film industry. Similarly, *Dimensions*, an American magazine featuring fat women wearing lingerie, has been labelled pornography. Kipnis questions "what really separates a preference for fat bodies from those 'normal' fetishes, like a preference for in-shape bodies with buns of steel ... or for breasts ... or washboard abs – other than prevailing fashion?"[76]

Applying Kipnis's analysis to *Canada WYDE* would suggest there was nothing untoward about advertisements seeking specific physical qualities. By comparison, Marcia Millman might see the *Canada WYDE* ads as emblematic of longer-standing stereotypes about fat women's sexuality. In *Such a Pretty Face*, Millman argues that fat women have been limited to two roles "the mother (with whom men can be weak, demanding, dependent, infantile) or the whore (with whom men can be abusive or violently sexual without obligation or guilt)."[77] Millman sees FA culture as problematic because it focused so much on physical largeness and provided fat women with "none of the privileges of being desirable" for other reasons.[78] *Canada WYDE* editor Helena Spring was herself critical of FAs. She described NAAFA conventions in the United States as "basically a fuck fest" and joked that FA stood for "fucking awful."[79]

An alternative reading could be that the personal advertisements offered fat women an opportunity to assert their sexuality. Women sought pleasure through *Canada WYDE's* personals section.[80] The ads indicate that some men and women were willingly and playfully conforming to the fat/saucy/female and FA roles. Rachel Colls has made a similar observation of "LargeLife," a monthly fat acceptance nightclub event held in London, England. Colls argues that women have limited power in FA culture because it reproduces the power dynamics of "regular" heterosexual relationships, in that men have tended to control such encounters.[81] Nonetheless, she observes that fat females attending the club night embraced the "sexualised subjectivities" that such spaces permitted, because it allowed them to "make friends and find lovers."[82] It is possible that, like the butch and femme roles played out by lesbians in the 1950s and early 1960s, these roles have offered fat women and FAs a way to make their preferences visible to each other.[83]

Conclusions

Fat feminist activists like LG5 and Christine Donald developed a network of support and a debate among lesbians that crossed national and linguistic boundaries. Fat lesbians believed that slenderness was as much a heterosexual ideal as were make-up and other trappings of feminine culture. The connection to gay and lesbian liberation was clear, fat lesbians argued, because fat women were excluded and marginalized due to something over which they had no control. They found other lesbians did not necessarily support this view. What followed from fat lesbian critiques of sexuality was quite different from discussions of the topic by fat acceptance groups: fat lesbians wanted to politicize sexual desire.

Fat acceptance groups, more so than fat lesbians, sought strategies to reconcile members' conflicted feelings about femininity and sexuality. At workshops like Facing Your Fat, as well as the aerobics classes and fashions shows described later in the book, these groups focused on helping women think through, and live in, their bodies. This model encouraged fat women to find ways to access the same kinds of things – clothing, make-up, dating – as any woman. Fat acceptance activists often embraced feminine norms, which on the surface appeared quite different from their fat feminist sisters. But it was similar because all fat activists refused to accept that they were fundamentally different or less worthy of pleasure than their thin counterparts. Many fat activists were "sex positive." Their emphasis on pleasure was not a part of, but echoed, feminist debates about sexuality and pornography of the era.

The word "complex" might best describe a fat activist approach to sexuality and relationships, since women expressed feelings of rejection from partners alongside expressions of rebellion and self-acceptance. Interviews with self-identified fat women show that sexuality and femininity were difficult topics to broach, whether within a group or with a potential partner. Women had difficulty finding ways to articulate why fat oppression was unfair when applied to such deeply personal experiences as sex and relationships.

LG5 and other fat lesbians politicized femininity and sexuality by relating oppression to homophobia as well as heterosexual social norms. Christine Donald's poetry, like LG5's activism, spoke to fat oppression among lesbians at the same time as she encouraged women to "rise" against body norms.[84] Members of LAL talked about sexuality and relationships but refused to do so publicly, removing their name from newsletter stories on the topic. In interviews conducted more than twenty years later, many LAL members continued to avoid directly talking about sexuality and relationships. *Canada WYDE* offers a rare glimpse inside a fat-positive singles culture from the 1980s, though we cannot know how representative the ads were of fat women's dating experiences, nor whether the ads successfully matched people together.

Feminist critiques of femininity and sexuality shaped fat activists' understanding of their experiences. Fat feminist activists drew on lesbian critiques of heterosexuality to challenge women to rethink beauty standards. The predominantly heterosexual members of fat acceptance groups did not want to challenge definitions of beauty per se. Rather, LAL sought to give women the tools to empower themselves. Fat lesbians wanted other lesbians to think differently and to realize that no woman should have to change her appearance to try to meet sexist beauty standards. For all women, however, feeling attractive was a difficult battle. Some women were able to reconcile their bodies with their selves and feel comfortable in their own skin. For others it was and is an ongoing struggle.

4 Dr Fullovitt, MD: Fat Women's Experiences with Doctors and Dieting

"Dr Fullovitt" was a fictional MD depicted in the December 1982 issue of the *Bolster*, the monthly newsletter of Large as Life (see figure 10). In the cartoon, a portly Dr Fullovitt advises his patient to "make an effort to lose some of that weight."[1] The Dr Fullovitt vignette satirized a common experience of the self-identified fat women interviewed for this book: being advised to diet by their doctor. Physicians who prescribed weight loss to patients but did not appear to follow their own medical advice were lampooned in this cartoon. The doctor's name, "Fullovitt," also takes aim at the frustrating, ineffective, and (often) unwelcome diet tips many of my research participants received from their physicians. Doctors did not have a clear understanding of weight loss and were "full of it." Fullovitt also tapped into some women's belief that the "the medical profession" had a negative view of fat people. Activists wanted to prove that they were not the "uncooperative, weak-willed, ugly and backward" patients their doctors made them out to be.[2] They especially sought to counter the assumption that being fat was a result of lack of willpower or ignorance about nutrition. Most members of fat women's organizations did not think they ate more, exercised less, or understood nutrition any differently than slimmer family members and friends.

Activist experiences with doctors and dieting are examined in this chapter. It focuses on two sites where women shared their experiences: Large as Life (LAL) Vancouver and Beyond Dieting (BD), a public health program for chronic dieters based in Toronto. Most activists had tried dieting, many times over, and wanted their doctors to understand that diets did not work. They sought out medical research to explain, and validate, their claims.[3] Together, shared experiences and empirical evidence helped to legitimize activists' critique of medicine: diets did not work, and doctors did not fully understand "obesity."

Figure 10. Dr Fullovitt, MD cartoon, "Big Giggles," 1982. From the *Bolster*, December 1982, 16. Courtesy of Suzanne Bell.

Criticisms of doctors and dieting are another example of the web of connections between feminism and fat activism. Activists encouraged women to "re-examine and redefine health and body issues" from an experiential perspective – a strategy that built on the feminist Women's Health Movement (WHM).[4] Since the 1960s, WHM described a range of activities intended to give women greater authority over their bodily health.[5] WHM activists believed that women gained "personal power through knowledge" about their bodies.[6] WHM wasn't necessarily a repudiation of Western medicine so much as a demand that women have a greater say in their care and for more health-care delivery options, like midwifery.[7] Fat activists built on the basic WHM principle of shared medical authority: fat women should learn about health for themselves, and decisions about their weight and diet should be guided by their own experience.

The difference between WHM and fat activism lay in the way they understood the relationship of body to self. WHM activists saw their bodies as their "primary and essential selves through which they related to the world."[8] But, for self-identified fat women, claiming that the body should be a primary site of knowledge about oneself was problematic. Most people saw fat as inherently unhealthy. Challenging the idea that fat was unhealthy and asserting their healthy behaviours was a way for activists to counter negative assumptions about their bodies. In the 2010s activists like Fat Girl Food Squad rejected this approach because it failed to challenge stereotypes about being fat. But members of Large as Life and Beyond Dieting tried to do both: they asserted that fatness could be healthy *and* critiqued the diet industry. As subsequent chapters will show, this combination of social critique with action was a hallmark of fat acceptance activism in Canada. After reviewing the medical history of obesity and self-identified fat women's frustrated accounts of their encounters with doctors, this chapter will show how activists worked to redefine health by rejecting dieting and weight loss surgeries and encouraging "normal" eating.

Weighing and Measuring the Body

The activism documented in this chapter occurred at a time when "healthism," an increased emphasis on self-discipline and personal responsibility for health, was on the rise. Since the 1980s, scholars argue, health has been understood through the lens of personal responsibility. Individuals who maintain a certain lifestyle – namely, a low-fat diet, lots of exercise, and low alcohol intake – are "healthy." Unhealthiness, it follows, is the result of poor choices and the wrong lifestyle. Emphasis on individualism and the avoidance of hazard reflects a neo-liberal approach to health that ignores socio-economic factors.[9] Critical obesity scholars argue that the "obesity epidemic" is a "healthist" response to individuals who "fail to regulate their weight."[10] Fat activism of the 1980s and 1990s was embedded in, and a response to, healthism.

Medical interest in weight developed in the nineteenth century. Belgian physician Adolphe Quételet created the first height-weight tables in the 1830s. He determined that a man's ideal weight in kilograms was his height in centimetres minus one hundred. This data was based on Quételet's observations of patterns of height and weight and was not intended as a measure of body composition.[11] Nonetheless, height-weight tables became a standard for measuring patient health. Quételet's work represents a major turning point in the history of obesity in Western nations.[12]

In North America, insurance companies were at the forefront of using height and weight as a way to measure the health (and cost benefits) of potential clients. Dr George C. Shepherd produced the first American height-weight table in 1897, based on the measurements of 74,162 Canadian and American men who had been accepted for life insurance coverage. The average weight for a man who was 5'8" tall and thirty years old was 154 pounds. A 1908 study modelled on Shepherd's method revealed that women who were 5'4" and thirty years old weighed an average of 130 pounds.[13] These data were used to estimate life expectancy and to assess risk among life insurance clientele. In 1923, this data indicated that overweight male insurance claimants had a slightly shorter life expectancy than average weight men.[14]

Mortality statistics led to a revision of the chart, and in 1940 the Metropolitan Life Insurance Company began to publish tables based on *ideal* weights. The charts no longer documented health in relation to the average population but rather against statistically determined ideals. The company's position was that "mere averages did not necessarily furnish appropriate standards." According to their data, the lowest mortality rates were associated with the ideal weights published in their tables.[15] An ideal weight for men 5'8" and 30 years old was between 136 and 166 pounds. For women 5'4" and 30 years old, an ideal weight was between 116 and 142 pounds.[16] The Metropolitan Life tables were widely used by doctors in the United States and Canada through the twentieth century. Ian Hacking has argued that in the twentieth century "normality" came to be understood as "how things ought to be" rather than how things are.[17] Many height-weight tables reflect this convergence of norms with ideals. Body weight tables document what could be instead of what is happening among the general population.

In Canada, L.B. Pett and G.F. Ogilvie undertook a height-weight study in 1952. Pett and Ogilvie believed that tables developed by insurance companies, as well as height-weight data from the military and public schools, were inadequate because they focused on "special groups ... and could not be applied with any accuracy to the Canadian population."[18] They claimed that clearly defined Canadian standards for height and weight would provide an important "reference guide to doctors, nurses and others concerned with weight control."[19] Data on the average weight of Canadian men and women was remarkably similar to the averages established by Shepherd in 1897. Pett and Ogilvie found that the average weight for a Canadian man who was 5'8" and 30 years old was 166 pounds, and for women 5'4" and 30 years old it was 133 pounds.[20] Pett and Ogilvie obtained Canadian numbers, but the data did not reveal anything new.

The fascination with knowing the body through measurement must be situated within a sociohistorical context wherein the body was seen as an index for the person within. As Elizabeth Grosz has suggested, Cartesian dualism has left its traces on contemporary Western ideas about weight. Healthism, building on several decades of medical debate about weight, suggests that human beings have control over their bodies. As a result of this assumption, the body has been seen to be a reflection of a person's choices.[21] Peter Stearns argues that American attitudes about fatness took on a particularly moralistic tone in the early twentieth century. Americans exhibited a particular zeal for self-control through weight management, which Stearns connects to the Protestant work ethic and emphasis on discipline.[22]

Building on Stearns's research, Amy Erdman Farrell's *Fat Shame* (2011) argues that prohibitions against fatness in America were shaped by the notion that some people are primitive and uncivilized. Farrell shows how eugenics shaped nineteenth- and twentieth-century texts that catalogued bodies and human traits.[23] Thinness was a marker of those who were thought to be higher on the evolutionary scale.[24] Wealthy women who were fat were denigrated for being out of control and unable to manage their consumption, while immigrant and working-class women were represented as fat, coarse, dumb, and, echoing contemporary debates about the "obesity epidemic," unable to properly care for their children.[25]

Racism and colonialism were also embedded in Canadian approaches to health and the body. Building better citizens was one of the primary goals of early twentieth-century public health campaigns.[26] In the 1920s, 1930s, and 1940s, health and welfare programs strove to maintain the ideal of a clean, white, and able body through physical fitness, proper nutrition, and sleep hygiene.[27] In the 1940s L.B. Pett, co-author of Canada's first height-weight study, undertook experimental research on Indigenous children in residential schools. Pett's subjects were chronically malnourished children, some of whom were intentionally fed a low-nutrient diet. Among other things, the research was intended to assess the progress of "modernity" in Indigenous communities.[28]

Nutrition and weight reform programs also targeted new immigrants. After an influx of over 2.5 million immigrants in the post-war era, Canada underwent a crisis of identity that resulted from a diversifying population and the shift of white, middle-class women into the workforce.[29] Indigenous peoples and new immigrants were encouraged to adopt a "better" diet and more closely follow Canada's food guide.[30]

Canadian women were also targets of government, medical, commercial, and social reform movements of the twentieth century. Demand for weight maintenance programs grew in the post-war era with the perception that Canadians were less fit and physically prepared than they had been in the past. Commercial diet programs aimed at women were advertised in newspapers and in the *Canadian Medical Association Journal*. Doctors, unable to offer any medical solutions to weight loss, prescribed diet pills and meal replacements.[31] By the 1970s, diet programs were big business in the United States and Canada. Weight Watchers was started by "formerly fat housewife" Jean Nidetch in 1961 and was returning $39 million dollars in profits by 1977. Nutri-System profited $48 million dollars in 1981, allowing owner Harold Katz to buy the Philadelphia 76ers basketball team.[32] In the absence of concrete membership numbers for Canada, the profits of commercial diet companies provide anecdotal evidence of their popularity.

The rise in commercial dieting in post-war North America coincided with a general proliferation of dieting and body projects that has been documented by historians. Growing social interest in *women's* weight emerged in different ways. Some scholars have attributed the body projects of women to a "beauty myth" that encouraged women to locate their self-worth in their bodies.[33] Other researchers have connected the imperative to be thin to women's liberation. Women have responded to their own liberation by becoming more boyish or androgynous.[34] Conversely, Susan Faludi has argued that the "backlash" against women's liberation led women to compensate by looking thinner and more feminine.[35]

This book shows that there is no single factor influencing body norms, but multiple social forces that shaped women's understanding of weight. In Canada body norms were also shaped by post-war efforts to improve the health and welfare of the population. As Douglas

Owram and Mona Gleason have observed, parents of the baby boom era were more focused than ever on the psychological health and stability of their children. Psychologists, nutritionists, doctors, and health nurses offered parents advice on how to bring up the "normal" child.[36] These pressures were evident in my research participants' answers to the question: "Have you ever been on a diet?"

Doctor and Dieting Stories

Doctor and dieting stories rolled easily off the tongues of my research participants.[37] Individually, these narratives reflect a lifetime of attempts to lose weight. Collectively, these stories reveal fat activists grappling with a disjuncture between "ideal" bodies and their experiences with weight. Only four of the forty-nine self-identified fat women interviewed for this book were not regular dieters.[38] The rest began dieting in their teens and twenties, sometimes earlier. Some began at the suggestion of mothers and doctors who told them they needed to watch their weight.[39] Many, like LAL's Jan Mindlin, "lost and gained thirty pounds more times than [she] cared to count."[40] The cycle of weight loss and gain became predictable. LAL's Joan Dal Santo recalled that it always felt good in the beginning but then "you plateau or you slide off and cheat and it feels bad ... there is that guilt and shame stuff ... it's very defeating."[41] To avoid embarrassment about regaining weight, some women moved between different Weight Watchers groups.[42] Suzanne Bell of LAL joked that she had joined a hundred times, sometimes "under an assumed name."[43] Jan Mindlin was certain that she had spent so much money on Weight Watchers that she "could be a shareholder."[44]

Women who became involved with fat activism also used diet pills. In the 1960s Benzedrine was the most common diet pill, but in the 1970s D-Amphetamine became a more popular way to reduce the appetite and increase the energy of patients.[45] Doctors recommended and prescribed diet pills, but there is plenty of evidence that patients also asked for these medications. Despite the fact that the drugs were potentially addictive and had to be taken continuously, amphetamine-based pills were prescribed to some of my participants when they were between the ages of eight and thirteen.[46] These women recalled that the amphetamines had a "buzz" effect. Plus-size clothing storeowner Monica Sieben-Kuhn was given the pills when she was eight years old. The pills "wound" Sieben-Kuhn up "tighter than a top," so her mother decided to take her off the drugs.[47] Sieben-Kuhn was one of four women interviewed who did not take diet pills by choice but were prescribed amphetamines at the request of their parents.[48] Joyce Cusack, a LAL Calgary member, went on the drugs shortly after she was married but quit because they "drove [her] nuts" and made her heart race.[49] Claudia Savage also took amphetamines as an adult, but she stopped taking the pills because they "wired you up for sound."[50] Despite such side effects, a teenaged Andria Siegler requested more of the drug from her physician. To stay slim Siegler knew she would have to take more and more pills.[51]

Dieting became a way for women to prepare for particularly important passages in their lives. Sandy Friedman, therapist and LAL member, did the Atkins diet in the early 1970s when she was moving to Vancouver to "start a new life" and therefore felt she "had to be on a diet." The Atkins diet required Friedman to "pee ... on a little stick" to ensure her body was in ketosis. Ketosis occurs when there are not enough carbohydrates in the body to produce glucose and the body turns to stored energy to function. According to Atkins's theory, using stored energy can burn fat and lower the appetite. Ever diligent, Friedman continued to do these checks "in the bushes" as she "camped across Canada" on her way from Montreal to Vancouver.[52] Two women dieted to get into nursing school. In the 1960s NAAFA/CASA's Helena Spring lost about thirty pounds "to get into nursing school because nobody would accept [her] fat."[53] Mrs O's member Lynne Grauer also worked hard to maintain her weight for nursing school. Grauer was informed that 170 pounds was too heavy to be a nurse and was advised by supervisors to "try and lose some of the weight."[54] Though is no Canadian-specific data, other researchers have shown that "weigh-ins" were a common practice in nursing schools in the United States in the 1960s.[55] Activists also dieted in order to get jobs,[56] life insurance,[57] and, of course, to attract potential partners.[58] Many succeeded in finding jobs, meeting partners, and getting insurance, but none of these women succeeded in losing weight permanently.

Doctors came up frequently in response to my questions about dieting. Jan Mindlin recalled being told at fifteen years old (c. 1960s) and 130 pounds that she was "disgusting."[59] As a teenager (c. 1960s), Sue Masterton's doctor mocked her for asking if she should take her shoes off before stepping on a scale. His response was "you can take your lipstick off if you think that will make a difference." Masterton complained that "in the medical profession they still think its calories in, calories out ... it's not that simple. And one day, one day, they're going to discover" that obesity is much more complex.[60] LAL member Evelyn Booth recalled feeling annoyed by a female doctor (c. 1980s), who was surprised to learn that Booth was a swimmer and complimented her for not being "ashamed to be seen in a bathing suit." Booth felt this was a clear example of anti-fat bias and noted that the doctors would never comment about race.[61] Booth reiterated the oft-repeated claim by activists that fat, unlike racism, was an "accepted" prejudice in the 1980s. This distinction does not have any grounding in fact, since black Canadians faced (and continue to face) discrimination in many social settings. What she was describing might more helpfully be understood as a bias based on visible identity. Linda Alcoff argues that in contemporary society "the reality of identities often comes from the fact that they are visibly marked on the body." Visible signifiers have tended to "achieve the status of accepted truth" about a person.[62] Doctors were making assumptions about the health of fat women based on what they looked like, not their physical symptoms.

Self-identified fat women reported that, at some appointments, their doctors focused on weight loss rather than the presenting health issue. Joyce Cusack of LAL Calgary recalled a visit to a doctor for a sciatic nerve problem (c. 1980s). He told her she was not helping herself by being overweight. Leaning over Cusack, who was lying down with a sheet covering her partially dressed body, he said, "you're fat." Cusack cried on her way home in the car. She refused "to put up with" such treatment and switched doctors over the years when she felt they overemphasized weight as an issue.[63] Therapist Doris Maranda believed that her weight was used as an excuse to deny her full coverage after a car accident. A doctor for ICBC insurance noted in his file of Maranda (c. 1990s), then a forty-year-old *woman*, "this girl needs to lose weight." Maranda was furious because the implication was that "weight had to do with the whiplash in my neck. It was bullshit." Because of this and similar experiences, Maranda and fellow therapist Sandy Friedman offered a "list of doctors and psychiatrists and people that were more progressive" to their clients.[64]

Activists' experiences with doctors echo many of the complaints expressed by WHM activists: doctors did not listen, they did not fully understand women's bodies, and they had a condescending and sexist attitude towards their female patients.[65] Self-identified fat women's experiences were evidence of the rise of healthism at the end of the twentieth century. They also confirm research undertaken since the 1990s on health professionals' attitudes towards obese patients. Authors of this literature have found that nurses and doctors tended to stigmatize obese patients and assume they were unhealthy.[66]

Fat Liberation and Health

Critiques of doctors and dieting first articulated by Llewellyn Louderback and the Fat Underground (FU) influenced Canadian fat activism. American activists argued that medical approaches to weight were shaped by aesthetic and moral distaste for fatness. Soon after FU's formation in 1973, Lynn Mabel-Lois taught fellow members to search through medical databases for information on fat and health.[67] In 1974, this research led to a burst of pamphlet writing by the FU. These pamphlets articulated the basic contours of fat activists claims against doctors and dieting.[68] In "Health of Fat People: The Scare Story Your Doctor Won't Tell You," Aldebaran accused doctors and medical researchers of being biased against fat people. She argued that medical research studies did not include healthy fat subjects. A second and related issue outlined in this pamphlet was the FU's belief that prescribing diets was a form mistreatment and abuse by doctors. The "reason why doctors rarely see healthy fat people," Aldebaran argued, "is because doctors prescribe diets which make fat people sick."[69] This claim reflected the influence of Louderback's *Fat Power*, which argued that physicians were ill-informed and hung on to the idea that "reducing is somehow possible ... with irrational tenacity."[70] Here Louderback referenced a series of medical studies that indicated that dieting led to malnutrition,[71] weight gain, reduced life expectancy,[72] and heart damage.[73] Louderback concluded that obesity had become "a handy wastebasket diagnosis" for a medical establishment that had failed to undertake "basic research into the condition."[74]

The FU applied Louderback's critique to women's health.[75] In "Health of Fat People: The Real Problem," the FU related their "furious realization" that doctors prescribe diets not for health but because they "value chiefly our looks, in the way of all sexist males."[76] The "99% failure rate" of dieting was evidence of "the medical establishment trivializing women's health issues and lack of regard for the safety of female patients generally."[77] The FU staged an event at Los Angeles's Women's Equality Day in 1974 to illustrate their point. Collectively, group members marched on to an open mic stage and held a symbolic funeral for musician "Mama Cass" Elliott (a.k.a. Naomi Cohen) who had died of a heart attack a few weeks earlier. The FU claimed Elliott's heart attack was the result of a doctor-prescribed diet. The "medical establishment" was guilty of murdering Cass.[78] Referring to the erroneous rumour that Cass had died from choking on a ham sandwich, the FU proclaimed that "Naomi Cohen choked on the culture, on the stale empty air and worthless standards of our conditioning. But Fat Power/Pride and love of sensuality is being reborn and is here to stay!"[79] In this dramatic protest the FU connected women's oppression to dieting. Mama Cass was a symbol of society's tragic emphasis on looks over talent.

Critiques of dieting articulated by Louderback and the FU tended to travel alongside fat activism itself, crossing geographical, ideological, and linguistic boundaries between the United States and Canada.[80] Members of LG5, LAL, and Hersize were inspired by the FU's critique of dieting and medical professionals.[81] The FU influenced or shared sources with other important books from the era like Marcia Millman's *Such a Pretty Face: Being Fat in America* (1980), *Shadow on a Tightrope: Writings by Women on Fat Oppression* (1983), and to a lesser extent Susie Orbach's bestselling *Fat Is a Feminist Issue* (1978), all texts with which many activists were familiar.[82] Louderback's and FU's research was cited in *Radiance: The Magazine for Large Women* (circulated in North America, 1984 to 2000), which counted at least two of my participants as readers. *Radiance* later published profiles of two Canadian activists and one group: Suzanne Bell and Jody Sandler, and Hersize.[83]

Activists tended to read this information through the lens of their personal experiences, which accounts for the subtle changes in messaging between groups. Canadian activists were particularly invested in the idea that fat people could be healthy. The activists of LAL Vancouver (1981 to 1985) and professionals behind Beyond Dieting (1986 to 1996) provide examples of the ways that Canadians worked to improve the well-being of fat women. Drawing on their experiences, activist approaches, and medical research, fat women in Canada worked to improve their knowledge of diet and exercise and wanted to find ways to be fat and healthy. While they did not reject healthism outright, their actions and activism reflect what Dorothy Smith has described as a point of "of rupture between experience and the relations of ruling."[84] Women used their personal histories as the grounds from which to test out new ways of being healthy – they stopped dieting, took up exercise, and tried to let go of their guilt about being fat.

"obesity: facts & fiction" (1984)

LAL founder Kate Partridge became interested in the pitfalls of dieting when she worked as a facilitator for a diabetes support group at Vancouver's Lions Gate Hospital. She observed that most participants were able to keep to a regular exercise routine but their diet programs never worked.[85] This pattern was one Partridge had observed in her life, and so she began to research the relationship between weight and health, taking time out from her doctoral research on standardized psychological testing.[86] Bits and pieces of Partridge's research began to appear in the *Bolster* and were discussed at LAL meetings in 1981 and 1982.[87] Partridge brought this information together for the 1982 meeting of the Women and Psychology section of the Canadian Psychological Association, and she published an abbreviated version of the research in a pamphlet called "obesity: facts & fiction."[88]

Partridge argued against the idea that "slimness and good health" were synonymous.[89] Fatness was seen as "morally wrong because it signifies either a weak will and a lack of self-control, or a wilful disregard of social values."[90] This stigma also resulted in discrimination in housing and jobs. As a consequence, women engaged in high-risk diets and supported a "dangerous" dieting industry. Here she pointed out that diets had a low success rate: "while any other disorder with a treatment success rate of 5% would probably be considered more or less incurable, it is still maintained that something can be done to lose weight permanently."[91] Partridge placed some of the blame for this problem on medical professionals who have "considerable power in determining how obesity is viewed in our culture."[92]

Obesity, Partridge continued, was a complex problem, not easily controlled by the conscious will.[93] Her experience and research suggested that weight management was not just a question of mind over matter. The greatest threat facing fat people was to their emotional well-being, since there was an "extraordinary social distaste for fatness and general obsession with slimness in our culture."[94] The result of such social pressure was shame and fear of "social rejection and humiliation." Dieting could actually make you fatter because "when you deprive yourself of food during a crash diet, your metabolic rate slows down, resulting in a decrease in overall energy expenditure." The solution was to get off the binge cycle altogether, eat normally, and get regular exercise.[95]

Next, Partridge outlined a series of treatment goals, urging doctors to take social and psychological factors into consideration when treating fat patients. Among Partridge's ideas was "an assessment of the client's true state of physical health – taking her past weight history into consideration – without untested assumptions based solely on the fact that the client is 'overweight.'" Instead, she encouraged doctors to promote "cardiovascular endurance, suppleness and strength" through a regular exercise program.[96] Partridge outlined a fat women's exercise program based on Large as Life's aerobics program, which will be discussed in chapter 5. She also encouraged "promoting the acceptance of large women" through the media as well as groups like "Large as Life."[97] She concluded her paper with a final entreaty to doctors to "include improvement in physical and emotional well-being in ways that are not dependent on weight loss" in their approach to obese patients. Focusing on health rather than weight loss was particularly important since there was no known cure for obesity and patients were likely to remain overweight.[98]

"obesity: facts & fiction" was unique because it paired the medical literature supporting the idea that fat could be healthy with a plan: education and self-help. She wanted fat women to use each other's experience and expertise as resources. "Obesity: facts & fiction" urged women to work with their doctors to improve their health. Partridge's vision was that a woman's experience and knowledge of her body would dictate her approach to wellness. Her woman-to-woman approach reflected the WHM's focus on self-education and the primacy of personal experience in that movement.

Evidence that LAL members were reading and applying ideas from "obesity: facts & fiction" can be found in the *Bolster*. The newsletter featured a regular "Ruffled Feathers" column that critiqued cultural messages about weight.[99] The April 1983 Ruffled Feathers write-up took aim at an advertisement for a "Weight Loss Clinic" chain that encouraged clients to "join the thinner circle." Editor Ingrid Laue underlined particularly egregious passages in the ad, including a testimonial reading, "I never knew that living could be so enjoyable and exciting until I discovered the Weight Loss Clinic. By the way, this thank you is seconded by my husband."[100] Laue took exception to the claim that life was more "enjoyable and exciting" after weight loss and seemed particularly annoyed by the suggestion that men preferred slimmer women. This column and similar features in the *Bolster* show LAL members were disillusioned with doctors and commercial diet programs.

Bariatric Surgery

While LAL provided a framework for women to critique fat oppression, debates in the newsletter show that members did not always agree on health issues. In January 1982, not long after the group formed, bariatric surgery became a hotly contested topic. Bariatrics is the umbrella term given to surgeries that treat obesity, including the surgery Sue Masterton underwent in the mid-1980s. Among these procedures were intestinal and gastric bypass and gastric banding, a.k.a. "stomach stapling." Candidates for the surgery had to be between eighteen and fifty years old, at least one hundred pounds overweight, with a healthy heart. They also had to undergo a psychiatric evaluation to make sure they were prepared for the procedure.[101]

Fat activists have generally been critical of bariatrics. Data from the 1970s indicated that up to one of every ten people who had the surgery died from complications.[102] Citing a NAAFA study by Paul Ernsberger,

Carla Rice of Toronto's Hersize suggested that between 2 to 9 per cent of bariatrics patients died within the first few months of their surgery. According to Ernsberger, a professor in the Department of Nutrition at Case Western Reserve University, 12 per cent of all bariatrics candidates died within seven years of having bariatric surgery.[103] Canadian diet and weight loss experts Janet Polivy and Peter Herman put this number somewhat lower, at between 5 and 10 per cent for the intestinal bypass procedures performed in the 1970s and 3 per cent for the gastric banding procedures introduced in the 1980s.[104] For activists, high mortality rates were evidence of the risk that doctors were willing to take in order to get their patients to lose weight. They likened bariatric surgery to cosmetic surgery because the risks were high and the health benefits questionable.[105]

In the pages of their newsletter, LAL members rigorously debated the pros and cons of bariatric surgery. LAL member Barbara Berry started the conversation on bariatric surgery with a January 1982 piece titled "'Naturally, the Choice Is up to You.'" Berry proudly proclaimed herself to be a "255 lb borderline diabetic" who controlled her blood sugar levels without insulin. Through diet and exercise she maintained a healthy heart, lungs, and blood pressure. For this reason, she was shocked when her doctor suggested that she consider obesity surgery. Initially the sceptical author's response was "No!" She told her doctor that research showed such surgeries to be unsafe. Still, she agreed to consider it and undertake further research if her doctor would do the same. Berry reported that she had already discovered surgeries could cause diarrhoea, liver damage, and kidney failure. She told readers that she was "off to the UBC Library" and promised to "share" her "findings with" readers."[106]

Members' responses to Berry about the benefits and pitfalls of bariatric surgery were published in the newsletter.[107] LAL member Laurie Kahn had the surgery and made this assessment: The diarrhoea was "annoying rather than debilitating. Some of my hair has fallen out, but the doctor assures me this will pass. Meanwhile, I should eat more protein. I still tire easily, but each week I have more energy." Overall, Kahn was pleased and said that "the weight just magically comes off, a little each month," and she was satisfied that her weight was down to close to two hundred pounds.[108] For Kahn, the risks and side effects of the surgeries were worth it because she had significantly improved her quality of life. Her experience was very different from that of Sue Masterton for whom the side effects of the surgery had been life-threatening.

Barbara Berry reported back to members that her research trip to UBC library was "shocking." She had found ten to fifteen articles on the surgeries in each monthly issue of the *Index Medicus*. She reviewed titles she found "most relevant for me – about 42 in all." A number of phrases in these articles "leapt out" at Berry: "skeletal abnormalities, arthritis/dermatis syndrome, foetal abnormalities of pregnancy during the malnutrition stage." Reviewing the articles, Berry found that most did not take an active position for or against the surgeries, focusing rather on how to minimize side effects. She felt this "seeming detachment" dehumanized fat patients. This research trip helped Berry to make up her mind not to have the surgery, despite the temptation to fit into the "size 12 clothes hidden at the back of" her "closet."[109] For readers who wanted more information, Berry listed articles from the *International Journal of Obesity* and *American Surgeon* at the end of her article. Notwithstanding these findings, Berry encouraged members to evaluate the medical evidence for themselves.

Bariatric surgery was contentious for some LAL members because it undermined the claim that fat women could be happy and healthy. For these members bariatric surgery seemed more like a cosmetic than a life-saving medical procedure. *Bolster* editor Ingrid Laue challenged this view in her own piece on bariatrics; she warned readers that more evidence was needed to understand the complications around the surgery. Herself a PhD candidate in Germanic studies and married to a medical doctor, Laue may have felt compelled to publish this note because of her own commitment to scholarly research or to medicine. Or, perhaps Laue sided with Kahn and felt that readers should make up their own minds about the process. This example shows that "experience" was not uncontested among LAL members. As Kathy Davis has argued, women considering body modification surgeries "always have at least some degree of awareness about their situation as well as the consequences of their actions."[110] Members of LAL compared medical, experiential, and anecdotal evidence in their discussions about the merits of weight-loss surgeries.

The debate by LAL members about bariatric surgery has some parallels to responses to *Our Bodies, Ourselves* – readers frequently wrote to the editors with suggestions and corrections to the text.[111] As Kathy Davis and Wendy Kline have shown, readers did not treat the editorial leadership as "undisputed authorities on women's health" but rather engaged with this leadership by writing them letters, and using the text in conversation with communities of women.[112] LAL members used the *Bolster* in a similar fashion, as a sounding board for personal opinions and perspectives on health issues. Berry concluded, based on her experience, that she was sufficiently healthy to forgo the surgery, whereas Kahn's experience told her that the surgery was the right choice.

Experience was not only a lens to understand weight science but also empowered LAL members to make up their own minds about doctors and dieting. Doctors were not the explicit target of criticism or action in Partridge's model. Instead, her framework assumed that women should take an active role in decisions about their health. LAL members needed to learn to differentiate between authoritative and authoritarian knowledge,[113] which meant that members should evaluate the advice offered by their doctors rather than accept that it was the only approach to health. LAL's approach implicated both doctors and patients in the redefinition of fatness as (potentially) healthy. Reflecting LAL's orientation towards fat acceptance, Partridge was encouraging members to think about how they could improve their personal experiences and everyday lives.[114] Provided they were at peace with their weight, members should choose the course of action that made them feel best.

While LAL permitted fluid understandings of fat acceptance within the group, their use of scientific expertise was idiosyncratic. Doctors emerged as villains or heroes, depending on how they approached women's weight. "Bad science" was that espoused by doctors who shamed fat people and found in medical journals whose scientific "neutrality" belied the pain and suffering experienced by overweight patients. "Good science" was that which incorporated and reflected the personal experiences of members. Other criteria that may have been important, including the scientific authors' qualifications, their philosophy of weight loss, or even the number of articles that repeated a particular claim, were less important than finding research that did not take a moralizing or shaming approach towards fat people. The assertion that diets do not work and fat people can be healthy is now well documented and increasingly widely accepted. But at the time activists were selective in choosing their evidence.[115]

In the last two years of its existence, LAL's approach to health shifted. This change coincided with the increased prominence of Gail Bell, a lawyer who became editor of the *Bolster* in January 1984 and assumed the presidency of the group after Suzanne Bell (no relation) left to pursue her aerobics and fashion business. Gail Bell wanted to take a more explicitly political stance on fatness and focus more specifically on "educating" doctors. For example, in the newsletter she profiled two pregnant members, Pat and Jane, who had been told by their doctors that being overweight was a "disaster" for their babies.[116] Pat and Jane had subsequently found new doctors who were described as "easy to talk to" and praised for "never bringing up the topic of weight." The following month, March 1984, the *Bolster* printed the names of physicians whom "various ... members find comfortable to deal with."[117]

Gail Bell also personally critiqued doctors' "Johnny-one-note view of treatment for the ills of large people":

> We owe it to ourselves not to be silent, not to make excuses for them ... And in the interests of getting their attention, we owe it to ourselves to try to talk a language they are able to comprehend. We must present our knowledge not as our belief, based on heaven knows what sources, but as the result of our reading of the research of their own colleagues. Be specific. Cite the title and name of the respected medical researchers who are more and more often stating that weight loss is not to be seen as snake oil to the ills of the large.[118]

Accompanying this article were two editorial cartoons of a male doctor, perhaps a colleague of Dr Fullovitt. In one, the doctor leans over a fat patient in a body cast telling her, "if you'd lose some weight your hair would stop falling out." This time, his patient talks back: "According to whom? Polivy and Herman say dieting causes loss of hair ... and energy, gall bladder, and libido."[119] In the second, the doctor exclaims, "I didn't know that!" (see figure 11).

Bell's cartoons referred to *Breaking the Diet Habit*, a 1983 book by Canadian researchers Janet Polivy and Peter Herman. Polivy and Herman's thesis was that "dieting and weight gain may be responsible for serious health problems usually attributed to overweight," such as high blood pressure. The researchers argued against those doctors "who urge weight loss for the sake of health." They believed that many doctors did not know that "weight loss can be actively harmful" and can lead to complications such as gallstones, low blood pressure, muscular aching, abdominal pain, kidney stones, anaemia, headache, cardiac problems, and depression.[120] Where Polivy and Herman departed from research previously presented in the *Bolster* and earlier fat activist texts was in their claim that "stable, lifelong overweight is probably the natural and optimally healthy state for many people."[121]

Polivy and Herman use set-point theory to make their case against dieting. Set-point theory suggests that a person's metabolism will adjust to changes in calorie intake in order to defend their set point, that is, their "natural" weight.[122] Bodies have different set points, and some are naturally larger. The body regulates "appetite and metabolism to defend the set point and prevent large fluctuations in weight," making weight loss and gain difficult.[123] Polivy and Herman further argue that weight gain might be physiological in origin. People who ate too much might in fact lack "natural regulatory signals of hunger and satiety."[124] Building on this research, Jerome P. Kassirer and

Figure 11. Cartoons from the *Bolster* explaining Polivy and Herman's dieting research, March 1984. Courtesy of Suzanne Bell.

Marcia Angell have argued that, while it is possible to "temporarily override the set point" through extensive dieting, afterward "weight generally returns to its pre-existing level." Set point theory explains individual variations in weight and why diets don't work. It also added scientific and professional authority to what self-identified fat women already suspected: that the logic behind dieting was flawed.[125]

Beyond Dieting

Polivy and Herman's book was part of a wave of Canadian research about the impact of body ideals on women. By 1985, crash diets, where a person drastically changed their eating habits and lost a large amount of weight in a short period of time, and yo-yo dieting, characterized by ongoing cycles of weight loss and gain, were such pervasive phenomena that the Canadian federal government formed an expert group to help develop a new "national strategy to promote healthy weights and prevent weight problems."[126] The 1985 expert group included three researchers with links to fat activism in Canada: Janet Polivy, one of the experts cited by Gail Bell; John Hunt, who had hired Kate Partridge of LAL in 1981 to facilitate a diabetes support group at Lions Gate Hospital; and David Garner, the eating disorder specialist who went on to form Hersize.[127]

"Promoting Healthy Weights" was the 1988 discussion paper that came out of the expert group. Even though government initiatives like ParticipACTION and the Canada Fitness Survey had contributed to increasing awareness of body weight and shape in the 1970s and 1980s, the expert group placed blame for the epidemic of "weight preoccupation" on the media and commercial dieting programs.[128] Seventy per cent of women surveyed in the study admitted to a desire to lose weight, which accounted for the problematic rise in "fad diets, and the sale of weight-loss gimmicks" that were "frequently exploitive."[129] "Personal and societal acceptance of a range of healthy weights and variations in body size ... encourage Canadians to develop and maintain appropriate eating habits and physical activity patterns" was recommended by the expert group. They also asked that the government support "services that are directed towards the promotion of healthy weights and the treatment of weight problems."[130]

"Promoting Healthy Weights" shares similar ideas with WHM and the fat activism of the 1980s and may have been influenced by them. Both "Promoting Healthy Weights" and "obesity: facts & fiction" deemed dieting unhealthy and suggested that the psychological impact of being overweight had serious consequences. Both texts argued it was necessary to make clearer distinctions between ideal and healthy bodies.[131] Both texts also identified stigma as a social problem, because of the physical and psychological impact of stereotypes about fat people.[132] Lastly, fat activists and health researchers were both concerned with the health impact of public (and private) pressure on women to be slim.

Anti-dieting messaging was an area where fat activism, WHM, and medical approaches to weight overlapped. In the 1980s feminist activities in Canada began to develop programs to encourage self-esteem and healthy eating. Whereas in the 1970s Canadian WHM activists focused on reproductive health, in the 1980s the impact of feminine norms was also a site for organizing.[133] Women's health clinics like the National Eating Disorder Information Centre, the Winnipeg Women's Health Clinic, and the Vancouver Women's Health Collective developed "body image" awareness and support programs across Canada. These organizations developed clinical interventions to help women stop dieting and develop greater self-esteem.

Beyond Dieting was the most enduring of these body image and self-esteem programs. Donna Ciliska, then a doctoral candidate at the University of Toronto, designed the program.[134] Ciliska wanted to build on Garner and Polivy's findings about the negative impact of dieting, and so she decided to "develop and actually test an alternative for large women, to see if their weight could be stabilized as opposed to continuing" to "yo-yo."[135] The program's goal was to get overweight women who were chronic dieters to re-establish normal eating, improve self-esteem, and learn to "become accepting of all different weights and sizes, especially" their own.[136]

A handful of men responded to the newspaper ads and articles about the Beyond Dieting program, but they were refused participation.[137] Ciliska believed that largeness in men was associated with power and not as highly stigmatized as it was in women.[138] Although she did not think all fat women had low self-esteem, Ciliska believed there was a relationship between chronic dieting and poor self-image.[139] Beyond Dieting shared three fundamental assumptions with fat activism: medical science had failed to find an effective approach to weight loss, it was important to find ways to ease the negative impact of fat oppression, and weight was primarily a women's issue. While Beyond Dieting was not an activist group per se, Ciliska's approach and her premise echoed both feminist fat liberation and fat acceptance practices.

Beyond Dieting started as a clinical study at the University of Toronto in 1986. Soon thereafter the National Eating Disorder Information

Centre began to offer the program, versions of which continued to be available at Toronto General Hospital until 1996.[140] The program also became the model for similar initiatives in feminist women's health clinics across Canada, including L'obsession de la minceur (Verdun) and Getting Beyond Weight (Winnipeg), as well as public health interventions like the Healthy Weight Program (Halton Region), among others.[141] Weight loss was not the goal of the ten- to twelve-week program. Instead, anti-dieting workshops aimed to get women to "normalize" their eating and follow the Canada Food Guide: "Three meals a day and two snacks, so that you are eating every couple of hours and you stop when you are satisfied, not when you are stuffed ... to not skip meals, but just get into a routine of eating ... It doesn't give ... time to get ravaged or hungry so you overcompensate and binge."[142] "Normal" eating was the antidote to "weight preoccupation." Similarities to Hersize's approach to fatness should be apparent, since the group borrowed the notion of "weight preoccupation" from clinical practitioners like Ciliska. Ciliska believed that weight preoccupation should be understood as a continuum of behaviours ranging from dieting to overeating to compulsive eating to anorexia and bulimia. Such behaviours were destructive to individual women, and, collectively, a waste of the energy and potential of all women.

Ciliska's workshops were aimed at persuading women that they could be healthy at any size and sought to educate participants about normal eating, body image, self-care, and self-acceptance.[143] Beyond Dieters were taught that caloric restriction and diet foods were not effective. Rather than limit food intake, Ciliska felt it was important to follow the Canada Food Guide and enjoy a range of food groups. Ciliska also informed participants that yo-yo dieting could do as much damage to their health as being overweight.[144] Participants' expectations of Beyond Dieting and their motivations for signing up for the program were quite different from those who joined activist-oriented groups like Large as Life. Information circulated differently because Beyond Dieting was a therapeutic environment that relied on the leadership of an expert whose role was to persuade participants to experience a diet-free lifestyle.

Prior to joining Hersize, Mary Frances Ellison participated in Beyond Dieting. She remembered that participants in Beyond Dieting were very apprehensive in initial sessions: "Giving up dieting and the whole idea of eating whatever you wanted and not being on a diet was very frightening. I mean the fear in the room was amazing ... there were women for whom that had been their lifestyle, that had been their life. They were in their forties or fifties or sixties and they had a whole lot invested in that belief system ... they were ... really not wanting to believe what they were hearing ... not wanting to give up the dream of 'someday, I'll be thin.'"[145] Ellison described a subdued, even fearful, environment. By comparison, LAL members described feeling "fired up" at their first meeting.

One of the first steps Ciliska used to get Beyond Dieting participants to let go of the "dream" was to add up the money they had cumulatively spent on weight-loss programs. Ciliska was aware that many women came to Beyond Dieting as a last resort – they had tried everything else. She remembered in particular a woman was so frustrated that she joined Weight Watchers, a local Toronto weight-loss clinic, and Beyond Dieting all at the same time. Beyond Dieting was free, but this woman had spent $3000 in one week. Ciliska reported that another participant owned her own weight-loss franchise. A few weeks into the program she admitted to the group that she "made a lot of money" from her franchise but was "not able to be successful on her own weight-loss program."[146]

Ciliska used participants' frustration to persuade them to try normal eating. She soon realized her task was made more complicated by the fact that she herself was not fat. It was hard for some participants to hear that diets did not work from someone who, by her own admission, had never struggled with her weight.[147] Where groups like Big Dance and LAL relied on the recognition of common experiences between all members, Beyond Dieting participants could not see themselves in Ciliska.

In response to this problem, Ciliska recruited self-identified fat women who had "graduated" from the program.[148] Andria Siegler, who succeeded Ciliska, believed that participants were "more willing to give [Beyond Dieting] a chance if it was coming from someone who lived it."[149] Remembering this decision in a 2006 interview, Ciliska felt that having a person who was "a graduate of the program" and had been following the non-dieting "philosophy for years and years" and was "still big" was more effective. Siegler's body size hit "them in the face" and helped participants to "deal" with the issue of dieting and health more effectively.[150] Ciliska's expertise was not always enough for Beyond Dieting participants. Women in the program wanted to hear from someone who looked like them. Perhaps they were sceptical because Ciliska looked just like any other medical professional they had dealt with in the past.

Beyond Dieting departed from the other forms of activism discussed in this book in several significant ways: Weight preoccupation personalized the problem of fat oppression, rather than seeing it as a societal issue. It represented a redirection of women's weight concerns back towards questions of food intake and away from critiques of social norms and the medical profession. Despite these shortcomings, weight preoccupation incorporated feminist critiques of health into new, government-supported and woman-centred models of care.[151] I include Beyond Dieting in my analysis of fat activism because it was part of what Miriam Smith has described as the "web of associations and overlapping connections" that characterized Canadian social movements in this time period.[152] These associations remind us that some women moved between roles as health professionals and activists, perhaps even that an activist stance towards weight was not incompatible with government-supported health-care programs.[153] Beyond Dieting reflected what Charlotte Cooper has called "political process fat activism." It achieved change through engagement with "the processes of state power."[154] Activists had to use dominant ideologies to gain access to the system.[155] Greater influence in the health-care system was achieved, but it did not have the radical edge of feminist fat activism.

Experience also shaped Beyond Dieting in much the same way it did in other fat activist groups. Women who came to the group wanted to see their struggles reflected in the experiences of other women in the room. It did not occur, or even matter to them, whether this issue impacted all women. They came to Beyond Dieting for personal reasons and did not expect anything other than individual solutions to their dilemma. Demographically, the average participant of Beyond Dieting had a lot in common with members of LAL. Ciliska reported that the average participant in the original Beyond Dieting program was between twenty and sixty-seven years old, with an average age of thirty-nine.[156] Data on the ethnicity of participants was not taken, but Ciliska and others interviewed suggested that the women were predominantly, though not exclusively, white.[157]

Even if the program was in a clinical setting, Beyond Dieting participants interviewed for another study reported similar outcomes to those of fat activist groups. These results included increased self-esteem and quitting dieting.[158] Mary Frances Ellison of Hersize offered a similar assessment. Her understanding of healthy weight changed after completing Beyond Dieting. Twenty years on, the concept of normal eating was influencing her approach to child-rearing. Ellison was attempting to impart a "health at any size" message to her children.[159] Ciliska found it most rewarding when Beyond Dieting was "freeing" for participants. Her goal was to see people "accept themselves, to believe that they are valuable people."[160] Beyond Dieting can be seen as a trajectory of earlier feminist and WHM efforts to bring women together to share their experiences and concerns about their bodies. It shows that women's health activism had an impact that reached far beyond feminist organizations and into the lives of women who did not see themselves as activists.[161]

Conclusions

They may not have had "good" bodies by the measure of cultural ideals, but fat activists believed they could have healthy bodies. In her study of the Boston Women's Health Book Collective and *Our Bodies, Ourselves*, Kathy Davis observed that the act of attributing "authority to women's embodied experiences" was "both individually and collectively empowering."[162] LAL members and Beyond Dieting participants similarly felt empowered through critical knowledge of doctors and dieting. LAL and Beyond Dieting also illustrate the ways that non-dieting approaches shifted over the course of the decade. Early in the decade the idea that fat people might be healthy was marginal and did not have a lot of currency. By the beginning of the 1990s the idea that women suffered from "weight preoccupation" and might be better off not dieting had permeated the mainstream. The path between fat activism, women's health, and government-supported health programs was not a direct one. Nonetheless, critical perspectives on dieting were helped along considerably by fat activists, who refused to accept that their weight was necessarily a problem.

While their critiques were similar, LAL and Beyond Dieting promoted identical strategies. The context in which these approaches developed mattered. Large as Life materialized in a climate where medical professionals assumed that fatness was unhealthy, and Beyond Dieting emerged at a time when concerns about the impact of yo-yo dieting had gained some legitimacy within the field of dietetics and public health. Although Beyond Dieting included discussions of fat oppression, the approach was necessarily different from that of organizations that were created by fat women, for fat women. If LAL was a case study for the circulation of medical information among fat women, then Beyond Dieting was a case study of the ways in which this message was incorporated into public health practices of the late 1980s. What was gained over this period was a greater understanding of the physiological and sociocultural dimensions of body weight. What was lost in this transition from the margins to the mainstream was the experimental and woman-to-woman approach of groups like LAL.

Analysing the ways that information circulated in LAL and BD shows that experience became an important lens through which fat women filtered medical information. Knowledge was built through exchanges of information among group members as well as between groups of activists in Canada and the United States. They learned that being fat was not necessarily unhealthy. Members of LAL began to rethink what their bodies could do. They began to organize aerobics, dance, and swimming classes for fat women only. Concurrently, some activists and self-identified fat female entrepreneurs opened clothing stores for fat women only. These by-fat-women-for-fat-women approaches to acceptance are evidence that activists were at least partially successful in persuading women that fat bodies could be "good" bodies.

5 "Let Me Hear Your Body Talk": Aerobics for Fat Women Only

Services created by fat women, for fat women are the focus of the next two chapters. Earlier chapters examined the relationship between feminism and fat activism. Was fat a feminist issue and how should women fight fat oppression? The remaining chapters look at how these ideas were put into practice by fat acceptance groups. Aerobics and dance classes, group swims, fashion shows, clothing swaps, and style workshops were places where women "did" fat activism.[1] The exercise programs analysed in this chapter, and fashion events discussed in the next, show that fat activism was productive. Feminist and activist ideas inspired new social sites and services. Bodies mattered, as Judith Butler so evocatively observed. Being fat was something activists did, rather than something that they were.

Aerobics for fat women flourished in Canada in the 1980s. This chapter traces the development of the classes and gives voice to the women who participated. Self-identified fat women took the analytic tools of fat activism and put them into practice in their weekly aerobics class. Many discovered themselves anew within these social spaces. Participants described pleasure and excitement in their ability to test themselves physically and at the sight of their fat female instructors and fellow aerobicizers. I also examine the commercialization of aerobics for fat women, arguing that such services were not incompatible with activism. Classes and products developed by and for fat women allowed participants to embody and enact the philosophy that fat people could be fit and healthy. Bodies talked. Aerobics helped many women feel that it was acceptable to be fat, and it inspired them to think differently about their bodies.

Not Jane Fondas

Aerobics combined callisthenic exercises with dance moves and set them to music.[2] The activity became popular in the post– Second World

Table 4. Aerobics for fat women in Canada, 1981–present

Years	Name	Location	Participants
1981–5	Large as Life Vancouver	Vancouver, BC	300 +
1982–5	Large as Life Calgary	Calgary, AB	100 +
1984–91	Suzanne Bell's Fitness (aka Suzanne Bell's Livin' Large, 1984–5)	Vancouver, BC	500 +
1985–present	Jody Sandler's In Grand Form (now known as Jody's Fitness)	North Vancouver, BC	300 +
c. 1987–9	Above Average	Prince Albert, SK	5
c. 1990	Jacqueline Hope's Big on Fitness	Toronto, ON	Unknown

War era, and their popularity accelerated in the 1980s. Jane Fonda was *the* icon of aerobics culture in the 1980s. Clad in high-cut leotards on the front of her bestselling *Jane Fonda's Workout Book* and aerobics videos, Fonda and her message of discipline as liberation were emblematic of the healthism of the period.[3] She was slim, but muscular; powerful, but feminine. *Jane Fonda's Workout Book* sold over 1.8 million copies in the United States in its first two years of publication. Fonda's three workout videos, released between 1982 and 1987, sold at least 4 million copies.[4] In 1986 Jody Sandler of Vancouver released *In Grand Form*, an aerobics video for larger women. She told a Vancouver journalist: "I'm not Jane Fonda ... I don't live in L.A. People are looking for a more down-to-earth approach." The headline of the article echoed this sentiment, describing Sandler's clientele as women who would "never be a Fonda."[5]

Critics charged that aerobics was a commodification of women's fitness programs that emphasized looks over strength.[6] Fonda, films like *Perfect* (1985), and advertisements from the period packaged the activity as sensual and feminine.[7] The convergence of aerobics and fat activism invites a re-examination of the connections between gender norms and physical fitness. Organizers of aerobics classes believed that they were challenging stereotypes about fat people and providing safe woman-centred spaces for women to exercise, goals which were consistent with sports feminist and WHM activism of this era. At the same time, participants in fat women's aerobics classes embraced the "feminization" of fitness. Fat women, like probably all women, participated in aerobics classes for a variety of reasons: fitness, fun, pressure to be "healthy," and sociality. Aerobics, like fat activism, was a reflection of late twentieth-century ideas about gender and the body. Mixed messages about fitness, femininity, and feminism didn't matter to participants, however. Pleasure was what kept women participating in aerobics classes and contributed to the classes' long-standing popularity in Canada.

For Fat Women Only

Aerobics for fat women were open to the general public, but the classes themselves were often organized by activists. Large as Life (LAL) Vancouver started the first fitness class for large women in Canada when they hired a "fitness instructor from the YMCA, a little skinny thing," who taught eight women at the Canadian Memorial Community Centre in fall 1981.[8] Classes lasted for one hour and were offered twice a week at a cost of forty-eight dollars for twelve classes, twenty dollars for five classes, or six dollars per class.[9] Initially, only a handful of women joined the class. After a few weeks, Kate Partridge hit upon the idea of getting LAL members themselves to teach the classes. Once large instructors began to teach, the program grew considerably. New classes were formed as demands in particular areas of the city warranted. By the end of 1984, LAL was operating fitness classes in ten different community centres across the Lower Mainland.[10]

Aerobics were also a critical part of the LAL groups that Kate Partridge established when she moved to Calgary, Alberta, in 1982, and London, Ontario, in 1997. LAL aerobics classes were offered through the Calgary Board of Education's evening adult programs at Connaught School for two nights a week, eight weeks at a time, for a fee of thirty dollars.[11] Partridge may have taught a few of these classes initially, but she was replaced early on by Pat Donaldson, a LAL member and physical education graduate of McGill University.[12] The aerobics classes in Calgary outlasted Large as Life itself. Partridge left the city in 1983, but former participants recalled that the classes lasted until 1985, if not longer.[13]

Carol Peat led LAL classes in London, Ontario. Peat was not a member of LAL as her predecessors in Calgary and Vancouver had been. She had a bachelor's degree in dance and was a certified fitness instructor with an interest in "special populations": the out of shape, the overweight, the elderly, and people with different physical abilities. Peat did not consider herself fat or thin. She described her figure as not "ideal" but physically fit. Some students were sceptical that she was not "big enough" to teach the class, but others told her that she looked "like a real person," which they found "motivating."[14] Peat believed she was able to "pass" among fat women because her body was perceived to be more "real" than a typical aerobics instructor – she was not Jane Fonda.

Outside organized aerobics programs for the general public, some self-identified fat women organized aerobics classes informally. Susan White, who had been part of a *Fat Is a Feminist Issue* CR group in Winnipeg in the late 1980s, met with three other women to do aerobics for a brief period at that time. White and her friends met in one woman's basement and worked out together to fitness videos.[15] Ruth Wylie Gillingham of NAAFA Canada also ran an aerobics group called Above Average for women in Prince Albert, Saskatchewan, in the late 1980s. Gillingham had been attending classes at the YWCA and asked an instructor to teach her some basic moves. She met other women in Prince Albert through her NAAFA activism. Gillingham stressed that she was not "qualified as an aerobics instructor" (it was not necessary to be so at this time) but told women "if you want to get together and do some fun stuff, routines that we've done at the gym, let's do it."[16] Five or six women joined with Gillingham as their leader, and they met regularly in the gym at a local youth centre for about a year.

As for longevity, aerobics for fat women had its greatest success in Vancouver. As Large as Life's activities in that city dwindled late in 1984, Suzanne Bell, the group's one-time president and long-term fitness coordinator, decided to start her own fitness business. Bell approached the group and LAL founder Kate Partridge about using the Large as Life name, which had been copyrighted. Partridge and others supported Bell's business but were wary of seeing Large as Life become a for-profit enterprise.[17] Consequently, Bell began teaching fitness under the name "Suzanne Bell's Livin' Large" (1984–5) and then "Suzanne Bell's Fitness and Fashion Enterprises" until her retirement in 2012 (see figure 12). Between September 1984 and January 1985, Bell took over responsibility for four existing Large as Life classes and also started new classes in twelve other community centres and schools in the Lower Mainland.[18] These early successes and a $10,000 loan from her parents allowed Bell to open an aerobics studio in September 1985.[19] In addition to the studio, Bell had a "pro-shop" where she sold the Suzanne Bell Collection, a line of activewear she had developed over the previous two years.[20] The studio lasted until 1992 when Bell decided to focus exclusively on clothing for large women. Although her aerobics classes were still popular, she did not find fitness to be as lucrative as fashion.[21]

Around the time Large as Life was winding down, Jody Sandler of North Vancouver also began to specialize in fitness for larger women. Sandler was not a LAL member, but she took over teaching responsibilities for one of their classes in 1985.[22] The class did not last much longer, but Sandler decided to stick with the concept of low-impact aerobics for larger women. She released her own bestselling fitness video, *In Grand Form*, in 1986, with *In 2 Grand Form* following in 1998, and she began to offer group fitness classes by the same name at local recreation centres.[23] During the 1980s and early 1990s, Sandler and Bell offered similar services, but both claimed they did not see each other as competition. In part, this was because Sandler's In Grand Form catered to the North Vancouver

Figure 12. Suzanne Bell's Fitness and Fashion instructors, c. 1985. Courtesy of Suzanne Bell.

market while Bell worked in Burnaby, Surrey, and Vancouver. The women also had different approaches to the fat and fit concept, reflecting different interpretations of fat acceptance. Bell was more explicit and vocal about fat acceptance in the 1980s and saw her business as a platform to share her views on the subject.[24] Bell wanted participants to understand that they could be fat and fabulous. Sandler was more interested in helping women to spiritually and physically "reconnect" with their bodies. Sandler continues to operate In Grand Form in North Vancouver, under the name Jody's Fitness. Her focus has shifted over the years. She moved from aerobic dance to "step aerobics" in the early 1990s. Personal training and outdoor fitness classes became the focus of Sandler's work with deconditioned adults in the 2000s.[25] Variations in approaches to being fat were reflected in the differences between Bell and Sandler.[26]

In addition to the grassroots work of Canadian activists and entrepreneurs, an American fitness chain, Women at Large, had branches in Alberta and British Columbia for a brief period in the early 1990s.[27] Women at Large was developed in Washington State in 1983 and went on to open twenty-nine franchises in the US and Canada before going out of business in 1988.[28] Runa Fiander of Big Dance briefly trained to be an instructor for Women at Large, but she dropped out because she was turned off by the chain's insistence that she maintain a feminine appearance by wearing pink clothing and full make-up at work.[29] While Women at Large's broader agenda was to "rebuild self-esteem" and self-worth among its clientele, the company rejected the language and politics of fat liberation.[30] Terms such as "fat" or "big" were avoided. Instead, Women at Large insisted on referring to members as "fluffy ladies," a term they erroneously believed lacked "demeaning connotation."[31] Women at Large departed from earlier efforts to organize classes by LAL in that it was for-profit and more explicitly feminized aerobics.

Canadian activists appear to have taken up aerobics earlier than their American counterparts. By 1985, however, aerobics classes were also a popular activity for fat activists across the United States. *Radiance: A Publication for Large Women* (1984–2000) was probably the most significant single resource for publicizing aerobics for large women in the US. Their spring 1985 "Celebrate Your Body" issue featured profiles of women in the San Francisco Bay Area who offered fitness classes for large women. These stories may have inspired other women to establish and attend aerobics classes. Subsequent issues featured classified ads announcing the arrival of "low impact aerobics for BBWs with BBW instructors" in Illinois, New York, Texas, and Virginia.[32] The concept of fat and fit also gained momentum with the publication of *Great Shape: The First Exercise Guide for Large Women* (1988). Found on the shelves of some of my interview subjects, this book argued that the pleasure and fun of sport and dance were for everyone, not just women who were already fit.[33] Sounding very much like their Canadian counterparts in Large as Life, they wrote, "most of us have finally come to the conclusion that picking a number on a scale and postponing our lives until we reach that number is never going to work."[34] In addition to guidance on starting a fitness program, the book had an extensive appendix listing aerobics programs, sources of fitness clothing, and exercise videos for large women. According to their listings in 1988, there were at least twenty-seven fitness programs for large women operating in ten different states.[35]

Aerobics for fat women only were central to activism in the 1980s. The phenomenon was significant in its own right, and it also intervened in the debate about the meaning of aerobics itself. By 1984 aerobics was one of "the most popular physical activities of North American women."[36] Sympathizers like Fonda saw aerobics as a way for women to "break the weaker sex mold," become "strong" and "healthy," and fulfil their "physical potential."[37] Detractors placed aerobics on an "axis of continuity" with a broader popular culture that had a negative impact on women's self-esteem.[38] Canadian sports historian Helen Lenskyj was an influential voice in the debate. She argued aerobics were an extension of beauty and fashion culture: "While its popularity signified greater female participation in regular physical activity, its association with the cosmetic and fashion industries made it, in many instances, another arena for women to compete for male attention. Like makeup and clothing, dance exercise produced more prescriptions for heterosexual appeal. The new requirements included thinness, muscularity and shapeliness, enhanced by fashionable and expensive sportswear."[39] Lenskyj saw aerobics as an aesthetic, rather than a health-promoting activity. Aerobics' associations with glamour and femininity undermined its health benefits.

For Lenskyj, aerobics were a setback from sports feminist gains of the 1970s, which saw increased levels of participation and funding for female athletes.[40] In Canada the Report of the Royal Commission on the Status of Women (1971) had recommended that the federal government take action to increase women's participation in sport. In the wake of this recommendation, Fitness and Amateur Sport Canada sponsored a 1974 conference on women and sport that led, after many years of lobbying, to the formation of Canadian Association for the Advancement of Women in Sport (CAAWS) in 1981. CAAWS's mandate was to "advance the position of women by defining, promoting and supporting a feminist perspective on sport and to improve the status of women in sport."[41] The organization received funding from Fitness and Amateur Sport Canada as well as the Secretary of State Women's Program, and it was, and is, run through a combination of volunteer work and paid staff. CAAWS's initiatives tended to focus on "liberal strategies aimed at equalizing access to sport and physical activity," like the National Coaching School for Women and a 1985 court challenge that gave Justine Blainey the legal right to play on a boys' hockey team.[42] Sports feminists in Canada were influenced by the conceptual and theoretical debates that fuelled the "second wave": activists believed that gender equality could be achieved by making sex differences less pronounced in all aspects of social life.

In Canada, sports feminist activism was concurrent with increased government interest in girl's and women's sport participation. The 1981 Canada Fitness Survey and 1984 report Changing Times: Women and Physical Activity revealed that boys ranked physical activity first among a list of factors contributing to well-being, whereas girls ranked it sixth.[43] When asked to rank reasons for undertaking physical activity, 51 per cent of women listed weight control as a "very important" reason, while only 33 per cent of men listed that as a factor.[44] A slightly smaller number of women, 44 per cent, listed "pleasure" as a "very important" reason for undertaking physical activity.[45] Socially prescribed gender roles were impacting women's choice of physical activity, and the authors of the study were concerned.[46] The Canada Fitness

Survey and *Changing Times* were evidence of increasing public sector interest in body weight and shape. Federal government studies and initiatives of the 1970s and 1980s like ParticipACTION were not neutral. Even if they had good intentions, they contributed to a moralizing climate that encouraged Canadians to modify their "bad behaviour" through diet and exercise.[47]

As Lenskyj's critique shows, early academic feminist assessments attacked aerobics from the perspective of media effects and sex roles, arguing that aerobics (in representation and in practice) reinforced unrealistic and dangerous feminine norms. In the 1990s, as theories about the totalizing impact of media images became less popular, feminist critics of aerobics began to analyse the activity through Foucauldian frameworks of discipline and biopower. Foucault's claim that "the body is invested with relations of power and domination" became the starting point for understanding the invisible ways in which power operated on women.[48] Although Foucault's theories overlook the gendered dimensions of biopower, other scholars have since explored how women's experience with power was different from men's.[49] For some, the female aerobic body became an emblem of the negative effects of a patriarchal and disciplinary society. Mona Lloyd describes aerobics as part of "a 'techno-political' register of power: a set of methods, techniques and practices for controlling the body."[50] Participation in aerobics could be understood through Foucault's notion of panopticism: a "system of permanent visibility that ensures the automatic functioning of power."[51] Women were self-disciplining subjects because they had "internalized" the male gaze and had begun to "surveil themselves."[52]

Numerous scholars have linked biopower, the male gaze, and late-twentieth-century bodily norms. Nina Loland argues that aerobics were part of a culture of display where women were encouraged to adopt appropriately feminine postures.[53] Audrey MacNevin suggested that aerobics constituted a "normative behaviour" women performed in order to achieve a slender and suitably feminine body.[54] Aerobics themselves were "geared toward the reproduction" of these "cultural standards of beauty."[55] Collectively, these studies concluded that women participated in aerobics in order to keep "their bodies in line with dominant messages about femininity."[56] Early feminist interpretations of Foucault pointed to media images and femininity as normative forces that reinforced women's disempowerment in contemporary culture. Aerobics became one way for scholars to explain gender inequality and women's ongoing adherence to feminine norms.

Studies of aerobics and women's physical fitness published in the 2000s have begun to re-evaluate the significance of the activity. Pirkko

Markula, whose initial assessment of aerobics was that women were less concerned with their overall health and fitness than with so-called "problem areas" such as their bums and thighs, has since changed her take on women's fitness practices.[57] Markula now argues that women's fitness classes can be seen as a "technology of the self" rather than just a disciplinary practice, as she and other scholars initially thought. Fitness activities focusing on an ethic of self-care can become a "feminist alternative politics under two conditions: they have to involve an active critical attitude and an act of self-stylization."[58]

Building on this rich debate about the meaning of aerobics, this chapter looks inside classes for fat women only. Rather than seeing women's motivations as a litmus test for whether aerobics were "good" or "bad," it examines what self-identified fat women took away from the classes. Pleasure and security emerge as key themes in self-identified fat women's narratives about training as fitness leaders, attending aerobics classes for fat women, and finding well-fitted leotards. Participants felt that classes reflected their embodied experiences; the atmosphere, the instructor, and the moves were all adapted to suit fat women's needs. Aerobics classes for fat women involved a more complex and subjective process of decision-making and feminine performance than the literature to date has allowed. Their worth cannot be measured against the extent to which they promoted femininity, but rather by the meanings that participants took away from the activity.

Bodies Talk

Kate Partridge realized that the body size of the instructor was critical to the success of aerobics classes as soon as she began organizing them for LAL Vancouver. Since there were no fat-identified instructors working in the city, she recruited LAL members to take the YWCA's fitness leader certification program. Suzanne Bell, Joan Dal Santo, and at least four others from LAL Vancouver went on to take this course. Pat Donaldson of Large as Life Calgary also trained as a fitness leader at the YWCA.[59] The twelve-week course cost $100. It included in-class theory lessons on physiology, anatomy, and basic nutrition. Later classes focused on practice, including how to warm up and cool down, planning a class, pre- and post-natal fitness, styles of leadership, and common injuries. Students were also expected to complete assignments. These included:

- filling out a nutritional analysis
- attending a fitness class and reporting back
- preparing and outlining a forty-five-minute class

- a midterm test
- a task that tested students on their knowledge of exercise technique
- doing a fitness assessment and "how to counsel after a fitness assessment"[60]

At the end of this involved process, which included thirty-five hours of instruction and training, students received a teaching certificate.

In spite of her leadership of LAL, Kate Partridge was nervous on the first day of the fitness leadership course. She scribbled "Get Binder; Nametag; Be Enthusiastic" on the first page of her notebook.[61] Partridge and other LAL members were nervous because no one else in the course was fat. Joan Dal Santo remembered feeling like an outsider amongst the "30 fitness Nazis with hard bodies" she encountered at the Y.[62] Dal Santo and Partridge felt as though other students perceived them as fat women. Suzanne Bell sensed that she was "not well received at all" by the "young women with bodies to die for" in her class. She also recalled noticing an older man and a black woman in her course and thinking that she was one of "three minorities in the class."[63] Pat Donaldson, who took the course in Calgary, realized that she was the only fat person in the class, the only Indigenous person, and, also, the only pregnant woman.[64] Partridge, Dal Santo, and Bell felt that their bodies differentiated them from the other trainees in the course. Donaldson, likewise, felt her body size and her pregnancy placed her in a different category from the "gorgeous little ladies and gentlemen in their exercise fitness clothes."[65]

The women had good reason to identify as outsiders. The five "S's" of physical fitness taught in the class were: "STAMINA – STRENGTH – SUPPLENESS – SLENDERNESS and SPIRIT."[66] A handout given to the students further detailed these principles. Stamina, strength, and suppleness were incorporated into exercises in order to build cardiovascular health and muscular strength. Spirit was the "'joie de vivre' that comes from feeling physically fit and mentally great!!!" Slenderness or "weight control" was the only category that included specific guidelines:

The balanced proportion of fat to muscle decreases effort in stamina activities and increases efficiency of movement:

In Women: 14–16% body fat is ideal
            16–20% body fat is acceptable
            Over 20% body fat is unacceptable.

In Men: 10–12% body fat is ideal
            12–16% body fat is acceptable
            Over 16% body fat is unacceptable.[67]

No doubt the LAL trainees' joie de vivre was tempered after being given a handout informing them that their levels of body fat were "unacceptable."[68]

Gradually, Dal Santo, Partridge, and Bell began to enjoy the YWCA course. They described this change in terms of gaining inner confidence. Dal Santo recalled "beginning to understand that I had a body that worked, and it was a good one."[69] Bell remembered thinking "oh my God, oh my God, I'm up here" when she had to demonstrate a technique to her classmates. Eventually she came to feel that the "whole scenario wasn't really about size," but about confidence.[70] Dal Santo, Partridge, and Bell also felt that their presence was having an impact on other participants' perceptions of fat exercisers. The YWCA was certainly convinced – Bell was invited back to subsequent graduating classes to talk about fitness for large women.[71]

The body size of the instructor was the first question most people asked before registering for LAL aerobics classes in London, Ontario. Instructor Carol Peat added the phrase "come out and be taught by someone who's not a size six" in LAL advertisements to try to assuage concern.[72] Aerobics participants interviewed for this study described feeling comfortable with LAL instructors. They were role models[73] rather than a "skinny person"[74] who might potentially "talk down" to larger women.[75] Large instructors became emblems for the potential of other women to be physically fit. In this respect, the appeal of classes for fat women may not have been so different from the appeal of Jane Fonda herself. Hilary Radner argues that Fonda was an example to her students rather than an unattainable idea. Her popularity was rooted in her ability to claim "membership within the group to whom she speaks." Fonda tried to underline her normalcy rather than her expertise.[76]

LAL instructors incorporated experiential knowledge into the approaches they learned from the YWCA. Suzanne Bell described the classes in the *Bolster*:

> The class begins with a long warm-up, slow-paced and lots of fun. This is designed to slowly warm the body and prepare the muscles for more action ... Now we are ready for a little up-paced movement. Don't panic – we are all in this together, and we won't be doing any Jigs! ... We slow the pace and stretch out our leg muscles, we continue to stretch other parts of the body until we have cooled down ... then we work on strengthening our major muscle groups ... We also spend time on exercises for the care of the back ... Finally, after our bodies are just about to groan, we relax and stretch to very soft music until we are cool and happy to leave, feeling great.[77]

Bell felt that participants returned to her class because she adapted the moves appropriately.[78] They could perform all of the moves that helped women feel safe and successful. Bell also modified the YWCA principles of physical fitness for her students. She omitted slenderness, teaching LAL participants that the *four* major principles of physical fitness were: strength, stamina, stature, and suppleness."[79] Contrary to the "feel-the-burn" and "no-pain-no-gain" image of aerobics classes from this period, LAL classes worked at a moderate pace. LAL's goal was to set up a class where women would not be afraid to test their physical limits.

Another important adaptation was to limit the amount of time students spent on the floor. Jody Sandler did this by having participants do their floor exercises standing up. Rather than performing sit-ups Sandler used belly dancing moves and pelvic tilts from a standing position. Limiting and eliminating the amount of time spent getting up off the floor put participants at ease. Susan White of Winnipeg had encountered this problem when she tried "regular" fitness activities. White found that even in classes for beginners, the combination of aerobics with floor exercises was hard on her back. White also tried yoga, a form of exercise she described as "not funny for fat people." In her opinion, the problem with yoga was that it was not adapted to suit women with large chests, stomachs, or legs. White laughed remembering trying different poses:

> I remember distinctly one called "the Plow" where you put your arm back and lift your legs and put them back over your head so your toes are touching the floor behind you. Okay good, I didn't have trouble getting into that position ... The only problem is that anybody in that position has their ... their nose, their face buried in their chest ... I remember one time being in that position and thinking to myself, I'm going to suffocate. I couldn't breathe, I had my face buried in my chest. So I didn't stick beyond that with the yoga.[80]

Ingrid Laue of Vancouver also found comfort in the format of LAL classes and in the absence of "skinny bodies who could do all the kind of stuff that you had trouble, really trouble, doing."[81] Sandler observed that once people became comfortable with basic aerobic dance movements, they began to be more comfortable in their workout. She remembered that participants would "start doing little gestures ... a little shoulder movement, a little smile or a little wink."[82]

Participants in aerobics classes were sometimes afraid of being laughed at or judged by non-fat people, so privacy became a priority.

Rooms needed to be windowless or have windows that could be covered. Women were welcome to participate in their first class for free and on a drop-in basis, but participants were not allowed to watch the class in order to decide whether or not they fit in.[83] One participant quoted in the *Bolster* noted, "I ... appreciate the fact that there are no 'spectators' allowed as I am very self-conscious about my 'size' – and the fact that I used to hate exercising in high school (nearly thirty years ago)."[84] Julie Levasseur, who briefly started an aerobics group for fat women with Susan White of Winnipeg, felt uncomfortable at fitness centres. She believed that large women, herself included, were perceived to be out of place at a gym. Levasseur described needing to psych herself up to go to a fitness centre and remind herself that she had a "right" to be there. As an Indigenous fat woman, she had legitimate concerns about being stereotyped by other exercisers. She noted, "there's a little bit of racism and stereotypes because people think maybe I drank too much, and I don't drink, but I feel like that's what people perceive."[85] Levasseur's ethnicity, class, and body size were factors that made it difficult for her to exercise in spaces that were dominated by white, middle-class, and slender people.

Gender was an unstated, but critical, dimension of fat women's desire for privacy. Two or three men participated in In Grand Form classes over the years, but aerobics classes for Large as Life and Suzanne Bell's, as well as the informal aerobics groups in Winnipeg and Prince Albert, were for women only.[86] A long-term client of In Grand Form, Sarah King, remembered that the presence of men in classes "upset people."[87] Former Large as Life participants were not able to articulate why men should be excluded. London instructor Carol Peat recalled that the one occasion when a man attended changed the atmosphere of the class. The "women weren't talking with each other, they weren't joking as much," despite the fact that this man was "very overweight."[88] Participants did not want men to be in spaces where they were working out because they felt vulnerable and exposed when they were exercising. Aerobics classes, much like organizations for fat women, assumed that being a fat woman was different than being a fat man. Men, even if they were fat, could not possibly understand what fat female participants experienced. In this way, gender shaped most aerobics classes for fat women, even though men were rarely present.

Along with gender, the main category for inclusion was that the participants be fat. Fat was a matter of self-identification, but imagery and words in advertisements helped to signal what the classes were about. Jody Sandler's pamphlets described her courses as "size-plus" fitness and included images of herself with two other full-figured women.[89] LAL and Suzanne Bell similarly used imagery to convey their idea

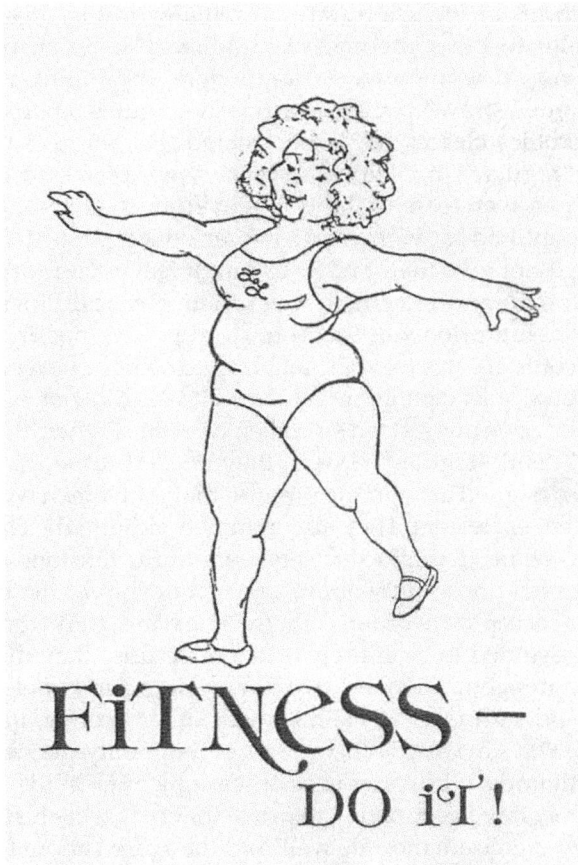

FiTNeSS –
DO iT!

Figure 13. "Fitness – DO IT!" Ingrid Laue drew this image for a LAL pamphlet in 1982. Courtesy of Suzanne Bell.

of "large" to a general audience. LAL used drawings created by the *Bolster* editor Ingrid Laue of large women in jogging suits and leotards. One such sketch captioned "Fitness – DO IT!" featured a smiling, curly-haired woman standing with one leg raised to the side. She wears a leotard emblazoned with a LAL logo (see figure 13). The woman's arms and legs look muscular, but three lines emphasizing the rolls of her full belly, and also a bump of thigh flesh protruding out from under the leotard, signal the prospective participant's size. In all cases, instructors and participants were identified as "large women" but there was no explicit definition of the terms by dress size or weight.

The categories of inclusion (fat and female) and exclusion (skinny or male) point to the sometimes contradictory logic on which aerobics classes for fat women were based. Here, the skinny women and all men became "straw" people – normative figures against which fat women's aerobics classes were constructed. Fat aerobics classes that disavowed "regular" or "skinny" women were premised on the idea that fat women were essentially different from their thinner counterparts. Self-identified fat women often overlooked the fact that thinner women might not love their bodies or might feel uncomfortable working out with men and uncertain about their physical fitness capacity. The implicit assumption was that thin women were passing judgment on their fat counterparts for their inability to achieve a slender body.

In interviews, participants in aerobics classes did not point to specific instances of being judged by other women. Rather, they felt that in order to attend "regular" classes, they needed to be thin. Standard classes were designed around the premise that fat women were delicate, even damaged, exercisers. They also assumed, despite the claim that fat people could be fit, that fat exercisers were unfit. Tensions and contradictions reflected uncertainty about the relationship of the body to the self within fat acceptance groups. On the one hand, thin women and all males were assumed to be entirely different because they did not experience fat oppression. Members of fat activist groups made their own judgments and normalizing claims about other groups and failed to reflect on the ways in which other norms of femininity, gender, ethnicity, or class might impact the experience of working out. On the other hand, fat women may have been trying to prove that they were just like everyone else: they exercised, they ate well, and they cared about their health.

Another one of the implications of special classes was that fat women's reasons for working out, or the satisfaction they gained from physical fitness, was different from other people's. Kate Partridge described LAL's goals as follows:

> We are ... running fitness and dance classes for large women. The purpose of which is not really primarily to lose weight. It's much more to get healthy; to start feeling better about your body to start understanding it; to move around more ... And I think that once people start moving that ... weight loss will be much easier if you choose to do that. But also just start to feel okay about yourself, you'll be able to present yourself better, you'll get a better response from other people. And, for goodness sakes, you'll be healthier.[90]

In this statement from a 1983 media interview, Partridge reproduced the distinction that sports feminists and media effects theorists made between aesthetic and health fitness goals. This may have been because, in Partridge's experience and research, exercise and weight loss were not causally linked. Alternatively, it may have been because Partridge was trying to distinguish the LAL program from the Jane Fonda, "feel-the-burn" aesthetic of "regular" aerobics classes.

While acceptance groups were successful because they focused on improving the material and day-to-day experiences of fat women, they did not mean that all participants let go of the dream of being thin. Few of the people I spoke to acknowledged that weight loss was one of *their* fitness goals. Instead, former instructors offered general comments about the students' expectations of the class. Nada Vuksic, who taught classes for both Suzanne Bell and In Grand Form, felt that "a lot of people came to the program anticipating that we were about weight loss and ... I think that's what ... probably drew a lot of people, and I think if I am honest with myself it probably drew me as well, is the idea that fitness would lead to weight loss."[91] Despite her belief that fat could be fit, Suzanne Bell recognized that many attendees were drawn to her program because of the potential to lose weight. She was not troubled by women's reasons for coming to her classes, perhaps because she saw acceptance as a process rather than an end in itself. In a study of fat exercisers in the United States, Dana Tealer and Lisa Schuster had similar findings: larger women had a variety of reasons for attending exercise classes. Some women came with the goal of losing weight, while others saw the classes as places they could be safe from weight-loss rhetoric.[92] Regardless of their motivations, Bell saw in every client an opportunity to "preach" the gospel of fat and fit, and "preach" she "did."[93] Bell did find that some people found relief in her message, and those exercisers said "thank God, somebody is finally speaking my language."[94] Not all participants in aerobics classes by LAL, Bell, or In Grand Form were LAL members, however. These women may not have been conversant with fat activists' critiques of dieting or they may not have bought into the "diets don't work" message. Each woman's reason for joining an aerobics class was, necessarily, different.

Perceived similarities in body weight and shape mattered most to participants in aerobics classes for fat women. Participants remembered feeling that everyone in the classes was like them, which they found exciting. Of Jody Sandler's classes, Sarah King remembered "the camaraderie and the other women in the class, and the laughing, and the social ... was almost more important than the class because as a large woman you find yourself isolated sometimes."[95] Fat women saw other fat women as allies. In the April 1982 issue of the *Bolster*, Sally Thompson described her "astonishment and delight" at exercising with "a group of my contemporaries – large women – who were starting from square one like me."[96] Janet Walker of LAL recalled this sense of security in their classes, "it felt wonderful to know you had a place you could go and people weren't going to be laughing at you."[97] Other former participants echoed the belief that fat women were out of place in "regular" aerobics spaces. Evelyn Booth remembered feeling "ashamed to be seen in" regular fitness centres, "ashamed of what their attitude would be." Whereas in Large as Life's classes, she felt "comfortable in the sense of, you're all the same."[98]

For participants, aerobics classes also became a way to challenge the stereotype that fat women were "lazy, stupid, underachievers, lacking in will power ... and out of control."[99] LAL members wrote stories and published editorial cartoons in the Bolster celebrating their physical fitness. One woman reported, "I weigh 255 lbs ... and I am a borderline diabetic. But I challenge anyone, slim or not, to keep up with me for even one day!"[100] Bolster editor Ingrid Laue chastised ParticipACTION Canada for their "Fat is NOT where it's at!" ad campaign. In her February 1982 interview, Laue charged, "fitness has little to do with body size, although it may take more effort, initially, to move 200lbs around the Stanley Park seawall than it takes to move 125lbs ... your slim friend who does not believe in exercising the body beautiful may have trouble keeping up with you."[101] Here, the physical and psychological benefits of exercise were emphasized. As Laue noted, "one FEELS so much better – not only in physical terms – when engaged in a program of regular exercise."[102] In Grand Form participant Sarah King was featured in a 1994 magazine article about fitness and weight. King told Maclean's, "I lift weights, I do aerobics. I'm in very good shape. Not for a fat lady – I'm in very good shape, period."[103] King saw herself as a model for the idea that fat can be healthy. Although aerobics had not substantially altered her body weight, her blood pressure and cholesterol levels remained in a healthy range into her sixties. She continued to exercise, usually in "regular" gyms and pools.[104]

Participants' ebullient accounts of their experiences offer a glimpse into the way that women responded to aerobics classes. By claiming aerobics as an activity for fat women, participants were taking control of the structural and social exclusions they had experienced in the past. Aerobics helped to illuminate how women "endure as well as react against discursive practices on multiple bodily, emotional, and intellectual levels."[105] Self-identified fat women named and challenged this oppression by creating affirmative social sites and services for other women. The affirmative focus of aerobics classes and emphasis on pleasure were different from other approaches to fat activism. A new activity for women was produced out of activists' critical observations about the limitations of "regular" fitness classes.

Commercialization

Aerobics classes for fat women also encourage us to ask different questions about the meaning of consumption. Commercialization was taken to mean that participants had a superficial commitment to physical fitness in analyses of aerobics from the 1980s and 1990s. Nancy Theberge argued that the benefit of aerobics was dependent on whether feminine ideals influenced classes. Those that focused on "the development of physical capacities such as strength and endurance are important additions to the opportunities available to women. Others, particularly among the TV and video versions and the more commercialized classes and programs, are clearly directed to the development of sexual attractiveness and appeal. Here, the feminization of the fitness movement represents, not the liberation of women in sport, but their continued oppression through the sexualization of physical activity."[106] Theberge, like Lenskyj before her, felt that the purpose and meaning of physical activity determined how beneficial it could be for women. She was concerned that women who participated in aerobics did not experience the same sense of empowerment as women who played sports. Aerobics seemed to be about individual achievement and looking good, and this goal was not satisfactory for scholars who saw sport as a way for women to liberate themselves from the constraints of femininity. For Theberge and Lenskyj, the meaning of aerobics was determined by the popular images of the activity on television and video and by icons like Jane Fonda.

Self-identified fat women were driving the commercialization of aerobics because they needed and wanted better options. Adam Lent describes commercialization as one of the "unforeseen consequences" of social movement activity in the post-war era.[107] Lent argues that commercialization transforms political activities into mere "acts of commercial consumption."[108] People who had been committed activists became more concerned with their bottom line. Fat activism suggests another reading. The production and consumption of goods can in themselves be political acts. Fat women felt that the producers of mass-market goods did not care about them and responded by creating what they needed. Suzanne Bell and Jody Sandler did not set out to become entrepreneurs but did so when they realized that there was a demand for plus-size goods that was not being met. Commercial activities developed by and for fat women did not run contrary to the goal of improving the material and social experience of fatness. Prior to Suzanne Bell's fashions, leotards, tights, headbands, and other aerobics gear were not readily available in sizes fourteen and up. This lack of access to consumables was a conundrum for participants for both practical and aesthetic reasons. On a practical level, women needed clothing to exercise in, and on an aesthetic level, they wanted to look good while doing it.

Some women saw leotards as a necessity and took pleasure in finding fun colours and fabrics, while others were primarily concerned with function. When the first aerobics classes for large women were introduced in the 1980s, participants remembered finding it especially difficult to find exercise clothing in plus sizes. Some crafted their own clothing. Jody Sandler made her own outfits by putting elastic around the bottom of yoga pants. Sandler wore long-sleeved leotards and sewed a vest that she wore overtop.[109] Ruth Gillingham of NAAFA Canada had her leotards made by a local seamstress because she was frustrated with having to work out in sweatpants. For many years Gillingham was not able to find fitness clothing in her size. She speculated that her appearance in homemade leotards in the late 1980s was probably the "first time" anyone "ever saw a fat lady walking in Prince Albert in a leotard."[110] Other women were happy to work out in sweats and homemade clothing because they were not interested in leotards. Tight clothing and spandex had a negative association for Joyce Cusack of LAL Calgary, who referred to aerobics leotards as "little chu-chu spandex things."[111] Julie Levasseur of Winnipeg similarly and succinctly explained of this period: "I didn't wear spandex."[112]

For those who were interested, it was initially a challenge to find plus-size aerobics leotards. The *Bolster* became a sounding board for LAL members as they sought out and tested different brands of tights. In February 1983 Suzanne Bell published an entire article comparing different types of tights, their fit, and where to buy them. Bell advised that "Danskin Outsize" tights were best, whereas "Phantom Queen" were unreliable. She listed three sources for the tights in Vancouver, "not much, but it's a start," and noted that neither Eaton's nor the Bay had any in stock. She advised that her preference, Danskin style number 85, was readily available in the US in a wider variety of colours.[113] Cross-border shopping in the United States was an essential source of clothing for plus-size women, which will be discussed in greater detail in chapter 6.

Suzanne Bell found pleasure in displaying, and flaunting, her big, beautiful body, and this enthusiasm drove her search for fashionable aerobics clothing. As Bell told one interviewer, "People notice me when I walk into a room. They can feel it: I really like me."[114] Bell's confidence level was undoubtedly critical to the success and appeal of her fitness classes for Large as Life and her business. It meant that she had a sense of entitlement to fashion that some others may have lacked. Bell was more experimental with her fitness clothing from the beginning. She laughed while remembering an early ensemble: "I had a purple leotard that I bought in the States and this wild top that was cut through with silver ... I mean, I was just a sight!"[115] Bell's fashion savvy also received notice in the *Bolster*, where Ingrid Laue described her as "very trendy in peach tights, black leotards, and colour-coordinated head-band."[116]

Within about a year of starting to teach fitness, Bell hit upon the idea of manufacturing fitness clothing for large women. Bell wanted other women to feel how she felt, and she wanted to profit from it. She approached a company that soon began to manufacture the Suzanne Bell Collection. Initially Bell began to sell the clothes "from the trunk of her car," and she later held home parties.[117] Photographs from the time show women wearing coordinated leotards and tights, in a wide range of styles in colourful fabrics. The Suzanne Bell Collection took off very quickly. By the fall 1985 opening of her fitness centre, the Suzanne Bell Collection had expanded to include a full range of fitness gear, including unitards, mesh cover-ups, bathing suits, headbands, and tights in a "range of colours."[118] Leaders from Suzanne Bell's Livin' Large and Suzanne Bell's Fitness and Fashion wore colourblock outfits with matching headbands and leg warmers.

Participants remembered their fitness clothing fondly. Joan Dal Santo of LAL remembered "getting into" leotards "in a big way. I started getting leotards that were coloured instead of getting leotards that were all black. I'd start getting coloured leotards with black tights, and I'd get some coloured tights with other coloured leotards. And, it was fun, it got to be fun."[119] LAL's Janet Walker likewise recalled a treasured pink leotard set: "I had gotten to a stage where I was exploring my body and being bolder. I loved to wear it under a black coat ... It was fun to begin to play."[120] Walker still owned the leotard at the time of our 2005 interview. Twenty-three years after its purchase, it remained in good condition. Wearing colour rather than black was an expression of confidence and excitement about the clothing, as well as the practice of aerobics. Fitness facilitated other pleasures and forms of self-expression for participants. It became fun and the safe environment where women tried on different forms of bodily expression.

Home videos were another element of aerobics that critics found troubling. By the mid-1980s aerobics videos were bestsellers. These and televised versions of aerobics classes were a second area of concern for sports feminist academics. The critique of videotaped exercise classes was that they individualized fitness. Sports feminists thought it was important for women to learn to work together, and women using videos were isolated in their homes. Another critique was that videos sexualized aerobics through camera angles and close-ups of bums, hips, and thighs. Margaret MacNeill referred to television programs like the *20 Minute Workout* as "sexually oriented (some would say pornographic)" because of their use of soft-focus lenses.[121] Here, consumption of women's popular culture was conflated with complicity to its messages. Aerobics classes were seen as part of a popular culture that was demeaning and damaging to its consumers. Popular culture representations in turn became dangerous for women, a "psychopathology" emblematic of all that was wrong with our culture.[122]

Services developed by fat women, along with oral histories from participants, challenge a straightforward reading of the relationship between consumption and popular culture messages. The meaning of commercialization for individual participants was not determined by representations of aerobics, but rather from women's use of these products. A handful of female entrepreneurs developed exercise tapes for fat women in the 1980s. These videos were marketed direct to consumers in the pages of *Radiance*, local newspapers, and women's directories. Aerobics videos offer an example of the ways in which fat women were negotiating and expanding the boundaries of the aerobics phenomenon. They are also suggestive of new ways to interpret all women's exercise practices, and the popularity of Jane Fonda in particular.

Jody Sandler hit upon the idea of producing her video when an unsupportive instructor in her fitness leadership course asked her if she knew where the business market for fitness services was heading. Considering her life as a working mother of two children, Sandler decided the "way that exercise had to go was it had to be done in people's own time, in their own homes, when they had time to do it."[123] With a $20,000 loan from her father, Sandler made the video. This process required becoming a limited liability company, auditioning two other "instructors" for roles in the video, and using friends and contacts to keep the production costs low. The result was a video, *In Grand Form*, which was touted as "a 30 min NO BOUNCE, LOW IMPACT aerobic program for full-figured adults, reaching forty and overweight or out of shape."[124] The video received positive reviews in the *Vancouver Sun* and *Radiance*, the latter of which recommended it "for absolute beginners who want to get a feel for aerobics in their own home[s]."[125] In 1986 alone Sandler's video sold two thousand copies, making it a bestseller in Canada. This feat was achieved primarily through woman-to-woman marketing and word of mouth.[126]

In Grand Form does not look like a Jane Fonda video. Sandler's video featured three women working at three different levels. Their dress was decidedly simple: jogging pants, T-shirts, and sneakers. There were no leotards, headbands, or tights. There was no soft focus lens in her video, and none of the cast ever looked seductively at the camera. Leaders smiled and encouraged participants to work at their own pace. Sandler's video suggests a need to rethink what was happening when a woman chose to work out in her home. Regardless of content, a woman's choice to use a fitness video may have been dependent on factors such as her work schedule, child-care arrangements, and budget. Commentary from fat and fit class participants earlier in this chapter also suggests that many women felt stigmatized and embarrassed working out in public. Videos also provided rural women and those living in smaller cities and towns with access to fitness classes. For this reason, the videos may have offered an alternative to, or a tool for, sedentary individuals interested in increasing their level of physical fitness. Sandler's video demands that we expand our analysis of the commercialization of physical fitness. Rather than catering to women's narcissism, commercial products were a tool used by people who could not or would not exercise outside the home. The popularity of Sandler's videos also shows that there was some demand among fat women for exercise tapes that was not being met through other exercise outlets. Producing videos became an extension of the movement because it carried the message that fat could be fit to new audiences.

Conclusions

In this chapter I have argued that aerobics for fat women are suggestive of a complex and subjective process of decision-making about fitness. The value of these activities was not determined by the extent to which they promoted health or femininity, but rather by the meanings that participants took away from the classes. The chapter has shown that the material experience of working out was transformative for participants in aerobics classes. Classes for fat women were both aethestic and health promoting – not just one or the other. Some self-identified fat women wanted their bodies to reflect their selves. At the same time, awareness that they were "not Jane Fonda,"[127] and probably never would be, strongly influenced participants' understanding of the activity. It is unlikely that aerobics participants had singular motivations that could easily be divided into good/bad or pro-woman/hegemonic reasons for exercising. Fat women, and potentially many women, participating in aerobics were critical and active consumers who created safe spaces in which to enjoy their bodies.

Shared experiences and a common identity as fat women structured aerobics classes. Experience dictated who should come to these classes (fat women) and who should not (everyone else). Knowledge claims about fatness also structured the classes themselves. Instructors used their expertise as fat women to design classes that best accommodated physically large bodies. Instructors understood that they were role models and wanted to teach their participants that they, too, could be fat and fit. This model was in itself normative in that it assumed all fat women had common embodied experiences, and that these experiences were qualitatively different from those of other women. Fat oppression, and the idea that fat women had special needs, was the justification for separate classes for fat women. A desire for exclusivity, and the notion that fat women were vulnerable to the judgment of other exercisers, brought aerobics for fat women into being. In reality, the anxieties fat women experienced about their bodies and beauty were likely not all that different from those of other women. Nonetheless, excluding non-fat women and designing classes specifically for larger bodies was appealing. Exclusivity, space, the instructor, and advertisements for the classes signalled that the classes were safe for fat women.

Aerobics classes were also a site of pleasure. Participants enjoyed the music and the camaraderie, and many also had fun finding well-fitted and flattering fitness clothing to wear to class. In aerobics classes, participants were literally embodying the ideas about fat and health that had been circulating among groups of fat women for the previous ten years. In this respect, aerobics departed from and added to the knowledge and knowledge practices built up by activists in Canada and the United States. Women experienced their bodies anew in aerobics classes, and, in turn, these social sites produced new kinds of social relations among fat women. In aerobics classes, women actually gained the sense of solidarity and bodily liberation that sports feminists envisioned. Aerobics classes were also productive in that they inspired entrepreneurship. Suzanne Bell and Jody Sandler harnessed their personal experiences to capitalize on a gap in the fitness market. The longevity of Bell's and Sandler's businesses may be a testament to their savvy marketing strategies, but their individual successes also confirmed the appeal of fat acceptance strategies. Most importantly, aerobics classes brought pleasure into fat activism. Pleasure did not eliminate the frustration some felt with being fat, but it did temper many women's sense of vulnerability and uncertainty. For participants, aerobics classes brought fat activism to life.

6 Bodies in Fashion: Buying and Selling Plus-Size Clothing

In snapshots from her 1979 wedding, Corrine is wearing a light pink chiffon gown. Stylish in that era, the gown has gathers at the wrist and waist and falls just below the bride's knee (see figure 14). Corrine's put-together appearance in snapshots from the day – signing the register, posing with the ring-bearer and flower-girl – belies the difficulty she experienced finding something to wear to her wedding. Corrine could not find any dresses in her size in Edmonton. She turned to Big & Beautiful Fashions on Eighty-Second Street for assistance. Owner Cindy Proskow came up with a sketch, purchased fabric, and arranged for a seamstress to make the gown. In an interview Proskow recalled helping Corrine prepare for her "big day" was a "joy."[1] Canada's first bridal salon for plus-size women opened thirteen years later in Toronto. Jackqueline Hope, owner of Big, Bold & Beautiful, opened the salon because of her own "demoralizing" experience shopping for a wedding gown. Hope believed that the experience of trying on a properly fitted gown was transformative for her fat clients. Trying on the right dress, Hope's clients saw "themselves for the first time" and ended up "picking a dress" that said "'here I am, look at me,' instead of settling for second-best."[2]

Fashion theorists generally think of the "constraints" placed on consumers in terms of "class, gender, location and income," but plus-size consumers have also experienced lack of choice and limited availability of clothing in their sizes.[3] Fit has been a long-standing emblem of privilege within fashion history, as only those with money could afford to buy tailored clothing.[4] Historically, inappropriate dress was a visible indicator of outsider status: "the embarrassment of such mistakes of dress is not simply that of a personal faux pas, but the shame of failing to meet the standards required of one by the moral order of the social space."[5] Plus-size consumers have also been limited in what

Figure 14. Custom wedding dress by Big & Beautiful Fashions, Edmonton, 1979. Courtesy of Cindy Proskow.

they were able to communicate about themselves through their clothing. Clothing has a capacity to "'say things' about the self" because it "frames what we see when we see another."[6] When clothes do not fit or are not appropriate, wearers become self-conscious, "vulnerable and embarrassed."[7]

In the 1980s and 1990s, fat activists felt constrained by the lack of clothing options in Canada. What women demanded was not uniform: it depended on their beliefs about femininity and sexuality, as well as practical concerns like cost and availability. This chapter looks at fat activists' experiences of buying clothing and the Canadian retailers that tried to meet their needs. It begins with a history of plus-size retailing in Canada. Fat activist experiences provide a lens through which to understand shopping for plus-size clothing in the 1980s and 1990s. It shows that that dressing required creativity and forethought. Their efforts blurred the boundary between fashion as something ephemeral, a "want," and clothing as something practical, a "need."[8] Plus-size retailing also blurred the boundaries of activism. In the context of fashion, staking a claim for plus-size women was a political act. The same issue inspired activists and entrepreneurs: lack of choice. A desire for choice shaped fat activist and plus-size approaches to shopping. Clothes were never just clothes. For self-identified fat women, as for women of earlier generations, fashion offered a way to assert a modern, empowered self-identity.[9] Fat women, like most consumers, wanted clothing that reflected their personalities, politics, sexuality, and style.

The History of Plus-Size Retailing in Canada

Canadian historical evidence suggests that large-sized clothing options have been limited since the introduction of ready-to-wear clothing in standard sizes in the late nineteenth century. Finding women's clothing in larger sizes required that one read the fine print and master a variety of "code" words for large. Between 1885 and 1975 the Eaton's catalogue, the most consistent Canadian source for information about clothing sizes, employed a variety of terms to delineate larger sizes. In this chapter I will employ the term plus-size to refer to clothing sized 16 and up. Plus-size was the term used most commonly in the 1980s by my research participants.

In the twentieth century, clothes for "the large woman" were consistently more expensive than those for her "slighter sister" at Eaton's.[10] From around 1905 extra sizes were offered to consumers who would receive their order two days later than other customers, at a markup of 10 per cent.[11] In 1905 the question "has the person any peculiarity of shape?" was added to the firm's measurement information form, suggesting that standardization had its limitations.[12] Over the course of the twentieth century, Eaton's varied the number of items it offered in plus sizes. In the 1885–6 "Fall–Winter Catalogue," "extra-sized" chemises and drawers were listed in the Ladies Sundries section, but no further information about the garments was provided.[13] Drawing attention to the (large) size of a garment became a more common feature after 1914–5 when Eaton's began to offer women's clothing "specially designed for stout figures."[14] This development was accompanied by an explosion of language to describe "big sizes for the extra large or stout figure"[15]: some items were "extra roomy"[16] and others "suitable for the short, stout woman who requires a general figure reduction and a moderate degree of abdominal support."[17]

After the Second World War, Eaton's catalogues increasingly emphasized the minimizing and figure-flattering quality of large-sized garments. "Generously proportioned dresses" were made to address particular types of stoutness. Corsets were also designed to meet a range of different concerns, from those that fit women who were "too heavy in the hip and thigh" to those that would "reduce and firmly support a heavy abdomen."[18] Promises mounted as new synthetic fabrics were developed in the 1940s. One model would "help eliminate that unwanted roll of fat at the waist,"[19] and another model claimed to be "the answer to the stout woman's figure problem because it's designed to help mould your bust, control your waist, abdomen and thighs in one combination."[20] Although corsetry was generally less common in the second half of the twentieth century, the garments continued to be offered for "the fuller figure" in the 1960s and 1970s.[21] Where other women's underwear stopped at size 46, corsets (by this time, girdles) were sold up to size 52 into the 1970s.[22] The cultural ubiquity of dieting in this period was reflected in a 1976 corset called "Subtract," which would "adjust to give firm control before, during and after dieting." Subtract corsets and girdles were sold for waist sizes 28 through 44 inches.[23] The diminishing prominence of corsets in the catalogue mirrored an overall shift in twentieth-century fashion. At the beginning of the century, corsetry and boning were used to manage and shape women's bodies from the outside in. By the late twentieth century, social norms had shifted, and women were expected to manage their physical bodies in order to display their figures to the greatest advantage.[24]

Mirroring this shift from the external management of the body through clothes to the internal management of the body for clothes, the variety of garments designed by Eaton's specifically for larger women decreased after 1960. In 1970 Eaton's introduced a new sizing system that divided women's clothing into three separate categories. Misses were "for the well-proportioned figure," women's clothing was "for the mature, well-proportioned figure," and half-sizes were for the "somewhat shorter from shoulder to waist than the women's mature size figures."[25] These classifications were a departure from the 1956 sizing categories of "regular and larger women."[26] A more limited range of sizes also accompanied this change. Sizes above a 46 bust were less common after 1950.[27] Women interviewed for this book expressed the sentiment that their bodies were out-of-fashion in a late twentieth-century context. The origins of this sentiment can be found in the cracks between these multiple sizing systems. Regular women's clothing in large sizes perhaps were not correctly proportioned for larger bodies, whereas half-sizes seemed to presume the wearer had a petite frame.

As the problem of being "outsized" became more apparent over the course of the twentieth century, specialty retailers emerged to cater to "stout" women. Lane Bryant was the first major American retailer to enter the market for larger-sized women's clothing. Lena

Himmelstein Bryant insisted that her decision to manufacture larger sizes was based on her own "firm belief that fashion was slighting such women ... Merely supplying 'large sizes' of current styles was entirely wrong. What the woman of ample figure wanted ... was a redesigning, a restyling of current fashions along slenderizing, beautifying lines."[28] Bryant's solution to this problem was a range of "slenderizing fashions," including stockings, pyjamas, undergarments, corsets, shoes, dresses, and outerwear.[29] The company went public in 1928.[30] By 1948 the company had twenty-two retail stores and a mail-order business with the majority of its $41 million in annual sales coming from clothing for large women.[31] Lane Bryant was acquired by a private investor in 1982 and has since changed hands.[32] The store was, and continues to be, an important source of clothing for Canadian women shopping in the US.

Canada's oldest retailer for larger women, Penningtons, was modelled after Lane Bryant. Owners William Drevnig and Albert Sherman began converting their "regular" women's clothing chain Cotton Town to Penningtons stores after the Second World War.[33] Penningtons' goal was to distinguish itself from plus-size garments offered at Eaton's and the Hudson's Bay Company by offering more stylish and "younger" clothing.[34] In a rare 1978 interview, Drevnig explained his inspiration to *Canadian Business*: "We went into large sizes ... because we sensed a pent-up demand among women. It was just like after the war when a woman would walk 12 blocks to find nylon stockings. These [overweight] women were traipsing from store to store for clothes that would fit them."[35] Penningtons offered larger-sized clothing for women "from the skin out" and sold "a complete range of underwear, lingerie, outerwear, dresses, suits, coats, sportswear."[36] Drevnig took it upon himself to oversee the selection and production of all garments and claimed to spend many of his Saturday mornings in store talking to customers about what they did and did not like about his choices.[37] The company went public in 1969 with nineteen stores, and by 1978 it had expanded across Canada, employing one thousand people.[38] By 1982 there were ninety-one Penningtons stores in Canada and ten sister stores called Liz Porter that were aimed at a younger market.[39] In 1979 the retailer expanded into the US under the name Penningtons du Canada.[40] After many boom years, finances took a downturn for Penningtons. Penningtons du Canada suffered in the competitive American market, closing in the early 1990s. Several attempts at restructuring were unsuccessful, and the company was sold to Reitmans in 1995. All divisions except Penningtons Warehouse were closed.[41] Presently, the chain is known as Penningtons: sizes 14 to 32.

Penningtons' customers had a love-hate relationship with the store.[42] The company's sympathy for its customers was mocked by Terry Poulton in a 1978 profile for *Canadian Business*.[43] She described Penningtons' attitude towards its customers as "unusually proprietorial, if not parental" and suggested that management glowed "the way one might glow helping Biafran refugees."[44] Poulton believed there was a "discrepancy between how Penningtons saw itself and how their customers saw Penningtons."[45] Some of the women who participated in this study echoed Poulton's sentiments, referring to the Penningtons of the 1980s as "polyester heaven"[46] and a place to buy "old women's clothes."[47] Others referred to the store affectionately as "good old Penningtons"[48] or "my home away from home."[49]

Regardless of how women felt about it, Penningtons was a critical source of clothing for fat women in Canada. Kate Partridge spoke frankly on this subject in a 1982 article for the *Bolster*, noting: "What would most of us have done without them over the years? At least for me, life would have been several degrees more difficult, since Penningtons were the only people that seemed to care about women my size."[50] Between the 1950s and the 1970s Penningtons was the only plus-size chain retailer available to many Canadians, and therefore it became an emblem of the promise and the limitations of the plus-size clothing industry. Although Penningtons provided plus-size consumers with more options, customers felt shame and embarrassment at having to enter the "fat lady store."[51] When plus-size clothing did not fit well, or was made of inferior fabrics, it exacerbated women's sense of being stigmatized and excluded by the fashion industry.

By the 1980s Penningtons' hold on the larger-sized women's clothing market in Canada was challenged by the introduction of two competing chains. Addition Elle opened in Canada in 1979 and was initially owned by Shirmax, which also owned the Shirley K Maternity chain.[52] Dalmy's chain of stores opened Antels "big and beautiful fashions" in 1981.[53] The *Bolster* reported on the opening of both stores. LAL members were enthusiastic about the arrival of more clothing options.[54] The entry of Antels and Addition Elle into the market was concurrent with overall growth in the plus-size fashion industry in the United States and Canada in the 1980s.[55] The explosion of interest in larger-sized women's clothing in the 1980s gave way to a reorganization of the marketplace in the mid-1990s. Lower-priced plus-size clothing started to be available through Cotton Ginny Plus, which opened forty-five stores across Canada between 1989 and 1991.[56] Budget plus-size fashion lines became increasingly available through retailers like Walmart and Zellers in the 1990s and beyond.[57]

This resulted in a reorganization of other stores. Reitmans bought Antels's parent company, Dalmy's, in 1995. They continued to operate Antels until 1999 when they closed the chain because it was not profitable.[58] In 2002 Reitmans bought the Shirmax chain, thus acquiring Penningtons' main rival, Addition Elle.

Finding, Maintaining, and Preserving Garments

Frustration with plus-size clothing prior was the hook that Kate Partridge used to draw women to the first LAL meeting in 1981. For about half of the forty-nine women interviewed for this study, the problem of finding clothing began in childhood. In Canada in the 1950s and 1960s, families with plus-size children had to travel long distances to buy clothes. Kate Partridge remembered that buying clothing was "fraught with anxiety and tension" because her parents had to make "special trips to special shops ... to find stuff to wear."[59] Helena Spring of NAAFA was driven thirty-five kilometres from Galt (Cambridge), Ontario, to Brantford, Ontario, to buy clothes. The experience was shrouded in secrecy because, "you know, in the Fifties it was disgusting to have a fat kid."[60] Even if their parents did not have to travel far to buy clothes, women recalled feeling stigmatized by having to shop in the "chubby section" of children's shops.[61] For Susan White, who participated in the "Fat Is a Feminist Issue" CR group in Winnipeg, school gym uniforms were the worst because she had difficulty finding the right size. The result was "so damn ugly and revealing" that she felt "very, very embarrassed to wear it."[62] Being a larger size as a child also meant wearing adult clothing earlier than one's peers. Margaret Burka, who later opened a plus-size clothing boutique, felt that she "always looked older" than other children, an experience Janet Walker of LAL said "didn't feel right ... didn't feel like ... the rest of the kids."[63] Participants' accounts of finding clothing as children echo Karen Jaffe's study of fat women and identity formation. Jaffe showed that childhood experiences of fat oppression had a negative impact on women. In tense interactions like those described above, children learned they did not measure up in the eyes of their families.[64]

Because of their difficulty finding clothing as children, some women learned to sew their own garments. Sewing was a way to emulate the same styles as their peers. Jan Mindlin and Susan White sewed their own clothes in order to get the right cut.[65] White began sewing in high school and was increasingly making her own clothes in her early twenties because she "couldn't find a size to fit."[66] Becoming a competent seamstress had its advantages. White and Mindlin, along with Lynn

Burzese and Claudia Savage, sewed well enough that they were able to alter or draft patterns to suit their needs.[67] Others in their teens and twenties who could not sew relied on their mothers and grandmothers to sew for them.[68] Later, when family could not perform these tasks, some of my participants hired seamstresses to craft special garments. Enthusiasm for this source of clothing varied due to both the quality and fit of the garments and their expense. Margaret Burka worked with a seamstress who was a former employee of Canadian fashion designer Alfred Sung. Burka was comfortable chatting with her seamstress about her desired fit, fabric, or collar design and was generally pleased with the results.[69] Sue Masterton was similarly satisfied with "a skirt, a jacket and a pair of pants" made for her by a seamstress in the 1980s. Although "they were absolutely beautifully made," Masterton felt that at $750, "they were very expensive."[70] Other women felt that custom-made clothing did not suit them any better than off-the-rack items. Lise Bergeron found that many seamstresses were not accustomed to sewing for larger bodies and did not understand how to "sew for people like me."[71] Ruth Gillingham found seamstresses unsatisfactory for a different reason: "the stigma of having your body measured" during which "you pretty much have to be in your underwear." Still, Gillingham relied on a seamstress to make garments she couldn't find in stores, including her aerobics leotard and her wedding dress.[72]

Self-identified fat women thought that the search for appropriate clothing was uniquely their problem. They felt that slim women, in particular, could not possibly understand their concerns about fashion. Part of the shame fat women felt was based on the experience of approaching thin sales staff to ask for hard-to-find items. Underwear was particularly embarrassing for Sarah King. She described "the fat ladies underwear department" as "soul destroying" because they did not have large women serving customers. Instead, "you had this little tiny girl who had no clue about the problem and ... you know, had attitude about fat people ... it was just ... nasty."[73] Claudia Savage found the problem of dealing with underwear so irritating that she began to make her own.[74] Commentary on seamstresses and underwear show that self-identified fat women believed that skinny women did not experience the same uncertainties about their appearance as larger women. Research indicates, however, that women of all sizes experience shame and frustration about their bodies.[75] Combined, research on female fashion consumers suggests that mass manufacturing and standardization of clothing sizes has drawn attention to embodied differences.

Size limitations led some plus-size women to purchase maternity clothes. Max Konigsberg, founder of Shirley K Maternity, attributed his decision to open Addition Elle in 1979 to the phenomenon of plus-size women buying maternity wear. Konigsberg wrote in his 2006 autobiography that Shirley K was one of "the only stores where plus-size ladies could find young, fashionable clothes to fit them. So many of them came to our maternity stores to shop" that "we realized that there was a need in the marketplace."[76] Sue Masterton bought her first maternity outfit at age sixteen. The fit of the garment worked because, as she recalled, "I carried a lot of my weight around my middle." Although Masterton knew at the time that "nobody else would have known it was maternity," she still remembered feeling it was "very embarrassing to have to wear."[77] Designer Jan Mindlin remembered feeling that the construction of maternity clothing was useful to her work. She bought a maternity bathing suit and used it as the basis for the design of a backless evening gown.[78] Mindlin was not embarrassed. The gown was "quite a hit" when she modelled it at a Large as Life fashion show in 1982.[79]

Women with more money extended their clothing search across the border to plus-size retailers in the US. It was a truism amongst my research participants that the US had a better selection of plus-size clothing. Lane Bryant was a favourite, but by no means the only source. As a teenager in the 1970s, Linda McKay-Panos recalled seeking out American "fat stores" because of their selection of pants. She wanted to be able to wear blue jeans like her friends and was only able to find her size in the US.[80] Suzanne Bell also found that shopping in the US allowed her to be more fashion-forward than her friends at school and to find clothing that no one else had. She recalled cross-border shopping and returning with "a madras shirt, which was huge" because no one else had one and she "did not want look like everybody else."[81] Later in life, women continued to use visits to the United States to find clothing. Pat Donaldson reported that when she was in the US she took the opportunity to approach "fat well-dressed women" to ask them where they bought their clothes. Donaldson even went so far as to go backstage to ask "male cross dressers" at a Las Vegas floor show where they bought their shoes.[82] Opportunities to cross-border shop were celebrated in *Canada WYDE* (the magazine of CASA) in the early 1990s, a period when Ontario's recession made such activities controversial. While many newspaper articles admonished Canadians to shop at home, articles such as "Let's Go Shopping!" celebrated the range of stores available just across the US border.[83] Marketplace listings of American stores were a regular feature in *Canada WYDE* and also the subject of occasional notices in the *Bolster* and Large as Life Calgary's newsletter.[84] Plus-size consumers felt they had no choice but to cross the border to find clothing.

Once a woman did find a garment she really loved, she took special care to maintain it and make it last. Sometimes this meant wearing clothing "until it had holes in it."[85] Pants were a particularly important find, and Pat Donaldson went to great lengths to preserve a few pairs of her favourites. One strategy was to take apart pants that were worn out and have a pattern made. Another tactic was to buy multiple versions of the same garment. Donaldson did this in the 1990s when one of her favourite stores was going out of business. She bought two pairs and, as of our meeting in 2006, had already worn out one pair of these pants. Donaldson said she was saving the second "as my final pair of gorgeous pants."[86]

Donaldson's actions show that certain garments were treasured and carefully maintained by their owners. Alexandra Palmer observed similar care of garments in her study of haute couture consumption in post-war Toronto. Palmer discovered that the garments she studied "repeatedly revealed evidence of wear."[87] She argued that consumers "bought with the intention of making their clothes last and were not about to pay unlimited amounts for their wardrobe ... Women were emotionally and aesthetically attached to their clothes and sought ways to extend their life."[88] Although the couture garments discussed by Palmer were rare and expensive, there is a parallel to be drawn with fat women's care for their favourite garments. For the wearer, clothing that fit right was invaluable, regardless of its source or its size. Canadian women with fewer resources likely relied on family members and clothing swaps to get by. More affluent women had their clothes made, and travelled across town, to nearby cities and across the border to find their clothing. Shopping strategy was not entirely determined by social class, however. All of the self-identified fat women who participated in this study sewed, travelled, and traded to meet their basic needs. What women wanted was often not available at all.

Feminism and Antifashion

While many women involved in fat acceptance groups saw the lack of affordable and appropriate plus-size clothing as a problem, most members of LG5 and Hersize did not. In this respect, there was a clear divide between feminist fat activists of the 1980s and early 1990s and fat acceptance groups of the same era. LG5 members saw their clothing as antifashion, even though their choice of plainer, less feminine clothing was in itself a style statement.[89] Wearing men's clothing was part of the "natural" look in fashion that was popular in the 1970s.

In this period many women rejected "mainstream" femininity, including confining undergarments, high heels, and styled hair in favour of a more "natural" aesthetic of jeans, overalls, and untreated hair.[90] Lesbian feminists of the 1970s, 1980s, and beyond adopted a distinct androgynous look of T-shirts and jeans to communicate their rejection of heterosexuality. In interviews with members of the Lesbian Organization of Toronto (LOOT), Becki L. Ross found that rejecting heterosexual femininity was seen as part of a broader symbolic rejection of sexism and male power.[91] Michèle Charland of LG5 confirmed this reading of her clothing choices. She wore men's clothing out of necessity but felt that it "wasn't that bad ... because at the time lesbians also were dressing like that."[92]

Fred Davis has argued that adopting a distinct "antifashion" look is not the same thing as being indifferent to fashion. Similarly, Valerie Steel has observed of this era that "fashion was not in fashion."[93] Antifashion is the adoption of particularly distinguishing forms of dress that is intended to make a claim.[94] Hersize, in comparison to LG5, believed that women should be indifferent to fashion because it was a waste of time, health, and comfort. Like other feminist groups of the era, the group saw fashion as a "principle means ... by which the institutions of patriarchy have managed ... to oppress women and relegate them to inferior social roles.[95] Hersize's position was that women invested too much time in beauty culture.[96] Lobbying for more and better fashion was, therefore, at odds with the group's critique of consumption. Member Mary Frances Ellison felt that Hersize did not take on fashion because "it wasn't seen as a feminist issue. It wasn't a political issue; it was a practical issue." Fashion choice was, however, an issue for Ellison. She researched how-to books and alternative fashion outlets in her own time.[97]

Members of Large as Life also wore men's clothing, but for different reasons than their feminist-identified counterparts. In the *Bolster*, LAL members traded tips on finding men's clothing that could pass as women's clothes. Designer Jan Mindlin encouraged readers of the *Bolster* to experiment with belts, noting, "I always buy men's belts, because they are generally more solid and don't squash when you sit down or move."[98] Several months later, another LAL member, Lori Wilson, published a column about buying clothing in the men's section of department stores. Wilson encouraged women to pick up unisex items, like sweaters and sweatshirts, in the men's section, because they were less expensive than the women's options.[99] Combined, the LAL and LG5 examples show that fat activists of the 1980s and early 1990s selectively used men's clothing to help achieve a particular look.

By the late 1990s a generational shift in attitudes towards fashion is apparent. Pretty Porky and Pissed Off viewed fashion differently from their feminist counterparts of earlier decades. In their rallies on Toronto's Queen Street in the mid-1990s, the group handed out flyers reading:

> We don't have time to seek out fatty specialty stores that may or may not have clothes which fit us.
>   Every fat girl knows the humiliation of looking in stores that do not, and will not carry our sizes. When you can't find anything that fits you feel alone and ugly.
>   **Fuck that shit.**[100]

Pretty Porky and Pissed Off's approach shared more with fat acceptance groups than feminists of earlier decades. PPPO believed that finding clothing that fit was an equity issue. The key difference was that PPPO identified itself as an "anti-consumerist" group. Lack of appropriate clothing was seen as the product of consumer capitalist societies that exploit women's body insecurities. The solution was twofold: First, draw attention to the limitations of corporate capitalist fashion system. Second, find alternative outlets for clothing.

In her 2004 study of fat identity politics, Kathleen LeBesco expressed scepticism about the growth of the plus-size fashion industry, reflecting a similar critique to PPPO. She feared that companies were capitalizing from fat women's desperation for clothing and the result was that the "objectification against which feminists have been arguing" had become the "new dream state of the fat female consumer."[101] While she conceded that fashion could be used as a means of resistance, LeBesco argued that ultimately the images of beautiful fat women presented by the industry presented a narrow view of attractiveness and that it was not appropriate to commodify social movements.[102] By contrast, in her study of plus-size fashion bloggers, Lauren Downing argued that the development of the plus-size industry was vital in "creating market equity, in undoing longstanding stereotypes and in crafting self-identity" for fat women.[103]

Finding clothing that fits is a necessity. For consumers challenged by a lack of options, the process of shopping is politicized. Fat activists interviewed for this book show how shopping helped to fuel their critiques of stigma. Sourcing appropriate clothing was a thoughtful process, and, as this chapter shows, women developed a number of creative solutions, from wearing men's clothing, to clothing swaps, to sewing their own garments. Echoing Downing's findings, then, this book shows that wearing fashionable clothing was not only an act of resistance to body norms but also a way to foster a positive self-identity.

Fashion Shows and Clothing Swaps

LAL's first event following their formation in 1981 was a fashion show and seminar called "Freedom to Be You – Now!" The event included instruction on make-up and wardrobe planning, followed by "a fashion show" that would "demonstrate how beautiful big can be!" Tickets cost ten dollars for LAL members and twelve dollars for non-members and included wine and cheese.[104] "Freedom to Be You – Now!" sold out the two-hundred-seat auditorium of the Robson Square Media Centre. The afternoon began with a panel discussion by representatives from the plus-size clothing industry. The retailers addressed common concerns of plus-size women, including the high cost of clothing. In turn the audience told the panellists some of their concerns, including that plus-size fashions cost more than other women's clothing, size ranges were limited, and garments were made of out cheap fabrics.[105] LAL gained a considerable amount of momentum from this event, which also helped to launch Evelyn Booth's Models Rubenesque and sparked Suzanne Bell's interest in fashion.[106]

LAL's fashion shows reveal that the group had a critical view of the fashion industry. Members were not content simply to have more options. They also demanded better cuts, a greater range of sizes, and affordability. The language used by LAL members to talk about fashion was telling. Appropriate clothing provided women "freedom" of choice and of movement. By the time they held their second fashion show, on 4 October 1982, the group was confident that fat women could be fashionable and knew where to find the right clothes. This show, called "Fabulous Fall Fashions for Big Beautiful Women," was held in conjunction with Antels, which was opening its first British Columbia location at the time. Like the previous show, this event featured fashions created by Large as Life member Jan Mindlin.[107]

Joan Dal Santo felt that the two shows differed in tone. With "the first one ... we were out to change people's way of thinking about large women and we wanted people to take us seriously." The second show, however, "wasn't subtle ... it was more in your face. Of course you take us seriously, we're wonderful."[108] This shift – from a tentative, formal fashion seminar to a splashy evening runway show – demonstrates a growing confidence among LAL members.

The process of organizing and participating in the show impacted members' sense of the possibilities for fat women.[109] Plus-size fashion became the "raw material" for LAL members to see themselves differently. As Joanne Entwistle has observed, "dress works on the body, imbuing it with social meaning, while the body is a dynamic field that gives life and fullness to dress."[110] Planning the fashion shows helped participants to see themselves and other fat women differently, as competent, beautiful, and fashionable. Joan Dal Santo modelled in the show and felt that "the audience was on our side, all the way." Kate Partridge described the atmosphere as "really exciting," and Ingrid Laue felt the day was a "howling success," particularly because LAL got "quite a few members as a result" of the event.[111] Seeing a model looking "well turned out" helped audience members to see themselves as potentially fashionable.[112] LAL members Janet Walker and Suzanne Bell met for the first time on their way to the "Freedom to Be You – Now!" show. Walker spotted Bell on the bus on her way to the show and thought "do I dare talk to her?" Walker admired Bell because "she dressed trendy ... she just looked fabulous no matter what she was wearing." Walker told me she "thought, whoa, I want to learn to be like that. Comfortable."[113] Interactions between women were important to the development of fat activism.

Camaraderie further developed between LAL members through their clothing swaps, held annually from 1981 to 1985. The atmosphere of the first swap was described as "giddy and fearful" by Janet Walker. Walker said women were giddy at being able to find clothing that fit at a reasonable price. Participants were fearful because the event was advertised and it was "public ... there was always that fear that people would come in and mock you, make fun of you."[114] The women present quickly overcame their fear and began to enjoy the opportunity to play around with fashion. Joan Dal Santo recalled groups of women gathered behind a curtain to try on each others' clothes:

> there were curtained off areas around the edges of the hall that we used as fitting rooms. They were not very private, and I remember that because nobody was worried about it. Here was a bunch of women that would go into a regular store and get into the fitting room and not want anybody to see them. And here we were, this bunch, behind a curtain and there would be four or five of us there just putting things on and off and saying, 'oh that looks good' of 'no, that one doesn't work.' We were just in various states of undress and very casual and comfortable with each other.[115]

Dal Santo also remembered one of her purchases from this swap quite vividly. She bought a dress from fellow LALer and designer Jan Mindlin (see figure 15), which she described as "kind of an ecru colour with

Figure 15. Jan Mindlin wearing one of her own designs, c. 1983. Courtesy of Suzanne Bell.

flowers on it ... it was gathered and extra long and it just kind of floated around me. Oh, it felt good."[116] Dal Santo's and Walker's recollections of the first clothing swap stand out from their earlier descriptions of "The Forgotten Woman" workshop, where they first met in 1979. While earlier both women had avoided relationships with fat women, two years later they took great pleasure in their interactions with members of Large as Life.

LAL fashion shows were an important tool to increase membership. By comparison, retailers who organized fashion shows had mixed reactions. Some felt that fashion shows weren't a very good return on their investment. The time taken to find the right fit, coordinate, and dress the models was not worth their effort and financial outlay.[117] One exception was Cindy Proskow, owner of Big & Beautiful in Edmonton, who organized fashion shows regularly in the early 1980s. Proskow relied on friends and clients to be her models. A grainy home video of one of these events shows four models and a dresser preparing the women to walk a catwalk placed at the centre of a conference room floor. Proskow acted as the master of ceremonies to her audience of approximately twenty women who were seated at tables around the runway. Iris, who was described as a "professional model," walked on to the runway wearing a long beach cover-up. As Iris gets to the end of the runway Proskow said, "the bathing suits that we carry lend themselves very nicely to the figures of our girls." At this point Iris pulled off her cover-up to reveal a flowered bathing suit. The women in the audience responded with whoops and applause.[118] The audience response reflected excitement about the display of a large woman's body. The hope of organizers, like LAL and Proskow, was that displaying fashionable fat female bodies would be productive, in the sense that it could encourage women to experiment with clothing.[119] Increasing fat women's access to clothing and the retailers' profitability went hand in hand. For the women in the audience, whether or not the fashion industry oppressed consumers was beside the point. Proskow's customers were excited by the possibilities that properly fitted clothing offered them.[120]

Another dimension of LAL's fashion activism was to teach women what clothing most flattered their bodies and to suggest strategies for building an affordable and versatile wardrobe. As with their work on aerobics, LAL members tended to favour working woman to woman to develop solutions to their concerns about fat oppression. They focused on strategies for addressing everyday problems like finding clothing and used their experiences as consumers as the basis for their activities. This woman-to-woman approach was used by LALers in a one-day seminar called "Largely Fashion: A Fashion Survival Workshop for Large Women." "Largely Fashion" promised to be a "fun and relaxing, yet stimulating workshop." Topics covered included:

- Changing your life (almost) with colour
- Coming to grips with your figure type
- Planning a figure flattering wardrobe
- Developing fashion consciousness, and uncovering your own personal style[121]

LAL founder Kate Partridge began the day by talking to participants about her personal fashion history. She offered herself as a "coping model" rather than a fashion expert. Participants then did a "lifestyle inventory" to assess what kinds of clothing they needed. They tallied what type of clothing was required for each activity such as "relaxing, housework, groceries, fitness, work, school, meetings, restaurants, entertaining, dancing, church, travel," and then assessed how frequently they used each particular type of clothing. A separate handout offered a breakdown of five different large women's figure types. These were rectangle, square, round, pear, and barrel. Subsequent handouts and discussion focused on what types of clothes looked good on the different figure types. Sample: "Avoid very wide sleeves as they add girth. Sleeves shouldn't end at the widest part of your body." Not all of the advice given by Partridge was focused on looking slim. For example, she urged women to let go of their fear of exposing flesh and to "liberate" their arms whenever possible.[122]

Ms magazine was an important feminist source of the 1980s that talked regularly about fashion. A semi-regular column called "Personal Style" offered women fashion tips on issues like how to dress to get taken seriously, developing a unique "personal style," and finding comfortable clothing, among other topics.[123] "Largely Fashion," much like *Ms*'s "Personal Style," did not wholly embrace femininity or the fashion industry. Style was framed as a personal and practical issue. LAL departed from *Ms*'s approach to personal style by linking it to fat acceptance. Partridge told the attendees, "You and I both **know** that we are as attractive, intelligent, sexy and so on, as any slim woman – we **know** this, but we may not **feel** it."[124] Partridge used rights talk and empowerment to frame her belief that fat women deserved to feel attractive. Activists like Partridge pushed feminist interpretations of personal style in new directions. Plus-size clothing revealed an axis of gender oppression that was not on the radar of other women's liberation groups.

Notably, "Largely Fashion" assumed that attendees knew what it meant to be attractive. Here, as elsewhere in fat activism, competing visions of beauty were not considered. Implicitly, "Largely Fashion" and LAL endorsed a typical feminine look by suggesting that fat women could and should look as good as "any slim woman."[125] Finding the right garment and developing a personal style from the options available to them could solve fat women's problems. The group was critical of the ways that the fashion industry privileged slim bodies, but it stopped short of taking on femininity more generally. Nonetheless, LAL's approach represents an important challenge to the feminist critique of femininity discussed in chapter 3. Feminists have tended to see femininity as problematic because norms establish a set of expectations about appropriate dress, demeanour, and actions. And yet members of LAL saw fashion as pleasurable. Femininity was defined not as repressive, but as a normal – and potentially empowering – cultural currency that should be available to all women.

Plus-Size Fashion in the *Bolster*

LAL was an important site for members to learn and share information about fashion. In the *Bolster*, women shared details about where
to find leotards, bras, jeans, and shoes. Between 1981 and 1984, the
Bolster contained updates about new local retailers who supplied larger-sized clothes. Carol Pierce's "Clothesline" feature for the *Bolster*
would appear every five or six issues. Pierce researched the availability of jeans as part of her work for the clothing committee of Large
as Life Vancouver, visiting a few local jeans stores and testing the
merchandise herself for a story called "Ample Jeans." She reported
that the store "Starbord Jeans" sold up to a size 38 waist and that customers should request larger sizes because they were not always on
display. The "Jeans Factory" had more promising results, with jeans
and corduroy pants available up to size 48. Pierce reported that that
"Jeans Factory" also had a good selection of jean jackets and all of their
clothing was very affordable.[126] Here, Pierce was acting as a friend and
expert to her fellow LALers.

In addition to exchanging information, newsletters became an
affordable source for advertising by local retailers. The *Bolster* began
to carry ads for Vancouver retailers including "Second Time Around:
Large Size Second Hand Clothes"[127] and later "Of Grand Design by
Jan Mindlin,"[128] "Alex's Mistress" lingerie,[129] "Southlands Ladies
Wear,"[130] and "Jaegal's Fashions."[131] Large as Life's most unlikely
advertiser was a company called SOFI (Sault Original Fashions Inc),
which was started in Sault Ste Marie, Ontario, in 1981. A 1983 advertisement for SOFI that appeared in the *Bolster* featured a woman in a
burka labelled "there's no need to continue patronizing Omar the tentmaker any longer – ask for fashions by SOFI!"[132] The ill-chosen "tentmaker" metaphor was intended by its author to make the point that
fat women's clothing was shapeless and colourless.[133] That this statement was considered harmless is an example of the narrow view fat
activists had on race and ethnicity. Fat was presumed to be a common
burden and differences of class, race, sexual orientation, and politics
were unexamined and unexplained in retail or other activist spaces.
The "Omar" advertisements further speak to a tendency within the
clothing industry to see the dress of "ethnic" groups as outside fashion. In Western nations, traditional religious or ethnic-identified clothing was seen as bland and ahistorical.[134] The burka-clad figure of the
"Omar" advertisement was supposed to contrast the modern, stylish
LAL woman. It shows that no one considered it possible for such a
woman to be a member of their group.

Table 5. Plus-size retailers interviewed

Store/Designer	Location	Years	Proprietor
Big & Beautiful	Edmonton, AB	1979–99	Cindy Proskow
Full Bloom	Winnipeg, MB	1983–2007	Lynn Schneider
Full Figure Fashions	Calgary, AB	1985–2019	Monica Sieben-Kuhn*
Jan Mindlin Designs	Vancouver, BC	1981–90	Jan Mindlin
Penningtons	Nationwide	1948–present	Sol Armel*
SOFI	Sault Ste Marie, ON	1981–4	Lynn Burzese
Suzanne Bell's Fashions	Vancouver, BC	1984–2012	Suzanne Bell
The Answer	Toronto, ON	1986–c. 2010	Margaret Burka*

*Indicates the founder of a store that is now under different ownership.

Inside Stores for Fat Women Only

Several independently run plus-size clothing stores for women opened across Canada in the 1980s. Women who opened these stores wanted customers to feel excited about fashion. Independent plus-size retailers were self-appointed experts in the clothing needs of fat women, and they designed their stores to appeal to this demographic. Many women opened their stores in the early 1980s, and their rise was coincident with the growth of fat activism. Most Canadian cities, and many towns, had at least one retailer that sold plus-size clothing. I tracked these retailers through fat activist sources, eventually interviewing five current and former owners.[135]

Plus-size retailers of the 1980s drew on the "shared experience" of "bodily trials and tribulations" to establish themselves as experts and friends to their customers. Kathy Peiss identified a similar woman-to-woman pattern of female entrepreneurship in her study of the early American beauty industry, which persisted across time and national borders.[136] In contrast to the frumpy chain store Penningtons and the gloomy department stores, female store owners claimed to truly understand the needs of consumers who were like them. Retailers took for granted that fat women had a common "problem," and that their store was the solution. Much like different branches of fat activism, plus-size retailers' understanding of body liberation was shaped by personal experience. Female entrepreneurs felt they had special knowledge of their customers. The merchandise, as well as the layout of the store, were intended to make fat women feel beautiful and glamorous. Even though they were commercial spaces, retailers often understood

Table 6. Other retailers mentioned by participants

Store/Designer	Location	Years	Proprietor
Big, Bold & Beautiful	Toronto	1979–97	Jackqueline Hope
The Forgotten Woman	United States	1987–2000	Nancye Radmin
Lane Bryant	United States	1907–present	Lena Himmelstein

their stores as special places for fat women only. Some owners had connections with groups discussed in this book. For others, opening a store was their fat activism.

An individual owner's decision to set up shop was usually inspired by her experiences with fashion, combined with a perceived gap in the clothing market. Designer and LAL member Jan Mindlin wanted to be the "Donna Karan of plus-size fashion." Mindlin did not want to compete with manufacturers to produce basics but instead wished to make "beautiful tailored clothing" using "fun fabric" with an eye to making women look "hot."[137] Entrepreneur Lynne Burzese wanted to provide "classic, clean lines" instead of the polyester, drab-coloured clothing she found in department stores.[138] Store owner Lynn Schneider travelled from Winnipeg to Chicago to find "beautiful lingerie" for the many women like her who had been "starved to death" because there was nothing "out there."[139] Monica Sieben-Kuhn opened a consignment store because cost was important to her.[140] LAL member Suzanne Bell began manufacturing aerobics leotards when she had difficulty finding such pieces in her size. She went on to open a retail store that focused on "soft dressing" in sizes 16 to 60. Bell was one of a few Canadian retailers who offered clothing above size 24, a decision that reflected her desire to dress women like herself, who belonged in the "queen-sized" market.[141] Two women, Burka and Schneider, were directly inspired by Nancye Radmin's The Forgotten Woman, an upscale plus-size clothing boutique that opened in New York in 1977. This memorable store, whose name Ellen Tallman borrowed for her 1979 workshop, sold designer clothes in sizes 16 through 24.[142] Winnipeg store owner Lynn Schneider described the store as "the best one" of the American retailers she had visited.[143] Margaret Burka and a friend decided to open a store after visiting a The Forgotten Woman shop in Boca Raton, Florida. She "thought, maybe ... in a small way there are enough people in Toronto that would appreciate this."[144]

The ability to open up shop reflected each retailer's class and financial background. Where the three co-owners of The Answer were blasé about the $25,000 each it cost them to get their high-end retail store started in 1984, Suzanne Bell relied on a loan from her parents to get started.[145] Sieben-Kuhn opened her store only after presenting a business plan to her husband.[146] This familial support minimized the financial risk Burka, Bell, and Sieben-Kuhn incurred by opening their shops. Women who did not have familial support, because they were single or came from a modest class background, struggled to get their businesses going. Lynn Schneider did not think her investment in Full Bloom was as secure as some other independent retailers in Winnipeg because she did not "have a husband that" had "money."[147] Jan Mindlin hinted that having the support of a partner might have helped her take her business further. Mindlin said she "always used to say, if I could've met an accountant ... they could handle the money and I could do my creative thing ... I think I have a good business head, but you need support, partnership."[148] Not having familial or a partner's support did not determine the course of a business, but it probably shaped the owner's ability to take financial risks.

Securing the financing to open a store was only the beginning for independent retailers. The next step was to fulfil the promise of something more for fat women. Many women discovered that buying clothing wholesale was not much easier for retailers than it was for everyday plus-size consumers. As a consequence, all of the retailers involved in this study decided to supplement merchandise they bought wholesale with garments manufactured specially for their stores. The decision to manufacture particular items resulted from a few different factors: there were no Canadian sources for a particular type of garment; the quality, cut, or colour of wholesale garments was found wanting; or manufacturers did not make large enough clothing. Cindy Proskow and Margaret Burka had patterns drafted based on the types of garments they felt were wanting in the industry. Proskow refused to refer to this as designing but conceded that she was "pretty good" at drafting patterns and had found a reliable team of seamstresses to work up garments for her.[149] The Answer co-owner Burka was a self-described "fabric freak" who enjoyed visiting a store in Toronto's garment district to pick her colours and prints. She had patterns drafted based on the body of a size 18 friend. Addressing one of many problems consumers had with plus-size clothing, Burka was careful to limit size increases to particular parts of the garment. Where length or waist size might increase by inches, she made sure that shoulders only went up one-eighth of an inch with every size. About ten versions of each pant and a smaller number of jackets were manufactured each season. The Answer sold these locally made, lined, wool pants and jackets at a cost of $270 for the pair.[150] Making a purchase from an independent retailer was often more expensive than shopping at chain stores like Addition Elle and

Table 7. Suzanne Bell's sizing chart, c. 1990

Suzanne Bell's Sizes	A	B	C	D	E
	S	M	L	XL	XXL
	1X		2X		
Bust (inches)	42–45	47–50	52–56	57–60	62–65
Waist (inches)	35–38	40–44	46–50	52–56	58–62
Hip (inches)	44–47	49–52	54–57	59–62	64–67
Thigh (inches)	26–27.5	27.5–29	29–30.5	30.5–32	32–33.5

Penningtons.[151] In return for this added cost, independent retailers claimed that customers got better quality, more fashionable clothing, with the best possible cut for larger figures.

Size was a key concern in Suzanne Bell's decision to begin manufacturing clothing under her own name. Bell had started by making aerobics leotards for Large as Life members, but she expanded her line because she could not find wholesale garments in the sizes she needed. She characterized her line as "soft dressing," a style of clothing she described as "not structured, it tends to be flow-y, it tends to layer-y, it tends to be not zipper-y with structured waists. It tends to be elastic waists, that kind of thing."[152] Like Proskow, Bell tended to see this line of basics as "manufacturing" rather than designing, requiring only seasonal changes in a collar, a colour, or a dart.[153] Bell was most particular about sizing. Like Burka, she had been frustrated by the inconsistency in women's clothing sizes. In the early 1990s Bell instituted an in-house sizing system. Clothing was advertised as available in sizes 16 through 60, but Bell also sold clothing using an A-B-C-D-E sizing system. The equivalences were listed, as shown in table 7.[154]

This useful chart offered equivalences between different plus-sizing systems. It was not only intended to guide shoppers but also to create a separate system so as not to stigmatize larger buyers. At the same time, the chart is savvy, adding in the less traditionally used thigh measurement to help customers determine the required size. This sizing system was also a way of taking control of the language of the politics of sizing – making plus-size customers the point of reference in place of the so-called "regular" size. All of these choices reflect Bell's personal knowledge of shopping for plus-size clothing. Bell's experiences, as well as those of LAL members and her long-time clients, guided her business decisions.[155]

Quality of fabric was the main problem SOFI founder Lynn Burzese identified in the plus-size clothing market. Burzese saw a gap in the higher-end, boutique plus-size clothing market. In 1979 she secured funding through the Sault Ste Marie Local Employment Assistance Program (LEAP), a Department of Employment and Immigration program, in the form of a grant to help women start small businesses.[156] SOFI designer Debbie Shuchat told a Canadian Press interviewer that a lot of plus-size clothing was manufactured cheaply because retailers saw being fat as a temporary state. Shuchat emphasized that there were very limited chances for permanent weight loss.[157] SOFI decided to try to distinguish the line through their choice of fabrics; they used real silk, wool, and cotton instead of polyester.[158]

Independent retailers' goals were to transform shopping for plus-size clothing – which many women found stigmatizing – into a pleasurable experience. Creating physically accessible, comfortable spaces was a strategy for promoting fat acceptance.[159] Entrepreneurs tried to do this through the design, layout, and atmosphere they created in-store. Suzanne Bell turned what was essentially a rectangular space into a fluid one, using curvy shapes in her store's furnishings and paint on the walls. Bell also customized the store to accommodate larger bodies, building spacious change rooms and specially constructing racks further from the walls with enough space in between to properly display the merchandise.[160] Cindy Proskow emphasized comfort and discretion in the planning of Big & Beautiful, believing her customers appreciated being able to drive up to a private store, park, and shop. Proskow felt that privacy was important for customers who felt embarrassed about going into a plus-size store.[161]

Shoppers were pleased that plus-size retail stores reflected a woman's needs. With the exception of Proskow, all of the retailers interviewed for this study were plus-size. They endeavoured to hire large women as sales staff because they knew plus-size women did not want to deal with "skinny" sales associates. This process was complicated because excluding candidates based on their size contravened employment law. Bell had a large pool of potential staff for her retail store as she had built relationships with clients and instructors when she owned her fitness centre.[162] Cindy Proskow, who herself was not plus-size, would not hire anyone less than "medium" sized to work in her store (see figure 16). She felt that it was not possible to "get into the soul of the big size person and feel their feelings and the depth of the person that they are," unless "to some extent" one had "been there, done that."[163] Monica Sieben-Kuhn likewise found that "someone who's smaller ... just makes a plus-size lady feel a little bit uncomfortable ... so ... always the girls had to be over size fourteen."[164] In fashion, as with aerobics, there was a sense that fat women understood the problems of other fat women.

Figure 16. Cindy Proskow and Joyce, a saleswoman at Big & Beautiful in Edmonton, 1981. Courtesy of Cindy Proskow.

Customers described independent plus-size retail stores as special places that reflected the needs of their consumers. Mary Frances Ellison of Hersize found this to be the case with her favourite plus-size store, Big, Bold & Beautiful in Toronto. She described the merchandise as "more trendy, more fashionable. More choice, it seemed. It wasn't all, you know, nylon muumuus and polyester and that sort of stuff. It was more with an eye to younger women, working women, suits, evening stuff."[165] Susan White, a client of Lynn Schneider's Full Bloom, also recalled that the store had items that were "different ... quite interesting, kind of neat."[166] Beyond the merchandise, White found Full Bloom had "a certain sense of community," reflected in the way Schneider treated customers.[167] Suzanne Bell's store was endorsed by *Canada WYDE* for its variety of clothing, range of sizes, and "hard-to-find" items like "lingerie ... exercise/swimwear ... business dress and outerwear."[168] Retailers met the desires of their clientele, and customers responded with enthusiasm to the unique garments they found in independent stores.

For some retailers, meeting consumer demand entailed travelling to smaller cities where the selection of plus-size clothing was not as good as in larger cities. The Answer provided this service to a client who lived in the Maritimes and was unable to visit the store. The client trusted Burka enough to have her pick out a selection of outfits and ship them to her.[169] Both Full Bloom and Big & Beautiful did occasional trunk shows in more remote communities to sell to clients outside Winnipeg and Edmonton. Proskow's goal was to "cover Alberta border to border." She travelled to cities like Red Deer, where local women would help her put on a fashion show and sale. She found this was "good PR" because the community was excited about being involved.[170] Lynn Schneider took an entire vanload of clothing from Winnipeg as far afield as Thomson and Flin Flon, Manitoba. She "rented ... a conference room, put the ads in their papers up north, and people would come." Schneider recalled happily that the "ladies from Flin Flon" loved "to buy."[171] She described these events as community gatherings, rather than a sales event, claiming that she was bringing women together for a common cause.

While individual stores became sites for community building, an air of discretion, secretiveness, and separateness characterized fat women's experiences with consumption. Plus-size clothing was difficult to find in department stores and specialty shops were often located far from regular retail centres.[172] Women had to travel, and did, to access this clothing. The pleasure of shopping did not necessarily eliminate the sense of stigma about going into a "fat store."[173] Women were proactive because they were disempowered and excluded from the mainstream, mass-marketed fashion industry.

Although the by-fat-women-for-fat-women concept was empowering for some women, it also had numerous limitations. Clearly, independent retail stores were directed mainly to an affluent clientele. Prices were often higher than in regular-sized stores, a problem that has also been documented in the United States.[174] Additionally, many of the stores catered to a particular kind of fashionable femininity that was not for everyone. Size was also an important limiter, as most of the stores described in this study, and many plus-size retailers today, offered sizes 16 to 24. The cost of clothing also limited who could shop in each store, along with the geographic location of the store, salespeople, and style of clothing available.

Fashion as Performance

All of the retailers discussed to this chapter sold women's clothing, but men sometimes shopped in the stores. This detail first came up in an interview with Margaret Burka. Burka was at first tentative on this subject, telling me "we had some male customers once in while." Unsure of what she meant, I followed up with the question "they would come in and buy for their wives?" To which Burka half-whispered, "they would come in and buy for themselves."[175] Subsequent interviews with Sol Armel, Cindy Proskow, Lynn Schneider, and Monica Sieben-Kuhn confirmed that men regularly shopped for women's clothing for themselves in plus-size stores.

We can't know the reasons men sought out the stores, and retailers of the 1980s lacked a vocabulary to describe a phenomenon they thought of as "cross-dressing." In response, however, each store developed policies for their male clientele. Penningtons and Full Figure Fashions did not allow male customers to use the dressing rooms. Former Penningtons executive Sol Armel believed that the practice of men shopping in Penningtons stores for themselves probably stretched back to the early days of the store. He became aware of the practice only in the early 1980s. By then Penningtons policy was that men "had every right to come in and buy," but they did not want men in the changing area. The store felt women would be offended by seeing men trying on the same size clothing as they were.[176] Monica Sieben-Kuhn of Full Figure Fashions disallowed men in the changing rooms for similar reasons. Instead she opened the store after hours for groups of men who shopped for themselves. It is unclear if or how these men knew one another or how they found each other. Sieben-Kuhn had one male customer who was annoyed with this policy, but no action was ever taken.[177] The Answer allowed men into their dressing rooms provided there was no one else trying things on. Burka believed that male shoppers were "just like anyone else. Make them welcome and feel happy and nothing unusual," though she conceded it "was unusual for those days."[178]

Full Bloom of Winnipeg and Big & Beautiful of Edmonton likewise let individual men shop after hours because they wanted to avoid the possibility of men and women using the store at the same time. Proskow was initially surprised when men came into the store, but she came to see herself as the bearer of their trust. She "felt very good about them believing that they could come to me ... and I could do some awesome things for them, you know? ... And that is not my place to question, I am not a medical person and I don't know ... in this world what a person is or isn't."[179] Lynn Schneider had mixed feelings about her male customers, primarily due to one bad experience with a customer who was sexually aroused by women's clothing. Schneider began to limit her services for men, but she did have a few clients she knew personally, to whom she would ship items.[180]

Men were treated differently by plus-size retailers than they were in other fat activist sites. Certainly, the stores offered services to men for practical reasons: for profit, and to avoid men and women shopping at the same time. Nonetheless, retailers' narratives focused on the vulnerability of their male customers who needed women's clothing that fit their bodies. This attitude towards men was more sympathetic and solicitous than what was found within the movement. Retailers' accounts of their male customers suggest they saw a parallel between fat women and men who were looking for clothing that accurately reflected the "truth" about their bodies. Even though retailers were sometimes wary of their male clientele, they went out of their way to be discreet and make these customers feel at home in their stores.

Retailers' belief that women would be offended by knowing that men could fit into plus-size clothing offers important insight into the gender politics of body size. Gender differentiation was (and is) one of the functions of fashion. Men's clothing does not conform to the same conventions of embellishment, cut, colour, and fabric as women's.[181] Historically, men's fashion has tended to emphasize their physical presence, broad shoulders, and angularity.[182] Fashions for women have tended to be softer in colour and in structure. When men's fashions have been popularized for women, they have tended to be a woman's version of a masculine garment, that is, the "dress for success" business suit of the 1980s that was worn with a lace collar.[183]

Fat activists' and retailers' approaches to fashion in the 1980s and 1990s appeared, on the surface, to reinforce essentialist notions of gender. Women wanted to look like women, and even men who wanted to look like women, could find garments that were gender appropriate. At the same time, fat activists' attitudes towards fashion echoed Judith Butler's assertion that gender is performative. Butler has argued that "gender is in no way a stable identity or locus of agency from which various acts proceed; rather it is an identity tenuously constituted in time – an identity instituted through stylized repetition of acts."[184] Fat acceptance activists argued that women were better able to perform the role of a confident and accepting person if they looked the part. Fat women who wanted to be in fashion further reflected Butler's claim that there is no essential "doer behind the deed" but rather the "doer is immanent and constructed through the deed."[185] Here, Butler is asserting that bodies materialize out of a combination of the social, cultural, and material conditions in which they are situated.[186] Activists were not seeking to recover a femininity that existed prior to or underneath their true selves. Rather, fashion was a tool that would help women to enact who they wanted to be.

Conclusions

Both Linda Scott and Elizabeth Wilson have rightly suggested that it is necessary to move beyond the assumption that a "woman's attempt to cultivate her appearance makes her a dupe of fashion."[187] Instead, we need to reconsider this anti-consumerist paradigm to contemplate the material and social conditions under which fashion was created and circulated.[188] This chapter has attempted to do that by situating the buying and selling of plus-size fashion in a broader social and historical context. Clothes were never just clothes because the process of finding, purchasing, altering, and making their garments was a challenge for plus-size women. As a consequence, clothing became an issue around which self-identified fat women mobilized. They did this as activists, at LAL events, and as retailers, by opening up stores for fat women. Although shopping is a commercial activity, this search for clothing was understood by consumers as part of a general marginalization of fat women.

The significance of fashion to fat activism lies in the relationship between the body and the self. Rather than understanding consumers as cultural dupes, fashion theorists suggest that clothing be understood as an expression and extension of the "self."[189] Fat women did not have (or did not think they had) the privilege of dressing in a way that reflected their personalities. As Ingrid Laue noted in the *Bolster*, many fat women had never "experienced the delight of wearing a smashing outfit, purchased because it was 'made for me,' and not because it happened to fit more or less well."[190] Finding the right garment could be transformative. After purchasing tailored clothing, Sue Masterton observed that it was "amazing how a piece of clothing, when you feel comfortable and nice ... it's amazing how that can make you feel so much better about how you look."[191] The fantasy garment was one that could be picked up off the rack and make the wearer feel like the best version of herself.

Women challenged the stereotype that being fat was unattractive, sloppy, and unfeminine through fashion. Referring to the role that fashion has played in the way Western societies understand the self, Fred Davis argues that "dress ... comes easily to serve as a kind of visual metaphor for identity and ... for registering the culturally anchored ambivalences that resonate within and among identities."[192] In the late twentieth century clothes were understood to "make" the woman. At the same time, Davis underlines "culturally anchored ambivalences," such as those about body size, which complicated the way that dressed bodies were read. This quotation captures a tension within fat activism.

Dress and the seen body have been understood to represent a person's identity. Not being able to find clothes that fit meant that fat women's clothes did not communicate who they thought they were and wanted to be. Self-identified fat women saw fashionable clothing as a way to bring their external, visible identity in line with their true selves. Buying and selling plus-size fashion was not just about reconciling the body and the self but also about belief in the importance of being oneself. A well-fitted, beautiful garment allowed women to wear their personalities on the outside and to put their bodies into fashion.

Conclusion: When We Rise the Earth Will Shake

All fat activism stems from a simple idea: it is okay to be fat. From this foundation, activists and scholars have built a multifaceted and heterogeneous movement. Groups in Canada and the United States have been loosely connected, sometimes through their activism, but more often through common texts like *Shadow on a Tightrope* and *The Fat Woman Measures Up*. To understand the significance of these activities as a whole, this book has identified two broad branches within the Canadian movement: fat feminist activism and fat acceptance groups. Fat feminist organizing was more explicitly connected to women's movements. Groups like LG5, Hersize, and Pretty Porky and Pissed Off sought to liberate women from feminine norms. Members of these groups had ties to other forms of feminist activism in these decades, and they helped to put fat oppression on the radar of Canada's women's health movement. Fat acceptance was a second, wide-ranging, approach to activism in the late 1970s through the early 1990s. Inspired by feminist critiques of femininity, fat acceptance groups put theory into practice in aerobics and dance classes, fashion shows, clothing swaps, and consciousness-raising groups. Like women of other generations who "broke the rules," these activists selectively adopted feminine norms and rejected others.[1]

Despite a lack of formal connections, all Canadian fat activists endorsed key concepts of their feminist contemporaries. These included the beliefs that looks-based oppression was primarily directed toward women and that male-stream medical authorities did not understand the experiences of (fat) women; fat activists also desired that women have greater knowledge and autonomy over their own bodies. In addition to being an example of the trajectories of feminism, fat activism is suggestive of its limitations. Many came to fat activism because they did not see their concerns reflected in the existing movement. Members of groups like LG5 and Hersize were connected to other feminist organizations and built their activism upon existing networks. By comparison, Large as Life and fat activist–inspired entrepreneurial activities created new activities and services to address issues not on the feminist agenda in the period under review.

Fat feminist and fat acceptance groups also overlapped in terms of the demographics of participants. Between 1977 and 1997 white women dominated the movement. Most were college or university graduates. Nearly all fat activism in this time was based in major cities, though documentary evidence shows women from more remote regions had contact with the movement. Within these categories there were important differences in terms of sexuality, marital status, and family. Fat activism also spread out across the country. Activists struggled to explain why there was limited ethnic and gender diversity within the movement. Indigenous and black women also varied in their opinions about why fat activism was dominated by white women. The limitations of the 1980s suggest a potential path forward for the movement: to recognize that people experience fatness in different ways.

Demonstrating the epistemological connections between fat acceptance groups and more radical approaches to the movement has been an important part of this work. I disagree with scholars who argue that acceptance and its successor, body positivity, is a depoliticization of fat activism or an example of a "breezy self-help" approach.[2] There is no right way to be fat. Just as there are multiple sites of fat oppression, there are multiple possible personal and political ways to challenge such discrimination. Intellectually, feminist organizing has developed and sharpened the critique of fat oppression. In terms of attracting members and sustaining activities, however, fat acceptance has been the more successful branch of the Canadian movement. To suggest a hierarchy between the two is to devalue women's choices and to ignore the ways that theory and practice work together to make change.

Being Fat has focused on the period between 1977 and 1997, but the story continues up to the present. Pretty Porky and Pissed Off signalled a shift in tactics in the movement. Post-1990s activists are working to queer the movement, that is, to challenge definitions of gender, sexuality, physical ability, and health. Judith Butler describes queering as a "reworking of abjection into political agency."[3] Fat Girl Food Squad is part of this shift. Refusing to be "good fatties," FGFS embraces food and eating. In a climate where fatness was deemed a crisis and obesity is considered a disease, these acts represent a radical refusal of healthism. FGFS is a contemporary example of the ways that fat activism changes to address new forms of oppression. Together with the other activism discussed in this book, FGFS helps us to see the obesity epidemic in historical context. Critiques of bodies perceived to be overweight or out of shape are not new. For decades governments, physicians, activists, and corporations have sought ways to better know and manage bodies.[4] Fat is a moving target. People don't like it, but the rationale for this antipathy has changed over time.

Paired with activist engagements by groups like FGFS, scholars of fat studies and critical obesity studies have developed a robust scholarly literature critiquing contemporary approaches to obesity.[5] These scholars argue that concern about obesity outstrips the actual problem it poses. Research by Elise Paradis compares weight trends to the dramatic increase in scientific research on weight. She has observed that academic publications have been "382 times greater than growth of weight trends" and argues that this is evidence of a moral panic around fatness that dwarfs "actual rises in population weights."[6] Michael Gard has challenged the very idea of an obesity epidemic in Canada. Data on Canadians' weight has often been based on self-reported data and has been drawn from studies using different methodologies, calling into question the accuracy of these numbers.[7] Additionally, BMI criteria for overweight and obese were lowered in the 1990s, meaning that, statistically, hundreds of thousands of Canadians became overweight overnight.[8] Gard argues the "obesity epidemic" is a "distinct historical event" that "harnesses the relatively recent and growing influence of risk factor medicine and epidemiology."[9]

With fat activism, as with any historical phenomenon, there was no single moment at which the movement was born. And yet many women came to fat activism around the same time and reported similar frustrations. In a time period when slenderness was paramount, thousands of women rejected fat oppression. In the context of other postwar women's liberation moments, this refusal should not be surprising. Representations of women in popular culture, women's social roles, their employment status, their sexuality, and their dress and demeanour were being re-evaluated at the end of the twentieth century. Women's movement activism, combined with the commercialization of dieting, public health investment in physical fitness, and the expansion of the mass media, set the stage for fat activism. Starting in the late 1970s, groups of fat women decided that there was nothing wrong with their bodies. When they did not find women's organizations to help them advocate for their concerns, they created their own. Regardless of the approach, the significance of this research lies in its core finding, which is that Canadian women engaged thoughtfully and critically with popular culture and body norms. In the process, women developed new ways of being fat and mobilized these ideas as alternatives to fat oppression.

APPENDIX A: RESEARCH METHODS

This book is inspired by my interest in femininity, fashion, health, and sport. Reading foundational feminist critiques of the body from the 1980s and 1990s, I began to wonder about women who could not, or would not, aspire to such ideals. What about women who are precluded from being seen as beautiful altogether? And what should we make of women who chose to be feminine, even as they chose non-traditional paths and challenged social norms? After spending two years studying advertising images of women in sport, it became clear that my next project would investigate personal and experiential histories of the body. Equally, this book is a political project aimed at writing women into the historical record, raising awareness of fat oppression, and valuing diverse forms of women's activism.

Autoethnography, that is, writing from experience and including one's experience in an academic text, has become a popular and useful way for writing about embodied health and social movements. In *Fat Activism* (2016) Charlotte Cooper argues that, ideally, fat studies scholars should be activists. While she acknowledges that such boundary policing is problematic, she believes that non-fat-identified, non-activist people do not belong. Deborah Lupton, author of *Fat* (2013) and numerous works on body image, says that limiting the field by body size is misguided. She counters that all people are impacted by anti-obesity discourses.[1]

As a historian I am attentive to the need to include the voices of the communities we study into our methods, and in our work. I've employed feminist methodologies, outlined below, to mitigate power differences with research participants, to ensure that different voices of fat activism are represented in this book, and to provide activists with an opportunity to reflect upon their interviews. I am not an activist, however. I have never participated in a group like the women in this book. I have been fat at some points in my life, and less fat at other points. All bodies change over time, and mine is no exception. I chose this topic because it helped shed light on the embodied experiences of Canadian women at the end of the twentieth century.

Coming across Large as Life's newsletters in the archives helped to focus the project on fat women's activism specifically. Prior to seeing the newsletters, it was not clear how I would analyse fat women's subjective experiences. Searching the Canadian Periodical Index led to further evidence of fat-centred women's organizing across Canada. Interviews with individual women yielded more textual sources, as my research participants shared photographs, newsletters, news clippings, videos, and letters. These documents, in turn, helped me to dig deeper into fat women's activism and find more participants.

Using printed sources as a starting point, I constructed a database of names and, when available, locations of women who participated in each group, as well as any service providers or experts who were connected to the groups. Some members were easy to locate through internet searches. Women who had moved or changed their name proved to be more difficult to find. I searched their names in newspaper archives and the white pages, cold-calling until I found the correct person or had no more leads to follow.

The project snowballed from these initial contacts. After my first round of interviews, conducted in Ontario and British Columbia between September 2005 and January 2006, I constructed a second database, dividing what I had found by province and location. Initially, I had few contacts in Manitoba, Quebec, and Atlantic Canada. At this time, I conducted searches of newspaper databases in English and French and sent messages to two internet "listservs" requesting assistance with the project. This search yielded further contacts and archival information in Quebec and in the prairie provinces, but no leads in Atlantic Canada. Between May and November 2006, I conducted additional archival research and interviews in Quebec, Manitoba, Saskatchewan, Alberta, and British Columbia.

Oral history interviews helped to connect the dots between Canadian groups and also to trace their intellectual links to the American activist movement. The primary goal of the interviews, however, was to consider how personal experiences shaped each woman's participation in fat activism. Experiential perspectives provided critical insight into interview participants feelings about Canadian society and culture, their families, and the impact of the movement on being fat.

The guiding principle of the interviews was that women were experts in their own lives.[2] Participants were asked to define the terms of the debate (fat, chubby, large, obese) so as to facilitate the translation of their experience to me as the researcher.[3] This approach was used to give them a voice in the research process.[4] It was also a way for me to show that I was open to different interpretations of events and did not have a preconceived definition of fat activism. This approach is common with feminist oral history researchers who want to mitigate possible power differentials with their participants. The methodological literature was important to helping me plan my interviews, but during the research process I sometimes encountered power dynamics different than those for which I was prepared.[5]

Time was set aside in advance of each interview to explain to participants my reasons for studying fat women, however, most people asked me to explain myself before I had the chance to do so. Because of their questions, interviews often began as or lapsed into conversations where I was asked to share some of my personal history with participants. Answering questions about myself seemed to contribute to a more relaxed atmosphere. I explained that my interest in fat activism is both personal and scholarly. I was a fat kid. While the work grew out of reflections on my own life, I quickly realized my experiences were different from those I was studying. Embodied experiences vary by time and place and are shaped by other privileges, like being white and middle class.

Each interview was semistructured. After the preliminary questions and language and self-identification, I followed a loose discussion guide, asking participants how they came to be involved in fat activism; what kinds of activities they participated in; and the extent to which they participated in beauty and fashion culture, exercised, and dieted. Participants were also asked to reflect on the impact of fat and fat activism on their personal and family lives. Despite my preparation, it was not uncommon for participants to reveal new and unexpected information to me during interviews. For example, I contacted Mary Frances Ellison to talk about her work with Hersize and found out during our interview she had also participated in the Beyond Dieting program. In this case a follow-up interview was scheduled.

Following the initial round of interviews, subsequent research was conducted on fat women and sexuality between 2008 and 2012. This research was intended to flesh out the story of fat/lesbian activism in Canada. Between 2006 and 2010 Christine Donald's papers were filed and accessioned by The ArQuives (formerly Canadian Gay and Lesbian Archives), offering me greater insight into the way that fat/lesbian critiques circulated between women. This extra time was also needed to study the transnational movement of fat activist ideas. Consulting repositories in Boston and New York led to interviews with two American fat activists. These women, Elana Dykewomon and Judith Stein, provided important insight into the way that fat/lesbian critiques travelled across the border, and between different linguistic groups.

This study documents the experiences of a group of primarily white women, who were "working" and "middle" class and born between 1940 and 1960. In total, I conducted interviews with fifty-five people: fifty-two women and three men. Of the three men, one was involved in fat organizing, one was a bariatric surgeon, and the third was an executive at plus-size clothing retailer Penningtons. Of the fifty-two women, forty-seven described themselves as fat, plus-sized, or another descriptive term for a large body. Cindy Proskow, Ellen Tallman, Donna Ciliska, Mary Dahonick, Caroly Peat, and Lynda Raino were fat allies.

I did not ask participants to fill out a questionnaire with their age, ethnicity, sexuality, or other possible identity categories. The goal of the interviews was to capture feelings and I felt that quantitative data wouldn't provide substantial insight into the movement. Rather, I allowed participants to share demographic information if and when it flowed from our conversations. Based on observations and comments made in our conversations, I estimate that at the time of the interviews, 18 per cent were seventy or older, 61 per cent were in their fifties and sixties, and 21 per cent were in their thirties and forties. The majority of these people would identify as white with the exception of two Indigenous women, Julie Levasseur and Pat Donaldson, and Jessica Carter, who is African Canadian.

As with ethnicity, participants had not thought of, or were reluctant to talk about, class.[6] At the time of their activism, many participants lived in urban centres including Vancouver, Victoria, Calgary, Prince Albert, Winnipeg, Toronto, Montreal, and London. Most of the women I spoke to were high school graduates with some post-secondary education. Occasionally women identified themselves as working class or poor, and I have indicated when they did so in the text. All but two women decided to participate under their own name. Most informants' names had already appeared in group newsletters and press stories about fat activism.

Each research participant was offered the option to review a transcription of our conversation. Two women requested that I omit the name of their employer. Another added supplementary information about her experiences in aerobics classes.

Five women declined to be interviewed for this project for reasons that were not always disclosed. Fat is a very personal topic and one with which the women who did participate continue to grapple. It is, therefore, not surprising that some messages and emails to potential participants also went unanswered. Fortunately, rich primary sources were available on most groups, documenting the experiences and opinions of Canadian fat activists from the 1970s to the 1990s.

APPENDIX B: DETAILED LIST OF RESEARCH PARTICIPANTS

Armel, Sol. Interviewed in Toronto, ON, 18 May 2006.
Armel was an employee for Penningtons for over fifty years. Armel began working with his cousin William Drevnig to convert their existing Cotton Town stores into Penningtons for larger-sized women in the 1940s. He worked for the company for the rest of his life and helped to take the company public in 1969. He was president of Penningtons in 1995 when the company was sold to Reitmans.

Atkins, Terryl. Interviewed in Kamloops, BC, 12 August 2006.
Atkins attended the first class of Big Dance in 1992 and joined the company in 1997. She was a social worker on women's issues when she joined Big Dance. She left the group c. 2002 to work on a PhD.

Beauchamp, André. Interviewed in Montreal, QC, 25 May 2006.
Beauchamp joined APOHQ in 1989 and took over as president of the organization after Gilles Leblanc passed away.

Bell, Suzanne. Interviewed in New Westminster, BC, 4 October 2005 and 16 August 2006.
Bell joined Large as Life in 1981 and worked as the group's fitness coordinator until 1983 when she assumed the presidency of the group. Bell left Large as Life in 1984 to start her own fitness and fashion company. She retired in 2012 and closed Suzanne Bell's Fashions at that time.

Bergeron, Lise. Interviewed in Montreal, QC, 23 May 2006.
Bergeron began to assist Gilles Leblanc with APOHQ in the late 1970s. She helped to found the activity centre that the organization ran briefly in the 1980s. Bergeron held executive positions with APOHQ through the 1980s and wrote an article about plus-size fashion for *Protect Yourself: A Magazine for Consumers* in June 1986.

Booth, Evelyn. Interviewed in Vancouver, BC, 11 October 2005 and 12 August 2006.
Booth helped to organize fashion shows for LAL. Booth went on to develop Models Rubenesque, a plus-size modelling school and agency that operated from 1984 to 1989.

Boschman, Lorna. Interviewed in Vancouver, BC, 30 April 2012.
Boschman published what is (probably) the first Canadian fat activist text, "Fat Liberation, a Wages for Housework Perspective" in the *Other*

Woman in 1975. She went on to work as a feminist video maker, where she sometimes explored fat people's issues, most notably with *Big Fat Slenderella* (1993) and *Fat World* (1993/1994).

Burka, Margaret. Interviewed in Toronto, ON, 14 February 2006.
Burka (1927–2009) opened The Answer boutique with two friends in 1985. Burka and her partners retired in the early 2000s and sold The Answer.

Burzese, Lynn. Interviewed in Toronto, ON, 11 April 2006.
In 1981 Burzese applied for a federal government grant to help establish a new business. Together with business partners, she manufactured "SOFI" plus size fashions. The business closed in 1984 due to a lack of financing.

Carter, Jessica. Interviewed in Toronto, ON, 16 January 2008.
Carter began modelling for Jackqueline Hope's Big, Bold & Beautiful in the 1980s. She went on to model in Chicago before returning to Canada and starting Lotus Creations, a series of beauty and fashion seminars for larger women. Carter also wrote on fashion for *Canada WYDE*.

Charland, Michèle. Interviewed in Montreal, QC, 22 October 2006.
Charland was active in the communist and feminist movements before forming a fat women's discussion group in 1984. This group became LG5.

Ciliska, Donna. Interviewed in Hamilton, ON, 11 January 2006.
Ciska developed the Beyond Dieting program as her PhD research at the University of Toronto. Ciliska worked with David Garner and Janet Polivy to develop this seminar program for overweight women who were chronic dieters. Beyond Dieting was later offered through the National Eating Disorder Information Centre. Ciliska's model for helping women break the diet cycle has been adopted by public health units and women's health centres across Canada.

Cusack, Joyce. Interviewed in Calgary, AB, 21 July 2006.
Cusack was a member of LAL Calgary and participated in their aerobics classes.

Dahonick, Mary. Interviewed in Toronto, ON, 13 February 2006.
Dahonick was part of the Toronto General Hospital political group, later Hersize.

Dal Santo, Joan. Interviewed in Sechelt, BC, 7 October 2005.
Dal Santo, a.k.a. Joan O'Brien, was a charter member of LAL. She met Kate Partridge at The Forgotten Woman workshop on Cortes Island in 1979. O'Brien contributed to the *Bolster*, organized a fashion survey of LAL members, participated in the groups' dance classes, and trained as a fitness instructor at the YWCA. O'Brien took over the presidency of Large as Life in 1982–3.

Donaldson, Pat. Interviewed in Empress, AB, 25 July 2006.
Donaldson a.k.a. Pat Bulcock a.k.a. Nokomis joined Large as Life in Calgary around 1982, eventually becoming a fitness instructor and co-ordinator for the group.

Dykewomon, Elana. Interviewed in San Francisco, CA, 22 March 2008.
Dykewomon was affiliated with women's liberation groups in Massachusetts before moving west and living as a lesbian separatist. During this time, she began to read pamphlets by the Fat Underground. Awakened to the notion of fat liberation, Dykewomon began writing and holding public readings about her own experiences as a fat lesbian. She later befriended Judy Freespirit of the Fat Underground and Louise Turcotte of LG5. She continues to write and publish about being fat.

Ellison, Mary Frances. Interviewed in Toronto, ON, 15 December 2005 and 25 January 2006.
Ellison joined Beyond Dieting shortly after finishing her degree at the University of Toronto. She was introduced to other Hersize members through Donna Ciliska. For Hersize, Ellison travelled around Ontario to talk to groups about weight preoccupation and images of women. Ellison continued to work with Hersize until its demise in 1992.

Fiander, Runa. Interviewed in Victoria, BC, 2 August 2006.
Fiander attended the first class of Big Dance in 1992 and performed with the company until the late 1990s when a heart condition prevented her from continuing.

Friedman, Sandra. Interviewed in Sechelt, BC, 7 October 2005.
Friedman trained at Antioch College in Ohio and interned for Dr Ellen Tallman. She assisted at Tallman's The Forgotten Woman workshop on Cortes Island in 1979 and went on to develop Facing Your Fat (later Learning to Love Yourself) workshops with Doris Maranda. Since the

early 1990s Friedman has developed a specialization in treating young women with eating disorders. Her publications include *When Girls Feel Fat: Helping Girls through Adolescence* (Toronto: HarperCollins, 1997) and *Body Thieves: Help Girls Reclaim Their Natural Bodies and Become Physically Active* (Vancouver: SaLAL Books, 2002).

Gillingham, Ruth Wylie. Interviewed in Prince Albert, SK, 27 July 2006.

After joining NAAFA-USA, Gillingham worked to build a Canadian branch of the organization. At one point she maintained a mailing list of the approximately one hundred NAAFA members in Canada. She sometimes worked with Helena Spring, another NAAFA member based in Toronto. In her hometown of Prince Albert, Saskatchewan, she formed an aerobics group called Above Average.

Grace, David Michael. Interviewed in London, ON, 10 April 2006.

Grace practised at University Hospital in London, Ontario, for twenty-four years. In that time, he performed nearly 1,500 bariatric surgeries. Dr Grace is an expert in the field of bariatrics in Canada and has provided testimony in medical malpractice cases involving the surgeries. He lives in London, Ontario.

Grauer, Lynne. Interviewed in Burnaby, BC, 8 August 2006.

Grauer joined Mrs O's Swimming Group in the 1980s as a young mother and continued to swim with them as of our 2006 interview. She also attended fat women's fitness classes in Burnaby in the 1980s, run either by Suzanne Bell or In Grand Form.

Henley, Kaca. Interviewed in Lindsay, ON, 8 March 2006.

Henley subscribed to the Hersize newsletter. To help large women increase their self-esteem, she later developed a personal development program called You*Nique. You*Nique sold self-guided affirmation tapes which she customized and sold to clients. Henley also volunteered with the National Eating Disorder Information Centre in Toronto on projects like "Foxy Fables and Facts About Dieting" (1996).

King, Sarah. Interviewed in North Vancouver, BC, 12 October 2005.

King grew up in California, where she was aware of the Fat Underground but never had any contact with the group. After moving to Vancouver, she joined Large as Life and then In Grand Form fitness classes. King continued with In Grand into the 1990s.

Laue, Ingrid, PhD. Interviewed in North Vancouver, BC, 3 October 2005.
Laue (d. 2010) was participating in a Lions Gate Hospital study on obesity when she met Kate Partridge c. 1980. She edited the *Bolster* from October 1981 to May 1983.

Levasseur, Julie (pseudonym). Interviewed in Winnipeg, MB, 14 July 2006.
Together with Susan White, Levasseur formed an aerobics group for fat women in Winnipeg, Manitoba, in the late 1980s.

Maranda, Doris. Interviewed in Vancouver, BC, 14 August 2006.
Maranda trained at Antioch College in Ohio where she met Sandra Friedman. Together they developed Facing Your Fat (later Learning to Love Yourself) workshops. Since the early 1990s Maranda has been in private practice, specializing in eating disorders.

Masterton, Susan. Interviewed in North Vancouver, BC, 11 October 2005.
Masterton was not officially a member of Large as Life, but she participated in their fitness classes, worked as a plus-size model for LAL member Evelyn Booth, and attended the second Forgotten Woman workshop for large women facilitated by Kate Partridge.

McKay-Panos, Linda. Interviewed in Calgary, AB, 18 July 2006.
McKay-Panos has twice made headlines in Canada. In 1991 she launched a lawsuit against Nutri-System diets because she developed gall bladder disease as a consequence of their program. Between 1997 and 2008, McKay-Panos led a complaint against the Canadian Transportation Agency based on discrimination she had experienced on an Air Canada flight. For this suit, McKay-Panos had to claim that obesity was a disability because there were no human rights provisions to protect against discrimination based on size. In 2001 the federal court ruled that Canadian airlines had to provide two seats for one fare for people who were functionally disabled by obesity. A 2008 attempt by the airlines to see this rule overturned was defeated. During this time McKay-Panos was director of the Alberta Civil Liberties Research Centre at the University of Calgary.

Mindlin, Jan. Interviewed in Burnaby, BC, 20 August 2006.
Mindlin was an active member of Large as Life who contributed to the newsletter. Her designs were featured in LAL's two fashion shows

and fellow members recalled her work fondly in interviews. Mindlin worked on and off designing clothes in the 1980s and 1990s.

Norman, Trudy. Interviewed in Victoria, BC, 3 August 2006.
Norman joined the Big Dance performing company in 1997 and toured semi-professionally as part of this group.

Partridge, Kate. Interviewed in Crediton, ON, 20 September 2005 and Exeter, ON, 16 April 2006.
Partridge (1945–2018) was the founder of Large as Life Vancouver (1981), Calgary (1982), and London (1997). Partridge was inspired to start LAL after she attended The Forgotten Woman workshop on Cortes Island in 1979.

Peat, Carol. Interviewed in London, ON, 17 June 2006.
Peat was a fitness instructor for LAL London who went on to develop a dance program for fat women in the London area in the 1990s. She continues to live and work in that city.

Proskow, Cindy. Interviewed in Edmonton, AB, 25 July 2006.
Proskow opened her plus-size clothing store in 1979. She sold the store in the late 1990s after suffering a stroke.

Raino, Lynda. Interviewed in Victoria, BC, 10 October 2005.
Raino was the founder of Big Dance. She led the classes and also the travelling group.

Rankin, Pauline. Interviewed in Vancouver, BC, 21 August October 2006.
Rankin's interest in fat activism was sparked by Christine Donald's poetry book, *The Fat Woman Measures Up.* She went on to run fat oppression workshops in Vancouver, which were modeled on anti-racism training.

Sandler, Jody. Interviewed in North Vancouver, BC, 5 October 2005.
Sandler got her start as a fitness instructor for Large as Life in 1985 and started her own business, In Grand Form, in 1986. Sandler continues to work in fitness under Jody's Fitness and LITE Squared.

Savage, Claudia. Interviewed in New Westminster, BC, 17 August 2006.
Savage joined Large as Life c. 1983. She initiated Mrs O's Swimming Group and continued to participate as of our 2006 interview. Savage was president of Large as Life in 1985 when the group began to disband.

Scheidt, Yuli. Interviewed in Toronto, ON, 26 May 2015.
Scheidt was co-founder of Fat Girl Food Squad. Together with Amanda Scriver, she blogged and led in-real-life meet-ups for women. She works as a photographer in Toronto.

Schneider, Lynn. Interviewed in Winnipeg, MB, 13 July 2006.
Schneider operated Full Bloom plus size store in Winnipeg from 1981–2007.

Scriver, Amanda. Interviewed in Toronto, ON, 22 May 2015.
Scriver co-founded Fat Girl Food Squad with Yuli Scheidt. Together, they blogged and led in-real-life meet-ups for women. Scriver is a freelance journalist who writes frequently on body image.

Sieben-Kuhn, Monica. Interviewed in Calgary, AB, 20 July 2006.
Sieben-Kuhn operated Calgary's Full Figure Fashions from 1986 to 2001. In 2006, she donated records from the store to the Glenbow Archives.

Siegler, Andria. Interviewed in Toronto, ON, 7 June 2006.
Siegler attended Beyond Dieting in the late 1980s and went on to lead Beyond Dieting groups for many years.

Smith, Lois. Interviewed in New Westminster, BC, 9 August 2006.
Smith was a member of Mrs O's swimming group at the time of our interview.

Spring, Helena. Interviewed in Toronto, ON, 5 January 2006.
Spring (1948–2009) joined NAAFA-USA and helped to organize NAAFA-Canada. She also formed CASA in 1994 and in 1996 started *Canada WYDE*.

Stein, Judith. Interviewed in Cambridge, MA, 14 April 2012.
Stein founded Boston Area Fat Liberation in 1979. She was a prolific voice for fat liberation in the United States in the 1970s, 1980s, and 1990s who helped to organize the first fat activists working meeting in Connecticut in 1982, among numerous other public events.

Tallman, Ellen. Interviewed in Vancouver, BC, 12 October 2005.
Tallman (1927–2008) was the leader of The Forgotten Woman workshop on Cortes Island in 1979. In the 1970s she worked with the Cold Mountain Institute as a therapist and then in private practice.

Thaw, Laura. Interviewed in Surrey, BC, 6 October 2005.
Thaw joined Large as Life in 1981 after reading about the group in the newspaper. Thaw wrote occasionally in the *Bolster* where she called on other members to see fat as a "political" issue.

Turcotte, Louise. Interviewed in Montreal, QC, 22 October 2006.
Turcotte worked on a film for lesbians only called *Amazones d'hier, lesbiennes d'aujourd'hui* in the 1980s. Together with Michèle Charland, she formed LG5 in 1984.

Vail, Diann. Interviewed in London, ON, 13 April 2006.
Vail was a member of LAL London and maintained the group's newsletter for the two years it existed.

Vuksic, Nada. Interviewed in Vancouver, BC, 14 August 2006.
Vuksic worked as an aerobics instructor first for Suzanne Bell and later for Jody Sandler's In Grand Form through the 1980s and 1990s. She also taught aquafit classes at the YMCA.

Walker, Janet. Interviewed in White Rock, BC, 6 October 2005.
Walker (1946–2008) attended The Forgotten Woman workshop in 1979 and moved to Vancouver in the early 1980s. She was an active member of LAL and wrote regular columns in the *Bolster*. Walker started the "Fat Lady Singers" (fun, awesome, talented) in 2000. The group sang at nursing homes, community, and business events in and around Vancouver.

White, Susan. Interviewed in Winnipeg, MB, 11 July 2006.
For two years White attended MACSW's *FIFI* group. She has since written and done talks about fat acceptance in Winnipeg.

Zatylny, Anne (pseudonym). Interviewed in Toronto, ON, 20 June 2006.
Zatylny shopped at Big, Bold & Beautiful while she was a graduate student in Toronto in the 1990s.

Notes

Introduction: Fat Women Are Not Few

1 Amy Erdman Farrell, *Fat Shame: Stigma and the Fat Body in American Culture* (New York: New York University Press, 2011); Richard Klein, *Eat Fat* (New York: Pantheon Books, 1996); Peter N. Stearns, *Fat History: Bodies and Beauty in the Modern West* (New York: New York University Press, 1997).

2 A. Finn Enke, *Finding the Movement: Sexuality, Contested Space, and Feminist Activism* (Durham, NC: Duke University Press, 2007), 2.

3 Frank Consentino and Maxwell Howell, *A History of Physical Education in Canada* (Toronto: General Publishing Company Limited, 1971), 13–14, 29.

4 Wendy Mitchinson, *Fighting Fat: Canada, 1920–1980* (Toronto: University of Toronto Press, 2018).

5 John J. Jackson, *Mr. 5BX Canadian Fitness Pioneer: A Biography of William A.R. Orban* (Victoria: Sono Nis Press, 1982), 43, 57.

6 Deborah McPhail, "What to Do with the 'Tubby Hubby'? 'Obesity,' the Crisis of Masculinity, and the Nuclear Family in Early Cold War Canada," *Antipode* 41, no. 5 (2009): 1031.

7 ParticipACTION, "Fat to Fit (Commercial)," 1979, accessed 5 June 2012, http://www.usask.ca/archives/participaction/english/motivate/early_video7.html.

8 McPhail, "What to Do with the 'Tubby Hubby'?; Elise Paradis, "'Obesity' as Process: The Medicalization of Fatness by Canadian Researchers, 1971–2010," in *Obesity in Canada: Critical Perspectives*, ed. Jenny Ellison, Deborah McPhail, and Wendy Mitchinson (Toronto: University of Toronto Press, 2016), 56–88.

9 Alexandra Palmer, *Couture & Commerce: The Transatlantic Fashion Trade in the 1950s* (Vancouver: UBC Press, 2001), 7.

10 Ibid., 26, 28, 130.

11 Ibid., 7.

12 Julia Ehrhardt, "You-Unlimited!: The Fat-Positive(?) Message of 1950s 'Plumps' Consultant Vinne Young" (paper presented at the Popular Culture Association [Fat Studies], San Francisco, 2008), 1.

13 Vinne Young, *It's Fun to Be Fat!* (New York: A.A. Wyn, 1953), 11.

14 Associated Press, "Big Girls: U.K. Housewife Campaigns for Fashion in Outsized Clothes," *Globe and Mail*, 11 November 1966, 13.

15 "Curves Have Their Day in Park; 500 at a 'Fat-In' Call for Obesity," *New York Times*, 5 June 1967, 54.

16 Llewellyn Louderback, "More People Should Be FAT," *Saturday Evening Post* 240, no. 22 (4 November 1967): 10.

17 William J. Fabrey, "What is NAAFA?," Pamphlet, (June 1969). Personal Papers of William J. Fabrey, Woodstock, New York.

18 Ibid.

19 Later, NAAFA would also work on litigation involving insurance discrimination against fat people. Anna Kirkland, "Representations of Fatness and Personhood: Pro-Advocacy and the Limits of the Law," *Representations* 82 (Spring 2003): 24–51.

20 Judy Freespirit and Vivian [Aldebaran] Mayer, "Fat Liberation Manifesto," in *Shadow on a Tightrope: Writings by Women on Fat Oppression*, ed. Lisa Schoenfielder and Barb Wieser (Iowa City: Aunt Lute Publishing Company, 1983), 52–3.

21 See for example Catrina Brown, *Getting beyond Weight: Women Helping Women. A How To Manual about the Development and Operation of Self Help Groups for Women Preoccupied with Weight* (Winnipeg, MB: Women's Health Clinic, 1987), 4; Centre de femmes de Verdun, *L'obsession de la minceur: Un guide d'intervention* (Verdun: Centre de femmes de Verdun, 1991); Vivian [Aldebaran] Mayer, "La grosse illusion ou le contrôle des corps comme forme de contrôle social," *Amazones d'hier lesbiennes d'aujourd'hui* 23 (December 1992): 53–70.

22 Elana Dykewomon, "Fat Liberation," in *Lesbian Histories and Cultures: An Encyclopedia*, ed. Bonnie Zimmerman (New York: Garland, 2000).

23 Charlotte Cooper, *Fat and Proud* (London: The Women's Press, 1998), 131–6; Dykewomon, "Fat Liberation," 290–2; Cooper, *Fat and Proud*. Cooper has revisited her 1998 analysis in a recent monograph. She no longer uses the pride/liberation distinction as emphatically, but she still argues there is a fundamental division between radical activisms inspired by the Fat Underground and more assimilationist approaches. See Charlotte Cooper, *Fat Activism: A Radical Social Movement* (Bristol, UK: HammerOn Press, 2016).

24 Farrell, *Fat Shame*, 171.

25 I've written a little about this elsewhere, see Jenny Ellison, "Not Jane Fonda: Aerobics for Fat Women Only," in *The Fat Studies Reader*, ed. Sondra

Solovay and Esther Rothblum (New York: New York University Press, 2009), 312–19. See also Sherri Krynski, "Celebrate Your Body!," *Radiance*, Spring 1985, 12–14; Pat Lyons and Debbie Burgard, *Great Shape: The First Exercise Guide for Large Women* (New York: Arbor House – William Morrow, 1988); Judith Stein, "Making a Big Splash: The Pleasures of Water Aerobics," *Radiance*, Spring 1997, accessed 26 April 2012, http://www .radiancemagazine.com/issues/1997/spring97_jstein.html.

26 Helena Spring, interview with author, digital recording (Toronto, ON, 5 January 2006); Ruth Gillingham, interview with author, digital recording (Prince Albert, SK, 27 July 2006).

27 Spring, interview with author; Jeff McKay, *Fat Chance* (Canada: National Film Board, 1994), accessed 27 December 2019, https://www.nfb.ca /film/fat_chance/.

28 Manitoba Action Committee on the Status of Women, "Fat Is a Feminist Issue," *Action: MACSW*, December 1981, 29; "We Are Organizing a CR Group," *Calgary Women's Newspaper*, July/August 1980, 6. Orbach's book will be discussed in detail in chapter 2.

29 Centre des femmes de Verdun, *L'obsession de la minceur: Un guide d'intervention*; Catrina Brown, "Self-Perceived Overweight Support Group," *Womanly Times: Women's Health Clinic*, February 1985; Donna Ciliska, *Beyond Dieting: Psychoeducational Interventions for Chronically Obese Women: A Non-Dieting Approach* (New York: Brunner/Mazel Publishers, 1990).

30 Laura Kipnis, *Bound and Gagged: Pornography and the Politics of Fantasy in America* (Durham, NC: Duke University Press, 1999), 106.

31 Pretty Porky and Pissed Off and Fat Girl Food Squad were not the only examples of fat activism of their time. About five years after PPPO ended a similar group, Fat Femme Mafia, performed cabaret in Toronto. Similarly, around the same time as FGFS there were other Canadian Facebook groups dedicated to fat activism, like "Fat, Awesome and Queer" and NAAFA-Canada.

32 Amanda Scriver, interview with author, digital recording (Toronto, ON, 22 May 2015).

33 Charlotte Cooper, "Fat Studies: Mapping the Field," *Sociology Compass* 4, no. 12 (2010): 1022; Sheena Starky, "The Obesity Epidemic in Canada," (Ottawa: Library of Parliament, Economics Division, 15 July 2005). BMI is calculated by dividing a person's weight in kilograms by the square of their height in metres (BMI = kg/m^2).

34 Jenny Ellison, Deborah McPhail, and Wendy Mitchinson, eds., *Obesity in Canada: Critical Perspectives* (Toronto: University of Toronto Press, 2016).

35 Paradis, "'Obesity' as Process"; Michael Gard, "Hearing Noises and Noticing Silences: Towards a Critical Engagement with Body Weight Statistics" in *Obesity in Canada: Critical Perspectives*, ed. Jenny Ellison,

Deborah McPhail, and Wendy Mitchinson (Toronto: University of Toronto Press, 2016).

36 For example, Rebecca M. Puhl and Chelsea A. Heuer, "The Stigma of Obesity: A Review and Update," *Obesity* 17 (2009): 941–64; Xuemei Sui et al., "Cardiorespoiratory Fitness and Adiposity as Mortality Predictors in Older Adults," *Journal of the American Medical Association* 298, no. 21 (2007): 2507–16; Raj S. Padwal et al., "Using the Edmonton Obesity Staging System to Predict Mortality in a Population-Representative Cohort of People with Overweight and Obesity," *Canadian Medical Association Journal* 183, no. 14 (4 October 2011): E1059–66; John G. Bruhn, "An Epidemiological Study of Myocardial Infarctions in an Italian-American Community: A Preliminary Sociological Study," *Journal of Chronic Diseases* 18, no. 4 (April 1965): 353–65; Dennis Raphael, "Social Justice is Good for Our Hearts: Why Societal Factors – Not Lifestyles – Are Major Causes of Heart Disease in Canada and Elsewhere," (Toronto: The Centre for Social Justice, 2002), 1–102.

37 Joan Jacobs Brumberg, *Fasting Girls: The History of Anorexia Nervosa* (New York: Penguin, 1989); Joan Jacobs Brumberg, *The Body Project: An Intimate History of American Girls* (New York: Random House, 1997); Estelle B. Freedman, *No Turning Back: The History of Feminism and the Future of Women* (New York: Ballantine, 2002); Kathy Peiss, *Hope in a Jar: The Making of American Beauty Culture* (New York: Metropolitan Books, 1998); Joanne Hollows, *Feminism, Femininity and Popular Culture* (Manchester: Manchester University Press, 2000); Lois Banner, *American Beauty* (Chicago: University of Chicago Press, 1983).

38 Joan Sangster, "Invoking Experience as Evidence," *Canadian Historical Review* 92, no. 1 (2011): 140; Joan Wallach Scott, "The Evidence of Experience," *Critical Inquiry* 17, no. 4 (Summer 1991): 793.

39 Scriver, interview with author.

40 In 1994, the National Film Board released a documentary about fat men joining NAAFA, the American activist organization. None of the activists I met with were familiar with the film, which outlines many of the same challenges named by fat activists in this book. See McKay, *Fat Chance*.

41 Yuli Scheidt, interview with author, digital recording (Toronto, ON, 26 May 2015).

42 Emily K. Abel, Joanne Leslie, and Antoinette K. Yancey, "Obesity at the Crossroads: Feminist and Public Health Perspectives," *Signs: Journal of Women in Culture and Society* 31, no. 2 (2006): 425–43; Stacy Ann Mitchell and Teri D. Mitchell, *Livin' Large: African American Sisters Confront Obesity* (Roscoe, IL: Hilton Publishing Company, 2004); Deborah McPhail, "Indigenous People's Clinical Encounters with Obesity: A Conversation with Barry Lavallee," in *Obesity in Canada: Critical Perspectives*, ed. Jenny Ellison, Deborah McPhail, and Wendy Mitchinson (Toronto: University of

Toronto Press, 2016); Jennifer Poudrier, "The Geneticization of Aboriginal Diabetes and Obesity," in *Obesity in Canada: Critical Perspectives*, ed. Jenny Ellison, Deborah McPhail, and Wendy Mitchinson (Toronto: University of Toronto Press, 2016), 89–121.

43 Jill Andrew and the Body Confidence Canada Awards, "#SizeismSUCKS! Help Make Size & Appearance-Based Discrimination Illegal in Ontario," Change.org, accessed 27 December 2019, https://www.change.org/p /sizeismsucks-you-can-help-make-size-appearance-based-discrimination -illegal-in-ontario-bodyconfidence.

44 Fat Girl Food Squad, "About," accessed 29 October 2019, https:// fatgirlfoodsquad.wordpress.com/about/.

45 Standing Senate Committee on Social Affairs, Science and Technology, Report, *Obesity in Canada: A Whole-of-Society Approach for a Healthier Canada*, (Ottawa: Senate of Canada, 2016), https://sencanada.ca/content /sen/committee/421/SOCI/Reports/2016-02-25_Revised_report _Obesity_in_Canada_e.pdf.

46 I'm referring here of the extensive literature on eugenics and race-based immigration policies of the twentieth century. See for example Constance Backhouse, *Colour-Coded: A Legal History of Racisim in Canada, 1900–1950* (Toronto: University of Toronto Press, 1999); Joan Sangster, *Girl Trouble: Female Delinquency in English Canada* (Toronto: Between the Lines, 2002); Barrington Walker, ed., *The History of Immigration and Racism in Canada* (Toronto: Canadian Scholars' Press, 2008).

47 Peiss, *Hope in a Jar*, 7.

48 Michael Ignatieff has described this phenomenon as "rights talk," a term I find helpful here. Michael Ignatieff, *The Rights Revolution* (Toronto: House of Anansi, 2000).

49 Sally Chivers, "Barrier by Barrier: The Canadian Disability Movement and the Fight for Equal Rights," in *Group Politics and Social Movements in Canada*, ed. Miriam Smith (Toronto: University of Toronto Press, 2008); Dominique Clement, *Canada's Rights Revolution: Social Movements and Social Change, 1937–1982* (Vancouver: UBC Press, 2008); M. Ann Hall, *The Girl and the Game: A History of Women's Sports in Canada* (Toronto: Broadview Press, 2002); Miriam Catherine Smith, *Lesbian and Gay Rights in Canada: Social Movements and Equality-seeking, 1971–1995* (Toronto: University of Toronto Press, 1999).

50 Brumberg, *The Body Project*, 97.

1 *FIFI*: Feminist Approaches to Being Fat

1 Susie Orbach, *Fat Is a Feminist Issue: A Self-Help Guide for Compulsive Overeaters* (1978; repr., New York: Berkley Books, 1979), xvi, 36.

2 Ibid., 6, 13, 14, 39, 48.

3 Susie Orbach, *Fat Is a Feminist Issue*, xv, xvii, xx.

4 Farrell makes a similar observation of the United States in this era. Farrell, *Fat Shame* 140–7.

5 Linda Trimble, "Coming Soon to a Station near You?: The CRTC Policy on Sex-Role Stereotyping," *Canadian Public Policy* 16, no. 3 (September 1990): 327.

6 Barbara Freeman, *The Satellite Sex: The Media and Women's Issues in English Canada, 1966–1971* (Waterloo, ON: Wilfred Laurier University Press, 2001), 93.

7 MediaWatch, *Tracing the Roots of MediaWatch* (Toronto: Mediawatch, 1993), 5.

8 Most notably the Canadian Coalition against Media Pornography and MediaWatch. Rose Potvin and Samantha Sanderson, "Adjusting the Image: Women and Canadian Advertising, Report of the National Conference on Canadian Broadcasting Policy" (Ottawa: MediaWatch, Canadian Coalition against Media Pornography, National Action Committee on the Status of Women, 20–2 March 1987).

9 Jennifer Brady and Jacqui Gingras, "'Celebrating Unruly Experiences': Queering Health at Every Size as a Response to the Politics of Postponement," in *Obesity in Canada: Critical Perspectives*, ed. Jenny Ellison, Deborah McPhail, and Wendy Mitchinson (Toronto: University of Toronto Press, 2016), 399–418.

10 Le collectif LG5, "Something to Think About," *Furie lesbienne/Lesbian Fury*, Summer–Fall 1986, 28. The version of the questionnaire I am using is an English translation published in *Furie lesbienne/Lesbian Fury* (Ottawa) in 1986. It is unclear if this is a translation from the original French undertaken by LG5 or by the editors of the journal.

11 Michèle Charland and Louise Turcotte, interview with author, digital recording (Montreal, QC, 22 October 2006).

12 Ibid.

13 Ibid.

14 Canadian Press, "444-Pound Man Loses 16 Pounds on Hunger Strike," *Globe and Mail*, 18 January 1978, 14; Jenny Ellison, "'Stop Postponing Your Life until You Lose Weight and Start Living Now': Vancouver's Large as Life Action Group, 1979–1985," *Journal of the Canadian Historical Association* 18, no. 1 (2007): 241–65.

15 Le collectif LG5, "Présentation," *Amazones d'hier lesbiennes d'aujourd'hui* 3, no. 2–3 (novembre 1984): 138.

16 Mayer, "La grosse illusion ou le contrôle des corps comme forme de contrôle social," 54.

17 Ibid., 61, 65, 67.

18 Le collectif LG5, "Présentation," *Amazones d'hier lesbiennes d'aujourd'hui* 4, no. 1 (juillet 1985): 81.

19 Marie-Michèle, "Une torche sert à éclairer; une 'grosse torche' à insulter
    ou C'est dans la tête qu'on est grosse! Hommage à LG5." *Treize* 3, no. 1
    (septembre 1986): 20.
20 Marie-Michèle, "Une torche sert à éclairer," 20.
21 For discussion of the early disability rights movement in Canada, see Lisa
    Vanhala, "Disability Rights Activists in the Supreme Court of Canada:
    Legal Mobilization Theory and Accommodating Social Movements,"
    Canadian Journal of Political Science 42, no. 4 (2009); Sally Chivers, "Barrier
    by Barrier."
22 Kathy Davis, *The Making of Our Bodies, Ourselves: How Feminism Travels
    across Borders* (Durham, NC: Duke University Press, 2007), 125.
23 AHLA, "Amazones d'hier, lesbiennes d'aujourd'hui," *Amazones d'hier,
    lesbiennes d'aujourd'hui* 1, no. 1 (June 1982): inside front cover. Emphasis in
    original. English translations here and elsewhere by the author.
24 Wittig, Monique, *The Straight Mind and Other Essays*, as cited in "Wittig,
    Monique: Novelist and Theorist," in *The Routledge Companion to Feminism
    and Postfeminism*, ed. Sarah Gamble (London: Routledge, 1998), 337.
25 Becki L. Ross, "How Lavender Jane Loved Women: Re-figuring
    Identity-Based Life/Stylism in 1970s Lesbian Feminism," *Journal of
    Canadian Studies* 30, no. 4 (1995): 111.
26 Smith, *Lesbian and Gay Rights in Canada*, 29; M. Julia Creet, "A Test of
    Unity: Lesbian Visibility in the British Columbia Federation of Women,"
    in *Lesbians in Canada*, ed. Sharon Dale Stone (Toronto: Between the
    Lines, 1990), 193; Alice Echols, *Daring to Be Bad: Radical Feminism in
    America, 1967–1975* (Minneapolis: University of Minnesota Press, 1989),
    212; Carmen Paquette, "Personal Reflections on Lesbian Organizing in
    Ottawa," in *Lesbians in Canada*, ed. Sharon Dale Stone (Toronto: Between
    the Lines, 1990), 226.
27 Echols, *Daring to Be Bad*, 211.
28 Charlotte Bunch, "Lesbians in Revolt," in *Feminist Theory Reader: Local and
    Global Perspectives*, ed. Carole McCann and Seung-Kyung Kim (New York:
    Routledge, 2003), 83-87. For a discussion of lesbian-feminist debates in
    the United States see Echols, *Daring to Be Bad*, 210–17. Canadian feminists
    experienced a similar tension around the subject of sexual orientation
    as discussed in Irene Demczuk and Frank W. Remiggi, eds., *Sortir de
    l'ombre: Histoires des communautés lesbienne et gaie de Montréal* (Montreal:
    VLB Éditeur, 1998). See also Creet, "A Test of Unity," 183–97; Paquette,
    "Personal Reflections on Lesbian Organizing in Ottawa," 221–9; Becki L.
    Ross, "The House That Jill Built: Lesbian Feminist Organizing in Toronto,
    1976–1980," *Feminist Review* 35 (Summer 1990): 75–91.
29 Ross, "The House That Jill Built," 88.
30 Ibid.

31 Charland and Turcotte, interview with author.
32 Jane O'Reily, "Click! The Housewife's Moment of Truth," *Ms*, Spring 2002 (1972), 5.
33 Charland and Turcotte, interview with author.
34 Rachel Bélisle, "Rapport des organisatrices du débat du 23 Novembre 1984," *Amazones d'hier lesbiennes d'aujourd'hui* 2, no. 4 (March 1985): 48–9.
35 Ibid.
36 Echols, *Daring to Be Bad*, 216.
37 Bélisle, "Rapport des organisatrices du débat du 23 novembre 1984," 49.
38 Le collectif LG5, "Bilan de notre intervention-surprise," 58. Emphasis in original.
39 Charland and Turcotte, interview with author.
40 Kim Chernin, *The Obsession: Reflections on the Tyranny of Slenderness* (New York: Harper and Row Perennial Library, 1981), 96.
41 Ibid., 99. Large as Life did not take a firm stance for or against the notion of an obsession and tyranny of slenderness. A review of *The Obsession* was reprinted in the *Bolster* followed by a caption that read: "We would be interested in your comments regarding Chernin's theory." See Judith Finlayson, "Not a Case Where Less is More," *Bolster*, February 1982, 6–7.
42 Chernin, *The Obsession*, 190.
43 Louise Turcotte, "Queer Theory: Transgression or Regression?," in *Canadian Woman Studies: An Introductory Reader*, ed. Nuzhat Amin (Toronto: Inanna, 1999), 57.
44 David S. Churchill, "Personal Ad Politics: Race, Sexuality and Power at *The Body Politic*," *Left History* 8, no. 2 (2003): 119.
45 Frank Zelko, "Making Greenpeace: The Development of Direct Action Environmentalism in British Columbia," *BC Studies*, no. 142–3 (2004): 214. See also Donald Stone, "The Human Potential Movement," *Society*, May/June 1978, 67.
46 References to, and advertisements for, *Fat Is a Feminist Issue*–inspired consciousness-raising groups were found in the following sources: Manitoba Action Committee on the Status of Women, "Fat Is a Feminist Issue," *Action: MACSW*, December 1981; "We Are Organizing a CR Group," *Calgary Women's Newspaper*, July/August 1980; Ellen Roseman, "Self-Help Groups Branching Out," *Globe and Mail*, 1 September 1983.
47 Manitoba Action Committee on the Status of Women, "Fat Is a Feminist Issue," 29.
48 Susan White, interview with author, digital recording (Winnipeg, MB, 11 July 2006).
49 Ibid. In our interview White did not make a distinction between *Fat as a Feminist Issue* and *Fat Is a Feminist Issue II*, although she did make clear that she had read and was referring to both texts interchangeably.

50 See, among others, Charlotte Cooper, *Fat Activism*, 22; Nicky Diamond, "Thin Is the Feminist Issue," in *The Body: A Reader*, ed. Miriam Fraser and Monica Greco (1985; repr., New York: Routledge, 2005), 115; Joan Dickenson, "Some Thoughts on Fat," in *Shadow on a Tightrope: Writings by Women on Fat Oppression*, ed. Lisa Schoenfielder and Barb Wieser (Iowa City: Aunt Lute Publishing Company, 1983), 39; Shea Pertman, "Being a Fat Woman in North America: A Theoretical Perspective on Fat Liberation" (MA thesis, Simon Fraser University, 1999), 5–6.

51 White, interview with author.

52 Doris Maranda, interview with author, digital recording (Vancouver, BC, 14 August 2006); Sandra Friedman, interview with author, digital recording (Sechelt, BC, 7 October 2005).

53 "Facing Your Fat," flyer, Maranda-Friedman, c. 1982, Vancouver, BC, Personal Papers of Sandra Friedman.

54 Maranda, interview with author.

55 Ibid.

56 White's recall on this activity is quite remarkable. Verbatim, her description was as follows:

"One of the exercises in the book was something like, close your eyes, imagine you are at a cocktail party. I don't remember the whole thing. But anyway, you were supposed to visualize yourself at the party and you're fat or your current size. Fine, so you draw the picture of yourself in the mind. Think about it, what are you doing? And then you were supposed to visualize the same party, and now you are quite a bit thinner, what are you doing?"

White has closely recalled Orbach's instructions, which were as follows: "imagine that you are at a party ... Set the scene and notice how you are feeling ... What are you wearing ... Now notice your behavior at this party ... I'd like you to imagine that you are getting fatter ... How do you feel at this size? ... What are you wearing and how do you feel about your clothes? ... What is your fat saying to others?" (Susie Orbach, *Fat Is a Feminist Issue II: A Program to Conquer Compulsive Eating* [1982; repr., New York: Berkley Books, 1984], 145–7)

57 White, interview with author.

58 Friedman, interview with author.

59 "Learning to Love Yourself: The Maranda Friedman Approach to Eating Disorders," flyer, Maranda-Friedman, 1987, Vancouver, BC, Personal Papers of Sandra Friedman.

60 Ellen Tallman, interview with author, digital recording (Vancouver, BC, 12 October 2005).

61 Nikolas Rose, *Governing the Soul: The Shaping of the Private Self* (London: Routledge, 1989), 246.

62 Tallman, interview with author.

63 Stone, "The Human Potential Movement," 66.
64 Cooper, *Fat Activism*, 144–5.
65 Lorraine Code, *What Can She Know: Feminist Theory and the Construction of Knowledge* (Ithaca, NY: Cornell University Press, 1991), 188.
66 Franceen Friefeld was a founding member who did not attend subsequent meetings. She went on to publish books on eating and healthy weight. Franceen Friefeld and Claire Friefeld, *The Healthy Weigh: Learn How to Eat, Not How to Diet* (Ottawa: Creative Bound, 1993); Franceen Friefeld and Claire Friefeld, *Fill Up, Not Out: A Healthy Approach to Weight Control for Life* (Ottawa: Creative Bound, 2004). See also Freedom from Eating Disorders (FED), "Meeting Minutes," 31 August 1987; Hersize, "Meeting Minutes," 4 October 1987, personal collection of the author.
67 Toronto General Hospital Political Group, "Meeting Notes," 17 August 1987, personal collection of the author.
68 Karin Jasper, "Body Image Dissatisfaction: A Personal or Political Problem?," *Hersize: A Weight Prejudice Action Group* (newsletter), c. 1989, 2.
69 David Garner et al., "Cultural Expectations of Thinness in Women," *Psychological Reports* 47, no. 2 (October 1980): 489.
70 Not long after he formed the "political group" Garner was fired from Toronto General Hospital. In February 1988, Garner's certificate of registration was suspended by the Ontario Board of Examiners in Psychology for two years after he pled guilty to "allegations of professional misconduct in that he had sexual intercourse with a client in 1979." Garner's name disappeared from Hersize minutes within months of these allegations surfacing. References to the psychologist appear occasionally in meeting minutes up to 1988, which contain citations like "ask David about government policy on weight" and another noting that Garner had revised a letter of complaint drafted by Hersize members. The only history of Hersize that has been recorded to date, by founding member Karin Jasper, excludes any reference to Garner and his role in starting the group. Several Hersize members have since gone on to work in the academy and in the field of eating disorders. Garner went on to work in the United States. He was hired by Michigan State University in 1989 and then dismissed when the Toronto scandal became public knowledge. He was subsequently hired to work as a professor in Ohio at the University of Toledo and Bowling Green State University and as director of the River Centre Clinic. In 2003 Garner again faced charges of sexual misconduct when he was accused of having an affair with a patient of the River Centre and buying her a condominium. In fall 2008 Garner was forced to cede

his licence to practice in Ohio after yet another allegation of sexual misconduct surfaced. As of September 2019, Garner is identified on the River Centre Foundation's website as the president and founder. See n.a., "Eating Disorder Expert Faces Sex Charges," *Edmonton Journal*, 12 December 2003, A10; Tracey Tyler, "Psychologist Fired in Metro Scandal Now Forced to Leave Job in Michigan," *Toronto Star*, 9 February 1989, A29; Hersize, "Meeting Minutes," 22 November 1987; Hersize, "Meeting Minutes," 16 May 1988; Karin Jasper, "Hersize: A Weight-Prejudice Action Group," in *Consuming Passions: Feminist Approaches to Weight Preoccupation and Eating Disorders*, ed. Catrina Brown and Karin Jasper (Toronto: Second Story Press, 1993), 421–8; Julie McKinnon, "Sylvania Psychologist Cedes License in Sex Charge, Female Patient Complained," *Toledo Blade*, 22 October 2008, accessed on 20 May 2009, http://toledoblade.com/apps/pbcs.dll/article?AID=/20081022/NEWS02/810220368; The River Centre Foundation, "Who We Are," accessed on 25 September 2019, http://www.rivercentrefoundation.org/about-the-company/.

71 Michele Landsberg, "Another Clinic Swallowed by Power Hungry Establishment," *Toronto Star*, 14 December 1991, G1; Toronto INDD Coalition and Tania Spencer [illustrator], *Foxy Fables and Facts about Dieting* (Toronto: NEDIC and the Toronto International No Diet Day Coalition: A Journey To Healthy Lifestyles, 1996).

72 Jeri Dawn Wine and Janice Ristock, eds., *Women and Social Change: Feminist Activism in Canada* (Toronto: James Lorimer, 1991).

73 Farrell, *Fat Shame*, 115.

74 Cooper, *Fat Activism*, 131.

75 Hersize, "Mailing List," c. 1990; Hersize, "Meeting Minutes," 5 April 1989, personal collection of the author; Mary Frances Ellison, interview with author, digital recording (Toronto, ON, 15 December 2005).

76 Hersize, "Mailing List."

77 Carla Rice, "Getting Cut Down in Size: How Cosmetic and Weight Loss Surgeries Harm Women," *Hersize: A Weight Prejudice Action Group* (newsletter), c. 1990, Canadian Women's Movement Archives.

78 Carla Rice, "Mediating Fat Phobia," *Hersize: A Weight Prejudice Action Group* (newsletter), c. 1988, 1–2, personal collection of the author.

79 Selma McGorman, *This Ad Offends Me! How to Write Letters of Complaint with Regard to the Objectionable Portrayal of Women in Advertising* (Windsor, ON: Selma McGorman, c. 1989), 6–7. This guide was among items anonymously donated to the personal collection of the author.

80 Hersize, "Letter to CBC Television Regarding 'Special K' Breakfast Cereal Advertisement," (Hersize, 1 October 1987).

81 Ellison, interview with author.

82 Summary and analysis of *Killing Us Softly* (1979) and *Still Killing Us Softly* (1987) can be found in Paul Rutherford, *A World Made Sexy: Freud to Madonna* (Toronto: University of Toronto Press, 2007), 150–2. Kilbourne later published books based on these lectures, including Jean Kilbourne, *Deadly Persuasion* (New York: The Free Press, 1999).

83 Hersize, "Exploding Media Myths: Women Reclaiming the Mirror," (Hersize, 24 October 1989). Personal collection of the author.

84 For example, Joanne Hollows, *Feminism, Femininity and Popular Culture* (Manchester, UK: Manchester University Press, 2000); Linda M. Scott, *Fresh Lipstick: Redressing Fashion and Feminism* (New York: Palgrave MacMillan 2005).

85 Naomi Wolf, *The Beauty Myth* (Toronto: Random House, 1990), 149. *Maclean's* hailed *The Beauty Myth* as "the most important feminist publication since *The Female Eunuch*," and one that had transformed its author, Naomi Wolf, into a "feminist icon." The paperback edition of *The Beauty Myth* spent more than two years on Canada's national bestseller list, hovering between number ten and number three on the list between July 1991 and January 1994. Mary Nemeth, "Who's Afraid of Naomi Wolf," *Maclean's*, 6 December 1993, 70; "National Bestsellers 6 July 1991," *Toronto Star*, 6 July 1991, F13; "National Bestsellers 12 October 1991," *Toronto Star*, 12 October 1991, K17; "National Bestsellers 28 March 1992," *Toronto Star*, 28 March 1992, K17; "National Bestsellers 9 May 1992," *Toronto Star*, 9 May 1992, G14; "National Bestsellers 23 May 1992," *Toronto Star*, 23 May 1992, H14; "National Bestsellers 6 June 1992," *Toronto Star*, 6 June 1992, H14; "National Bestsellers 28 November 1992," *Toronto Star*, 28 November 1992, K16; "National Bestsellers 20 March 1993," *Toronto Star*, 20 March 1993, K16; "National Bestsellers 17 July 1993," *Toronto Star*, 17 July 1993, G13; "National Bestsellers 7 August 1993," *Toronto Star*, 7 August 1993, K13; "National Bestsellers 29 January 1994," *Toronto Star*, 29 January 1994, J14.

86 Wolf, *The Beauty Myth*, 147. In the early 1980s *Ms* magazine published an article by Susan Squire suggesting eating disorders were on the rise. Eating disorders in this case refers to anorexia and bulimia. Susan Squire, "Is the Binge-Purge Cycle Catching? A New Outbreak of Eating Disorders," *Ms*, October 1983, 41–5.

87 Ellison, interview with author.

88 n.a., "Letter to Hersize," 25 October 1989, personal collection of the author.

89 Davis, *The Making of Our Bodies, Ourselves*, 132.

90 Ellison, interview with author; Jasper, "Hersize: A Weight-Prejudice
    Action Group," 427.

91 Hersize, "Meeting Minutes," 4 July 1989.

92 Hersize, "Hersize: A Weight Prejudice Action Group," in *Hersize: A Weight
    Prejudice Action Group* (newsletter), c. 1990, 4. Emphasis in original.

93 Michèle Barrett and Anne Phillips, eds., *Destabilizing Theory: Contemporary
    Feminist Debates* (Cambridge: Polity Press, 1992), 1–2.

94 See for example Barrett and Phillips, *Destabilizing Theory*, 4; Combahee
    River Collective, "A Black Feminist Statement," in *Feminist Theory Reader:
    Local and Global Perspectives*, ed. Carole McCann and Seung-Kyung Kim
    (1977; repr., New York: Routledge, 2003), 164–71.

95 Ellison, interview with author.

96 Judith Stein, interview with author, digital recording (Cambridge, MA,
    14 April 2012).

97 Arun Mukherjee, "A House Divided: Women of Colour and American
    Feminist Theory," in *Challenging Times: The Women's Movement in Canada
    and the United States*, ed. Constance Backhouse and David H. Flaherty
    (Montreal: McGill-Queens University Press, 1992), 166.

98 Combahee River Collective, "A Black Feminist Statement," 164.

99 Cooper, *Fat Activism*, 169–87 passim.

100 American data from the 1980s and 1990s show that women of colour
    are more likely to be obese and from lower socio-economic groups,
    which is why lack of diversity is troubling. See Esther Rothblum,
    "The Stigma of Women's Weight: Social and Economic Realities,"
    Feminism and Psychology 2, no. 1 (1992); Mitchell and Mitchell,
    Livin' Large; Carole M. Counihan, "Food Rules in the United States:
    Individualism, Control and Hierarchy," *Anthropological Quarterly* 65,
    no. 2 (April 1992).

101 Jennifer Poudrier, "The Geneticization of Aboriginal Diabetes and
    Obesity," in *Obesity in Canada: Critical Perspectives*, ed. Jenny Ellison,
    Deborah McPhail, and Wendy Mitchinson (Toronto: University of
    Toronto Press, 2016), 89–90, 100.

102 Ibid., 109.

103 Ibid., 110.

104 Deborah McPhail, "Indigenous People's Clinical Encounters with
    Obesity."

105 Donna Ciliska, interview with author, digital recording (Hamilton, ON,
    11 January 2006); Claudia Savage, interview with author, digital record-
    ing (Burnaby, BC, 17 August 2006).

106 Jessica Carter, interview with author, digital recording (Toronto, ON,
    16 January 2006).

107 Retha Powers, "Fat is a Black Woman's Issue," *Essence*, October 1989, 75, 78, 135–6.
108 Tamara Beauboeuf-Lafontant, "Strong and Large Black Women? Exploring Relationships between Deviant Womanhood and Weight," *Gender and Society* 17, no. 1 (February 2003): 112.
109 Julie Levasseur, interview with author, digital recording (Winnipeg, MB, 14 July 2006).
110 Pat [Bulcock a.k.a. Nokomis] Donaldson, interview with author, digital recording (Empress, AB, 25 July 2006).
111 Jennifer Poudrier and Janice Kennedy, "Embodiment and the Meaning of the 'Healthy Body': An Exploration of Aboriginal Women's Perspectives of Healthy Body Weight and Body Image," *Journal of Aboriginal Health* 4, no. 1 (2007): 17, 21.
112 See for example Daniel Francis, *The Imaginary Indian: The Image of the Indian in Canadian Culture* (Vancouver, BC: Arsenal Pulp Press, 1992); Sarah Carter, "In Sharp Relief: Representations of Aboriginal Women in the Colonial Imagination," in *Capturing Women: The Manipulation of Cultural Imagery in Canada's Prairie West* (Montreal: McGill-Queen's University Press, 1997), 158–93.
113 Elena Levy-Navarro, "Fattening Queer History: Where Does Fat History Go from Here?," in *The Fat Studies Reader*, ed. Sandra Solovay and Esther Rothblum (New York: New York University Press, 2009), 16.
114 Code, *What Can She Know*, 2.
115 Laura Kipnis, *Bound and Gagged*, 106.
116 Allyson Mitchell, "Pissed Off," in *Fat: The Anthropology of an Obsession*, ed. Don Kulick and Anne Meneley (New York: Penguin Group, 2005). 219
117 Founded by Allyson Mitchell, Mariko Tamaki, and Ruby Rowen, the group eventually came to include Abi Slone, Lisa Ayuso, Tracy Tidgwell, Joanne Huffa, and Zoe Whittall. See Mitchell, "Pissed Off," 215. Rowen left the group circa 1997 or 1998. A second group, the Fat Femme Mafia, also performed at cabarets and organized events in Toronto. Liz Worth, "A Big, Fat Revolution; The Fat Femme Mafia are Performance Artists, Cabaret Dancers and the Latest in a Budding Local History of Activists for Plus-Sized Women, Writes Liz Worth," *Toronto Star*, 7 November 2006.
118 Mitchell, "Pissed Off," 217.
119 Pretty Porky and Pissed Off, "Queen Sized Revolt," *Fireweed*, no. 67 (1999): 23. Emphasis in original.
120 In addition to American predecessors like Nomy Lamm, PPPO owed a conceptual debt to the Fat Lip Readers Theatre (FLRT), a performance art group that started in San Francisco in 1982. FLRT ran workshops, made short films, and performed publicly into the 2000s. FLRT's short film *Nothing to Lose* (1989) featured a choir of fat women singing "no more

diets" to the tune of *Frère Jacques*. Like FLRT, PPPO adapted traditional modes of artistic expression to make a political point. See Fat Lip Readers Theatre, "Fat Workshop: For Womyn of All Sizes," flyer, n.d., Winnipeg Women's Health Clinic Library, Winnipeg, MB, Mazer Lesbian Archives, Los Angeles, CA.

121 Mitchell, "Pissed Off," 220.
122 Josée Johnston and Judith Taylor, "Feminist Consumerism and Fat Activists: A Comparative Study of Grassroots Activism and the Dove Real Beauty Campaign," *Signs: Journal of Women in Culture and Society* 33, no. 4 (2008): 941–66.
123 Leah McLaren, "Porky Pride: Fat Lot of Good That Does," *Globe and Mail*, 27 January 2001.
124 Recent data on this phenomenon can be found in Paradis, "'Obesity' as Process," 56–88; Gard, "Hearing Noises and Noticing Silences," 31–55.
125 Kathy Davis, *The Making of Our Bodies, Ourselves*, 9.

2 Between Women: Fat Acceptance Organizations

1 Cold Mountain Institute, "Vancouver Workshops," *Cold Mountain Journal* (September–November 1979): 3. Personal collection of the author. Emphasis in original.
2 Joan [O'Brien] Dal Santo, interview with author, digital recording (Sechelt, BC, 7 October 2005).
3 Kate Partridge, interview with author, digital recording (Crediton, ON, 20 September 2005).
4 Janet Walker, interview with author, digital recording (White Rock, BC, 6 October 2005).
5 Tallman, interview with author.
6 Dal Santo, interview with author. See also Eve Rockett, "Five Days on a Fat Farm," Chatelaine, May 1980, 42, 136, 138, 140, 142, 146, 148.
7 Partridge, interview with author.
8 Ingrid Laue, interview with author, digital recording (North Vancouver, BC, 3 October 2005).
9 Partridge, interview with author.
10 Kate Partridge, "Dear Friends," *Large as Life* (newsletter), August 1981, 1.
11 Davis, *The Making of Our Bodies, Ourselves*, 139.
12 Ibid., 133.
13 Claudia Savage, "To the Membership," *Large as Life* (newsletter), October 1984; Claudia Savage, "Dear LAL Members," *Large as Life* (newsletter), November 1984.
14 Dal Santo, interview with author.
15 Walker, interview with author.

16 Evelyn Booth, interview with author, digital recording (North Vancouver, BC, 11 October 2005).
17 Evelyn Booth, follow-up interview with author, digital recording (Vancouver, BC, 12 August 2006).
18 Eve Kosofsky Sedgwick, *Epistemology of the Closet* (Berkeley: University of California Press, 1990), 75.
19 Ibid., 63.
20 Samantha Murray, "Doing Politics or Selling Out? Living the Fat Body," *Women's Studies: An Inter-Disciplinary Journal* 34, no. 3–4 (2005): 266.
21 Ibid., 269.
22 Ibid., 277.
23 Cooper, *Fat Activism*, 145.
24 "Large as Life," *Bolster*, September 1982, 2.
25 Laura Thaw, interview with author, digital recording (Surrey, BC, 6 October 2005); Laue, interview with author.
26 Booth, interview with author; Walker, interview with author.
27 Suzanne Bell, interview with author, digital recording (New Westminster, BC, 4 October 2005); Dal Santo, interview with author; Partridge, interview with author.
28 J. Rowntree, letter to the editor, *Bolster*, June 1982, 2. Emphasis in original.
29 Large as Life Action Group Executive, "Ah, There's Nothing Like Being a Winner! Introducing Your New Executive," *Bolster*, May 1982, 6.
30 Laura Thaw, "Political?," *Bolster*, September 1982, 6.
31 Patricia Bradley, *Mass Media and the Shaping of American Feminism, 1963–1975* (Jackson: University Press of Mississippi, 2003), 74–5; Freeman, *The Satellite Sex*, 81–3.
32 Ingrid Laue, "From Our Suggestion Box," *Bolster*, December 1981, 4.
33 Laue, interview with author.
34 Partridge, interview with author.
35 Jill Vickers, "The Intellectual Origins of the Women's Movement in Canada," in *Challenging Times: The Women's Movement in Canada and the United States*, ed. Constance Backhouse and David H. Flaherty (Montreal: McGill-Queen's University Press, 1992), 49.
36 Michelle Murphy, "Immodest Witnessing: The Epistemology of Vaginal Self-Examination in the U.S. Feminist Self-Help Movement," *Feminist Studies* 30, no. 1 (Spring 2004): 127.
37 Janet Walker, "October Meeting," *Bolster*, November 1982, 19.
38 Ibid.
39 Ingrid Laue, "Editor's Sphere," *Bolster*, September 1982, 21.
40 Laue, interview with author. The newsletter was not given the title the *Bolster* until the September 1981 issue. The first nineteen issues of the

Bolster (August 1981 to May 1983) were available in the Canadian Women's Movement Archives, Ottawa. These issues are between twelve and twenty-four pages in length. All issues after September 1983 were in the personal collection of Kate Partridge. These issues were ten to fifteen pages long and were edited by Sally Thomson and Gail Bell. After September 1984 the *Bolster* folded and a pamphlet-sized four- to six-page *Large as Life* newsletter was circulated to members by then LAL president, Claudia Savage.

41 "Next Meeting," *Bolster*, May 1982, 2.
42 "Next Meeting," *Bolster*, February 1982, 3.
43 Anna Hobbs, "Big Can Be Beautiful: Solving Fashion Problems When You're Size 16 and Up," *Canadian Living*, August 1982, 84–90.
44 Laue, "Editor's Sphere," 21; Partridge, interview with author. These questionnaires were thrown in the garbage some time after LAL Vancouver folded.
45 "BIG Can Be BEAUTIFUL," *Bolster*, September 1982, 11.
46 Anne Leslie, letter to the editor, *Bolster*, September 1982, 5.
47 Nancy L. Kaizer, letter to the editor, *Bolster*, October 1982, 4.
48 Shannon Andrew, letter to the editor, *Bolster*, October 1982, 5.
49 O'Reily, "Click! The Housewife's Moment of Truth, 5–8; Valerie J. Korinek, *Roughing It in the Suburbs: Reading Chatelaine Magazine in the Fifties and Sixties* (Toronto: University of Toronto Press, 2000).
50 Barbara Freeman, "'A Public Sense of Ourselves': Communication and Community-Building in Canada's LESBIANEWS/LNEWS, 1989–1998," *Westminster Papers* 8, no. 3 (December 2011).
51 Suzanne Bell, interview with author; Dal Santo, interview with author.
52 Savage, interview with author.
53 Claudia Savage, "To the Membership," *Large as Life* (newsletter), October 1984; Claudia Savage, "Dear LAL Members," *Large as Life* (newsletter), November 1984.
54 Savage, interview with author.
55 Calgary Board of Education, *Spring 1983 Program Calendar* (Calgary, AB: Calgary Board of Education); Nina Howe, *Large as Life* (newsletter), 7/8 ed., vol. 2 (Calgary, AB: Large as Life, October 1984). Although I was able to interview three women from Calgary LAL, all were primarily involved in the aerobics program and were unable to offer me any details about other events. The LAL Calgary newsletter was kept in the Calgary Status of Women Office and that the organization was still in existence in October 1984. Calgary Board of Education, *Spring 1983 Program Calendar* (Calgary, AB: Calgary Board of Education); Calgary Status of Women Action Committee (CSWAC), *Fat Issues: LARGE AS LIFE* (newsletters), Calgary Status of Women Action Committee.

56 Partridge, follow-up interview with author; Partridge, interview with author; Diann Vail, interview with author, digital recording (London, ON, 13 April 2006).

57 Partridge, follow-up interview with author.

58 Booth, interview with author.

59 Friedman, interview with author; Sandra Friedman, *Body Thieves: Help Girls Reclaim Their Natural Bodies and Become Physically Active* (Vancouver: Salal Books, 2002); Sandra Susan Friedman, *When Girls Feel Fat: Helping Girls Through Adolescence* (Toronto: HarperCollins, 1997); Hersize, "Mailing List."

60 Suzanne Bell's Fashions, *Coming Attractions*, June 2003.

61 Savage, interview with author.

62 Savage, interview with author; Lynne Grauer, interview with author, digital recording (Burnaby, BC, 8 August 2006); Lois Smith, interview with author, digital recording (New Westminster, BC, 9 August 2006).

63 Claudia Savage, letter to the editor, *Radiance*, Fall 1997, accessed 6 June 2012, http://www.radiancemagazine.com/letters/letters_98.htm.

64 Grauer, interview with author.

65 Smith, interview with author.

66 Grauer, interview with author.

67 Smith, interview with author.

68 Savage, interview with author.

69 Smith, interview with author.

70 Ibid.

71 Savage, interview with author.

72 Grauer, interview with author.

73 Mukherjee, "A House Divided," 197, 193.

74 Enke, *Finding the Movement*, 252–4.

75 Ibid., 62.

76 Davis, *The Making of Our Bodies, Ourselves*, 10.

77 Runa Fiander, interview with author, digital recording (Victoria, BC, 2 August 2006).

78 Bell, interview with author.

79 Vail, interview with author.

80 Booth, interview with author.

81 Levasseur, interview with author; Partridge, interview with author.

82 Jan Mindlin, interview with author, digital recording (Burnaby, BC, 20 August 2006).

83 Grauer, interview with author.

84 Booth, interview with author.

85 Charland and Turcotte, interview with author. Note that Christine Donald also uses the names C.M. Donald and Hilary Clare.

86 Masterton, interview with author.

87 Jeff McKay, *Fat Chance.*

88 Spring, interview with author.

89 Translation: "I have never seen the Metro." n.a. "Gilles Leblanc remplace la marche par le sit-in," *Le Devoir*, 25 July 1979, n.p., APOHQ archive, CDAT Montreal.

90 Madelaine Berthault, "Des insultes pour les obèses," *La Presse*, January 1978 (?), n.p. This article was pasted in the APOHQ scrapbook. APOHQ archive, CDAT Montreal.

91 Chivers, "Barrier by Barrier."

92 Smith, *Lesbian and Gay Rights in Canada*, 5, 7.

93 Coopératives et institutions financiers, Ministère des Consommateurs, "Lettres patentes par l'aide aux personnes obèses handicapées du Québec," 31 October 1978, APOHQ archive, *CDAT* Montreal.

94 n.a., "Photo of Gilles LeBlanc Ribbon Cutting with Jean Drapeau,"Aide aux personnes obèses handicapées du Québec, 1979? APOHQ archive, CDAT Montreal.

95 "Morbidly obese" is a medical term that refers to people who are more than one hundred pounds "overweight." Gouvernment du Québec ministère de la santé et des services sociaux, "Lettre de ministère de la santé et des services sociaux à l'aide aux personnes obèses handicapées du Québec," Ville de Québec: la ministère de la santé et des services Sociaux, APOHQ archive, CDAT Montreal.

96 Kenneth McRoberts, *Québec: Social Change and Political Crisis*, 3rd ed. (Toronto: McLelland and Stewart, 1988), 254.

97 Daniel Béland and André Lecouts, "Nationalisme et protection sociale: Une approche comparative," *Canadian Public Policy* 30, no. 3 (2004): 321.

98 Lise Bergeron, interview with author, digital recording (Montreal, QC, 23 May 2006).

99 Ibid.

100 André Beauchamp, interview with author, digital recording (Montreal, QC, 25 May 2006).

101 Lennard J. Davis, "Crips Strike Back: The Rise of Disability Studies," *American Literary History* 11, no. 3 (Autumn 1999): 506–7; Peter Freund, "Bodies, Disability and Spaces," in *The Body: A Reader*, ed. Miriam Fraser and Monica Greco (New York: Routledge, 2005), 183.

102 Davis, "Crips Strike Back," 503.

103 Michael Friscolanti, "Flyer Celebrates 'Significant Victory for Obese People,'" *National Post*, 13 December 2001, A2; Linda McKay-Panos, interview with author, digital recording (Calgary, AB, 18 July 2006).

104 Robert Remington, "Labelling Obese People Disabled an Insult: Group," *National Post*, 26 September 2001, A14; McKay-Panos, interview with author.

105 Friscolanti, "Flyer Celebrates 'Significant Victory for Obese People,'" A12.
106 McKay-Panos, interview with author.
107 Helena Spring, interview with author, digital recording (Toronto, ON, 5 January 2006).
108 Ruth Gillingham, interview with author, digital recording (Prince Albert, SK, 27 July 2006).
109 Ibid.
110 Ibid.; The Canadian Council on Social Development, "No More Fat Jokes: A Group That Helps People Carry That Weight," *Initiative: The Self-help Newsletter*, Winter 1990, 5.
111 Spring, interview with author.
112 Ibid.
113 My participants commented on Spring's abrasive personal style both on and off the record. Gillingham, interview with author; Kaca Henley, interview with author, digital recording (Lindsay, ON, 8 March 2006).
114 Canada WYDE, "You Are Invited to Participate in the Second Annual Canadian International No Diet Day," *Canada WYDE*, May 1998.
115 Korinek, *Roughing It in the Suburbs*, 179.
116 See "CW Marketplace," *Canada WYDE*, Summer 1996, 12; "Marketplace," *Canada WYDE*, Fall/Winter 1997, 2; "International No Diet Day Celebrations and Plus Size Fashion Show and Sale," *Canada WYDE*, Fall /Winter 1997, 12–13; "SHOPPING, SHOPPING, SHOPPING!," *Canada WYDE*, Fall 1996, 13; Jessica Carter, "Women's Fashion Tips," *Canada WYDE*, Summer 1996, 8–9; Fiona Shaw, "Fall Fashion Hints," *Canada WYDE*, Fall/Winter 1997, 7; Helena Spring, "Let's Go Shopping!," *Canada WYDE*, Summer 1996, 9; Jacquie Whyte, "Fashion Fun for Springtime Fanatics," *Canada WYDE*, Spring 1997, 7.
117 Spring, interview with author.
118 Gillingham, interview with author.
119 Constance Backhouse and David H. Flaherty, *Challenging Times: The Women's Movement in Canada and the United States* (Montreal: McGill-Queen's University Press, 1992).
120 Lynda Raino, interview with author, digital recording (Victoria, BC, 10 October 2005).
121 Terryl Atkins, interview with author, digital recording (Kamloops, BC, 12 August 2006).
122 Trudy Norman, interview with author, digital recording (Victoria, BC, 3 August 2006).
123 Fiander, interview with author.
124 Raino, interview with author.
125 Atkins, interview with author.
126 Raino, interview with author.

127 Atkins, interview with author.
128 Norman, interview with author.
129 Fiander, interview with author.
130 Atkins, interview with author.
131 Raino, interview with author; Atkins, interview with author; Norman, interview with author.
132 Atkins, interview with author.
133 Norman, interview with author.
134 Atkins, interview with author.
135 Fiander, interview with author.
136 Davis, *The Making of Our Bodies, Ourselves*, 139.
137 Norman, interview with author.
138 Atkins, interview with author.
139 Norman, interview with author.
140 Raino, interview with author.
141 Norman, interview with author.
142 Atkins, interview with author.
143 Norman, interview with author.
144 Atkins, interview with author.
145 Ibid.
146 Petra Kuppers, "Fatties on Stage: Feminist Performances," in *Bodies Out of Bounds: Fatness and Transgression*, ed. Jana Evans Braziel and Kathleen LeBesco (Berkeley: University of California Press, 2001), 278.
147 Raino, interview with author.
148 Norman, interview with author.
149 Rosemarie Garland-Thomson, "Introduction," in *Freakery: Cultural Spectacles of the Extraordinary Body*, ed. Rosemarie Garland-Thomson (New York: New York University Press, 1996), 5; Davis, "Crips Strike Back," 504.
150 Smith, *Lesbian and Gay Rights in Canada*, 9.

3 "If Only You'd Lose Weight...": Femininity, Sexuality, and Fat Activism

1 For a discussion of TOPS see Laura Fraser, *Losing It: America's Obsession with Weight and the Industry That Feeds on It* (New York: Dutton Books, 1997), 150.
2 Susan Masterton, interview with author, digital recording (North Vancouver, BC, 11 October 2005). Susan Masterton, follow-up interview with author, digital recording (North Vancouver, BC, 26 November 2007).
3 This type of complication was not uncommon in intestinal bypass patients prior to the 1980s, which have since been abandoned in favour of gastroplasties and gastric banding. Dr David Michael Grace, interview with author, digital recording (London, ON, 10 April 2006).
4 Susan Masterton, follow-up interview with author.

5 Becki L. Ross, *The House That Jill Built: A Lesbian Nation in Formation* (Toronto: University of Toronto Press, 1995), 16.

6 Atkins, interview with author; Bell, interview with author; Donaldson, interview with author; Dal Santo, interview with author; Ellison, interview with author; Fiander, interview with author; Grauer, interview with author; Henley, interview with author; Levasseur, interview with author; Masterton, interview with author; Mindlin, interview with author; Norman, interview with author; Partridge, interview with author; Jody Sandler, interview with author, digital recording (North Vancouver, BC, 5 October 2005); Savage, interview with author; Spring, interview with author; Laura Thaw, interview with author, digital recording (Surrey, BC, 6 October 2005); Walker, interview with author; White, interview with author; Anne Zatylny, interview with author, digital recording (Toronto, ON, 20 June 2006).

7 Simone de Beauvoir, "The Second Sex: Introduction," in *Feminist Theory Reader: Local and Global Perspectives*, ed. Carole McCann and Seung-Kyung Kim (New York: Routledge, 2003), 32–4.

8 Mary Russo, "Female Grotesques: Carnival and Theory," in *Feminist Studies Critical Studies*, ed. Teresa de Laurentis (Bloomington: Indiana University Press, 1986), 218.

9 Angela Stukator, "'It's Not Over until the Fat Lady Sings': Comedy, the Carnivalesque and Body Politics," in *Bodies Out of Bounds: Fatness and Transgression*, ed. Kathleen LeBesco and Jana Evans Braziel (Berkeley: University of California Press, 2001), 197.

10 LeBesco, Kathleen, *Revolting Bodies: The Struggle to Redefine Fat Identity* (Amherst: University of Massachusetts Press, 2004), 124.

11 Andrée Lévesque, *Making and Breaking the Rules: Women in Québec, 1919–1939*, trans. Yvonne M. Klein (Toronto: McLelland and Stewart, 1989), 12.

12 Carol Groneman, "Nymphomania: The Historical Construction of Female Sexuality," in *Deviant Bodies: Critical Perspectives on Difference in Science and Popular Culture*, ed. Jennifer Terry and Jacqueline Urla (Indianapolis: Indiana University Press, 1995), 223, 233.

13 Danielle Ramsey, "Second Wave Feminism," in *Feminism and Postfeminism*, ed. Sarah Gamble (London: Routledge, 1998), 173.

14 Ibid., 173–4.

15 Feona Attwood, "Pornography and Objectification: Re-Reading "the Picture That Divided Britain," *Feminist Media Studies* 4, no. 1 (2004): 7–8.

16 Ross, *The House That Jill Built: A Lesbian Nation in Formation*, 85.

17 MIT Panel on Sojourner Book, Personal Notes of Judith Stein, 8 March 1996, Judith Stein Fonds 2005-MIS8, Radcliffe Institute, Schlesinger Library, Cambridge, MA.

18 The Cambridge Women's Centre Statement from the Fat Lesbian Group, Judith Stein Fonds 2005-MIS8, Radcliffe Institute, Schlesinger Library, Cambridge, MA.

19 1983 Michigan Womyn's Music Festival Program, Lesbian Herstory Archives, SP COLL 2005–17, folder 3, Brooklyn, NY.

20 Ibid., 5.

21 Stein, interview with author.

22 Ibid.

23 1980 Program. Both OA and fat women's support groups were present in 1981 and every year up until 2010.

24 See, for example, "The Festival Land: Then … and Now Newsletter," 1990 Michigan Womyn's Music Festival, Lesbian Herstory Archives, SP COLL 2005–17 folder 5, Brooklyn, NY, 6.

25 1983 Michigan Womyn's Music Festival Program, 18.

26 Ibid., 14.

27 Charland and Turcotte, interview with author; Elana Dykewomon, interview with author, digital recording (San Francisco, CA, 22 March 2008); AHLA, "Dossier oppression de la grosseur," *Amazones d'hier lesbiennes d'aujourd'hui*, no. 21 (December 1992).

28 Smith, *Lesbian and Gay Rights in Canada*, 31.

29 Christine Donald, *The Fat Woman Measures Up* (Charlottetown, PEI: Ragweed Press, 1986), 31

30 Ibid., 19

31 1986 letter from Christine Donald to Jim from Windsor, Christine Donald Papers, CGLA 2005-090-1, Canadian Gay and Lesbian Archives, Toronto, ON.

32 Ross, *The House That Jill Built: A Lesbian Nation in Formation*, 85.

33 "Grant Agreement for Donald's Book Tour Letter from Canada House to Christine Donald," 9 June 1986, Christine Donald Papers, The ArQuives (CLGA) 2006-090/1 Shelf 20.1.2., Canadian Gay and Lesbian Archives, Toronto, ON; 18 January 1987 letter from Libby Oughton (Ragweed Press) to Christine Donald, The ArQuives (CLGA) 2006-090/1 Shelf s 20.1.2., Canadian Gay and Lesbian Archives, Toronto, ON.

34 30 August 1986 letter from Helen H. to Christine Donald, The ArQuives (CLGA) 2006-090/1 Shelf 20.1.2., Canadian Gay and Lesbian Archives, Toronto, ON. Emphasis in original.

35 27 May 1986 letter from Betty H. to Christine Donald, The ArQuives (CLGA) 2006-090/1 Shelf s 20.1.2., Canadian Gay and Lesbian Archives, Toronto, ON.

36 22 January 1987 letter from Judith Stein to Christine Donald, Christine Donald Papers, The ArQuives (CLGA) 2006-090/1 Shelf 20.1.2., Canadian Gay and Lesbian Archives, Toronto, ON.

37 Irene Neufeld, "The Fat Woman: Christine Donald Nurtures All and Sometimes, Too, the Thin," *Angles*, April 1987, 12

38 Pauline Rankin and Sage de Belle, letter to the editor, *Angles*, May 1987, 11.

39 Maranda-Friedman, "Facing Your Fat" (flyer).

40 Pauline Rankin, interview with author, digital recording (Vancouver, BC, 21 August 2006).

41 Smith, *Lesbian and Gay Rights in Canada*, 41.

42 Barrett and Phillips, *Destabilizing Theory: Contemporary Feminist Debates*, 4.

43 Rankin, interview with author.

44 A calendar fitting this description was found in the Lesbian Herstory Archives and is also described by Kathleen LeBesco. See LeBesco, *Revolting Bodies: The Struggle to Redefine Fat Identity*, 11; "Images of Our Flesh" by the Fat Avengers Calendar, 1983, Seattle, WA, Lesbian Herstory Archives, Fat Liberation Subject File 04700, Brooklyn, NY.

45 Charland and Turcotte, interview with author.

46 Sharon Chrismas, "Fun Fashion Nite – Sept 19th Meeting," *Bolster*, September 1983, 5–6.

47 Janet Walker, "January Meeting/February Meeting," *Bolster*, April 1983, 24.

48 "They'll Take Romance," *Bolster*, April 1984, 7.

49 A year after LAL folded a dating service designed to match larger men and women called "Ample Attractions" briefly operated in Vancouver. Carmen Cook was at that time an employee of Suzanne Bell. Newspaper profiles show that the service lasted for at least six months, and Cook reported that she had fifty clients, "and slightly more than half are women." The "club" cost $250 for six months or $400 for a year. Pene Horton, "Big Is Beautiful," *Woman to Woman*, May 1987, 27; Kathy Tait, "For the Big at Heart," *Province* 16 December 1986, 31.

50 "They'll Take Romance," 8.

51 Partridge, interview with author.

52 Fiander, interview with author.

53 Bell, interview with author.

54 Henley, interview with author.

55 Sarah King, interview with author, digital recording (North Vancouver, BC, 12 October 2005).

56 Mindlin, interview with author; Norman, interview with author.

57 King, interview with author.

58 Ellison, interview with author.

59 Masterton, interview with author.

60 Booth, interview with author; Norman, interview with author; Thaw, interview with author.

61 Brumberg, *The Body Project*, 97.

62 Dal Santo, interview with author.
63 Booth, interview with author.
64 Partridge, interview with author.
65 Mindlin, interview with author.
66 Bell, interview with author.
67 Sandler, interview with author; Mindlin, interview with author; Norman, interview with author.
68 "The Personals," *Canada WYDE*, Fall/Winter 1997, 17.
69 "The Personals," *Canada WYDE*, Spring 1997, 13.
70 Ibid.
71 "The Personals," *Canada WYDE*, Fall/Winter 1997, 1917.
72 "Personals and Penpals," *Canada WYDE*, Summer 1996, 10.
73 Ibid.
74 "The Personals," Fall/Winter 1997, 1917.
75 "Personals," *Canada WYDE*, Fall 1996, 14.
76 Kipnis, *Bound and Gagged*, 95.
77 Marcia Millman, *Such a Pretty Face* (New York: WW Norton, 1980), 192.
78 Ibid.
79 Spring, interview with author.
80 Stukator, "'It's Not Over until the Fat Lady Sings'," 197.
81 Rachel Colls, "Big Girls Having Fun: Reflections on a 'Fat Accepting Space,'" *Somatechnics* 2, no. 1 (2012): 32.
82 Ibid., 31.
83 A. Finn Enke suggests that lesbian bars were spaces where black women and lesbians fostered a visible culture. Enke, *Finding the Movement*, 29; Elise Chenier, "Rethinking Class in Lesbian Bar Culture: Living 'The Gay Life' in Toronto, 1955–1965," in *Rethinking Canada: The Promise of Women's History*, ed. Adele Perry and Mona Gleason (Toronto: Oxford University Press, 2006), 301–22.
84 Donald, *The Fat Woman Measures Up*, 17.

4 Dr Fullovitt, MD: Fat Women's Experiences with Doctors and Dieting

1 Barbara Warner, "Big Giggles No. 2," *Bolster*, December 1982, 16.
2 Kate Partridge and Large as Life, "obesity: facts & fiction" (Vancouver: Large as Life Association, 1984). Personal collection of the author.
3 Albert Stunkard, MD, and Mavis McLaren-Hume, MS, "The Results of Treatment for Obesity: A Review of the Literature and Report of a Series," *Archives of Internal Medicine* 103, no. 1 (1959): 79–85. Strunkard's study suggested that weight reduction programs were ineffective and sometimes harmful to patients because they experienced emotional disturbances when they were dieting.

4 Sheryl Burt Ruzek, *The Women's Health Movement: Feminist Alternatives to Medical Control* (New York: Praeger, 1978), 28.

5 Ibid., 143.

6 Cheryl Krasnick Warsh, *Prescribed Norms: Women and Health in Canada and the United States since 1800* (Toronto: University of Toronto Press, 2010), xiii.

7 Ruzek, *The Women's Health Movement: Feminist Alternatives to Medical Control*, 2, 11, 143, 147; Madeline Boscoe et al., "The Women's Health Movement: Looking Back and Moving Forward " in *Canadian Woman Studies: An Introductory Reader*, ed. Andrea Medovarski and Brenda Cranney (Toronto: Inanna Publications, 2006), 503.

8 Ruzek, *The Women's Health Movement*, 28.

9 Michael Gard, "Friends, Enemies and the Cultural Politics of Critical Obesity Research," in *Biopolitics and the 'Obesity Epidemic': Governing Bodies*, ed. Jane Wright and Valerie Harwood (New York: Routledge, 2009), 31.

10 Lee F. Monaghan, "Discussion Piece: A Critical Take on the Obesity Debate," *Social Theory and Health* 3 (2005): 311.

11 Jenn Anderson, "Whose Voice Counts? A Critical Examination of Discourses Surrounding the Body Mass Index," *Fat Studies Journal* 1, no. 2 (2012): 198.

12 Stearns, *Fat History*, 157, 211.

13 Emma Seifrit Weigley, "Average? Ideal? Desirable? A Brief Overview of Height-Weight Tables in the United States," *Journal of the American Diabetic Association* 84, no. 4 (April 1984): 418.

14 Hillel Schwartz, *Never Satisfied: A Cultural History of Diets, Fantasies and Fat* (New York: Anchor Books, 1986), 156.

15 Seifrit Weigley, "Average? Ideal? Desirable? A Brief Overview of Height-Weight Tables in the United States," 419.

16 Ibid., 420. The range of numbers was meant to reflect different "frame" sizes, even though the Metropolitan Life Insurance Company did not establish a method for determining frame size in their study. Adding "frame" was a scientific advancement that was supposed to be more accurately assess who was normal and in doing so maximize the insurance company's profit margins.

17 Ian Hacking as cited in Mariam Fraser and Monica Greco, "Introduction," in *The Body: A Reader*, ed. Mariam Fraser and Monica Greco (New York: Routledge, 2005), 16.

18 L.B. Pett and G.F. Ogilvie, "The Report on Canadian Average Weights, Heights and Skinfolds," *Canadian Bulletin on Nutrition* 5, no. 1 (1957): 1.

19 Ibid.

20 The Canadian Council on Nutrition, "A Dietary Standard for Canada," *Canadian Bulletin on Nutrition* 6, no. 1 (1963): 76.

21 Elizabeth Grosz, "Refiguring Bodies," in *The Body: A Reader*, ed. Mariam Fraser and Monica Greco (New York: Routledge, 2005), 50.

22 Stearns, *Fat History*, 6, 7, 248–9.

23 Farrell, *Fat Shame*, 59–61.

24 Ibid., 64.

25 Ibid., 68–80 passim.

26 Katherine Arnup, *Education for Motherhood: Advice for Mothers in Twentieth-Century Canada* (Toronto: University of Toronto Press, 1994); Denyse Baillargeon, *Un Québec en mal d'enfants: La médicalisation de la maternité, 1910–1970* (Montreal: Éditions du remue-ménage, 2004); Colin D. Howell, *Blood, Sweat, and Cheers: Sport and the Making of Modern Canada* (Toronto: University of Toronto Press, 2001).

27 Mariana Valverde, *The Age of Light, Soap and Water: Moral Reform in English Canada, 1885–1925* (Toronto: McLelland and Stewart, 1991), 17.

28 Ian Mosby, "Administering Colonial Science: Nutrition Research and Human Biomedical Experimentation in Aboriginal Communities and Residential Schools, 1942–1952," *Histoire sociale/Social History* 46, no. 91 (May 2013): 161–4.

29 Deborah McPhail, "Canada Weighs In: Gender, Race, and the Making of 'Obesity,' 1945–1970" (PhD diss., York University, 2009), 17.

30 Franca Iacovetta and Valerie J. Korinek, "Jell-O Salads, One Stop Shopping and Maria the Homemaker: The Gender Politics of Food," in *Sisters or Strangers? Immigrant, Ethnic and Racialized Women in Canadian History*, ed. Marlene Epp, Franca Iacovetta, and Frances Swyripa (Toronto: University of Toronto Press, 2004), 191, 205; McPhail, "Canada Weighs In," 17; Naomi Adelson, *Being Alive Well: Health and the Politics of Cree Well-Being* (Toronto: University of Toronto Press, 2000), 103.

31 Mitchinson, *Fighting Fat*, 108–9.

32 See Schwartz, *Never Satisfied*, 246–8; Jean Nidetch, *Story of Weight Watchers* (Winnipeg, MB: Signet, 1970).

33 Brumberg, *The Body Project: An Intimate History of American Girls*, 97–8; Schwartz, *Never Satisfied*, 327–8.

34 Sandra Lee Bartky, "Foucault, Femininity, and the Modernization of Patriarchal Power," in *Feminism and Foucault: Reflections on Resistance*, ed. Irene Diamond and Lee Quinby (Boston: Northeastern University Press, 1988), 64; Susan Bordo, "Anorexia Nervosa: Psychopathology as the Crystallization of Culture," in *Feminism and Foucault: Reflections on Resistance*, ed. Irene Diamond and Lee Quinby (Boston: Northeastern University Press, 1988), 102.

35 Susan Faludi, *Backlash: The Undeclared War against American Women* (Toronto: Doubleday, 1991).

36 Douglas Owram, *Born at the Right Time: A History of the Baby Boom Generation* (Toronto: University of Toronto Press, 1996), 6; Mona Gleason,

Normalizing the Ideal: Psychology, Schooling, and the Family in Postwar Canada (Toronto: University of Toronto Press, 1999), 4–5.

37 Most members of the Boston Women's Health Book Collective had a "doctor story" – "a tale about male physicians who were sexist, paternalistic, judgmental, or simply unable to provide the information that women needed." Davis, *The Making of Our Bodies, Ourselves*, 21.

38 Donaldson, interview with author; Levasseur, interview with author; Smith, interview with author; White, interview with author.

39 Ellison, interview with author; Friedman, interview with author; White, interview with author; Zatylny, interview with author.

40 Mindlin, interview with author.

41 Dal Santo, interview with author.

42 Friedman, interview with author.

43 Bell, interview with author.

44 Mindlin, interview with author.

45 Mitchinson, *Fighting Fat*, 147.

46 Walker, interview with author; Thaw, interview with author; Spring, interview with author; Andria Siegler, interview with author, digital recording (Toronto, ON, 7 June 2006); Monica Sieben-Kuhn, interview with author, digital recording (Calgary, AB, 20 July 2006); Savage, interview with author; Partridge, interview with author; Joyce Cusack, interview with author, digital recording (Calgary, AB, 21 July 2006); Bell, interview with author; King, interview with author.

47 Sieben-Kuhn, interview with author.

48 Walker, interview with author; Spring, interview with author; Siegler, interview with author.

49 Cusack, interview with author.

50 Savage, interview with author.

51 Siegler, interview with author.

52 Friedman, interview with author.

53 Spring, interview with author.

54 Grauer, interview with author.

55 Susan Gelfand Malka, *Daring to Care: American Nursing and Second-Wave Feminism* (Chicago: University of Illinois Press, 2007), 37. A reader of *Canada WYDE* also wrote to Helena Spring to tell of the pain she experienced when she was refused entry to nursing school because of her weight. See I.S., letter to the editor, *Canada WYDE*, Summer 1996, 2. There is also evidence that American colleges used weight as a criterion to judge potential candidates. See Judy Klemesrud, "There Are a Lot of People Willing to Believe That Fat is Beautiful," *New York Times*, 18 August 1970, 38; Rothblum, "The Stigma of Women's Weight," 67.

56 Spring, interview with author; Walker, interview with author. Appearance was an unofficial and official qualification for finding work. For example, the battle over appearance and age qualifications for flight attendants is documented in Eileen Boris, "Desirable Dress: Rosies, Sky Girls, and the Politics of Appearance," *International Labor and Working-Class History* 69 (2006): 132–42.

57 Charland and Turcotte, interview with author; Norman, interview with author.

58 Bell, interview with author; Masterton, interview with author; Norman, interview with author; Charland and Turcotte, interview with author.

59 Mindlin, interview with author.

60 Masterton, interview with author.

61 Booth, interview with author.

62 Linda Alcoff, *Visible Identities: Race, Gender and the Self* (New York: Oxford University Press, 2006), 6.

63 Cusack, interview with author.

64 Maranda, interview with author.

65 Davis, *The Making of Our Bodies, Ourselves*, 21.

66 See for example Jane Wright, "Female Nurses' Perceptions of Acceptable Female Body Size: An Exploratory Study," *Journal of Clinical Nursing* 7, no. 4 (1998); Lauren Vacek, "Perspective: Sensitivity Training for Nurses Caring for Morbidly Obese Patients," *Bariatric Nursing & Surgical Patient Care* 2, no. 4 (2008); E. L. Merrill, "Women's Stories of Their Experiences as Overweight Patients" (PhD diss., Texas Woman's University, 2007); C.A. Jeffrey and S. Kitto, "Struggling to Care: Nurses' Perceptions of Caring for Obese Patients in an Australian Bariatric Ward," *Health Sociology Review* 15, no. 1 (2006); Janet Cade and Shaun O'Connell, "Management of Weight Problems and Obesity: Knowledge, Attitudes and Current Practice of General Practitioners," *British Journal of General Practice* 41 (1991); Leanne Joanisse and Anthony Synnott, "Fighting Back: Reactions and Resistance to the Stigma of Obesity," in *Interpreting Weight: The Social Management of Fatness and Thinness,* ed. Jeffery Sobal and Donna Maurer (New York: Aldine de Gruyter, 1999), 57.

67 Sara Golda Bracha Fishman, "Life in the Fat Underground," *Radiance,* Winter 1998, 33. Most members of the FU adopted different names in the 1970s and have since reverted to their original names. Lynn Mabel-Lois is Lynn McAfee. She has continued to work as an activist, most recently with the Council on Size and Weight Discrimination.

68 Lisa Schoenfielder and Barb Wieser, "Preface," in *Shadow on a Tightrope: Writings by Women on Fat Oppression,* ed. Lisa Schoenfielder and Barb Wieser (Iowa City: Aunt Lute Publishing Company, 1983), xx; Minneapolis Fat Liberator Publications, Minnesota, Price List, n.d., Mazer Lesbian Archives, Los Angeles CA; Minneapolis Fat Liberator

Publications, Minnesota, Book List, 1980, Mazer Lesbian Archives, Los Angeles CA. Sales figures are not available.

69 "Health of Fat People: The Scare Story Your Doctor Won't Tell You," Pamphlet, Fat Underground, 1974, Mazer Lesbian Archives, Los Angeles, CA.

70 Llewellyn Louderback, *Fat Power: Whatever You Weigh is Right* (New York: Hawthorn Books, 1970), 136.

71 Ibid., 137.

72 Ibid., 139.

73 Ibid., 141.

74 Ibid., 158. Louderback's book did not contain footnotes. According to William Fabrey, they were removed as a cost-saving measure. Bearsville letter from Bill Fabrey, NY, to Jenny Ellison, Toronto, ON, 23 July 2008.

75 Fishman, "Life in the Fat Underground," 33.

76 "Health of Fat Women ... The Real Problem," Pamphlet, Fat Underground, 1974, Mazer Lesbian Archives, Los Angeles, CA.

77 Ibid.

78 Fishman, "Life in the Fat Underground," 34.

79 Sharon Bas Hannah, "Naomi Cohen Choked on the Culture," *Sister*, September 1974, 1.

80 Kathy Davis, "Feminist Body/Politics as World Traveler: Translating *Our Bodies, Ourselves*," *European Journal of Women's Studies* 9, no. 3 (2002): 242.

81 Re-published in 1992 as Vivian [Aldebaran] Mayer, "La grosse illusion ou le contrôle des corps comme forme de contrôle social," *Amazones d'hier lesbiennes d'aujourd'hui* 23 (1992): 53–70.

82 Dal Santo, interview with author; Partridge, interview with author; Thaw, interview with author; Barbara Berry, "'Naturally the Choice Is up To You,'" *Bolster*, January 1982, 11; "Plain Facts," *Bolster*, April 1983, 25.

83 White, interview with author; Henley, interview with author; Mary Hower, "From Indoor Exercise to Outdoor FItness: This Canadian Aerobics Enthusiast Brings Large Women a Grand Form," *Radiance*, Winter 1991, 8–11; Caffyn Kelley, "Talent + Skill x Action = Suzanne Bell," *Radiance*, Winter 1992, 6–7, 13; Ellison, interview with author.

84 Dorothy Smith, *The Everyday World as Problematic: A Feminist Sociology* (New York: Open University Press, 1987), 49.

85 Partridge, interview with author.

86 Partridge, follow-up interview with author.

87 Kate Partridge, "The Fat-Promoting Metabolism," *Bolster*, December 1981, 11–12; Ingrid Laue, "LAL Monthly Meeting, September 16th," *Bolster*, October 1982, 19.

88 Kate Partridge, "A Redefinition of Treatment Goals for Obesity" (paper presented at the Canadian Psychological Association Section on Women and Psychology, Montreal, QC, 1982). Personal Papers of Kate Partridge.

89 Partridge and Large as Life, "obesity," 1.
90 Ibid.
91 Ibid., 2.
92 Ibid., 3.
93 Ibid.
94 Ibid., 4.
95 Partridge, "The Fat-Promoting Metabolism," 12.
96 Partridge and Large as Life, "obesity," 6.
97 Ibid., 7.
98 Ibid., 8.
99 Consumer Reports, "No Diet Pill Works Harder to Help You Lose Weight," *Bolster*, June 1982, 15.
100 "Ruffled Feathers," *Bolster*, April 1983. Emphasis in original.
101 Janet Polivy and C. Peter Herman, *Breaking the Diet Habit* (New York: Basic Books, 1983), 94; Betty Shermer, "Intestinal Bypass," in *Shadow on a Tightrope: Writings by Women on Fat Oppression*, ed. Lisa Schoenfielder and Barb Wieser (Iowa City: Aunt Lute Publishing Company, 1983), 157; Grace, interview with author.
102 Shermer, "Intestinal Bypass," 158.
103 Rice, "Getting Cut Down in Size: How Cosmetic and Weight Loss Surgeries Harm Women," 3.
104 Polivy and Herman, *Breaking the Diet Habit*, 95.
105 Canadian bariatric surgeon David Grace, interviewed for this book, said that by the 1990s the mortality rate for bariatric procedures was 0.5 per cent. He did, however, acknowledge mortality rates were high for intestinal bypasses performed in the United States in the 1960s and 1970s. Ultimately, more study is needed because the sources I've found cited in activist literature are not Canadian and not always from peer reviewed medical journals. Not surprisingly, Grace felt bariatric surgery was a worthwhile procedure. Shermer, "Intestinal Bypass," 157–61; Rice, "Getting Cut Down in Size: How Cosmetic and Weight Loss Surgeries Harm Women," 1–6; Grace, interview with author.
106 Berry, "'Naturally the Choice Is up to You.'"
107 n.a., "'Stomach Stapling' Danger Cited," *Bolster*, November 1982, 12.
108 Laurie Kahn, "Personal Optimism," *Bolster*, June 1982, 14.
109 Barbara Berry, "Naturally, the Choice Is up to You (Part II)," *Bolster*, March 1983, 10–11.
110 Kathy Davis, "Remaking the She-Devil: A Critical Look at Feminist Approaches to Beauty," *Hypatia: A Journal of Feminist Philosophy* 6, no. 2 (Summer 1991): 33.
111 Davis, *The Making of Our Bodies, Ourselves*, 155; Wendy Kline, "'Please Include This in Your Book': Readers Respond to *Our Bodies, Our Selves*," *Bulletin of Medical History* 79 (2005): 91–101 passim.
112 Davis, *The Making of Our Bodies, Ourselves*, 155.

113 Code, *What Can She Know*, 185.
114 Stone, "The Human Potential Movement," 66.
115 Paul Campos argues that the "war on fat" is actually about gener-
     ating profits for the diet industry and research money for obesity
     scientists. Campos, and the other studies listed below, demonstrate
     that the notion that fat people can be healthy has some validity and
     that this idea is part of ongoing debates about obesity by medical and
     public health researchers, as well as the media. Paul Campos, *The
     Obesity Myth: Why America's Obsession with Weight is Hazardous to Your
     Health* (New York: Gotham Books, 2004), xix; Jerome P. Kassirer and
     Marcia Angell, "Losing weight – an Ill-Fated New Year's Resolution,"
     New England Journal of Medicine 338, no. 1 (1 January 1998): 52–5;
     Jacqui Gingras, "Throwing Their Weight Around: Canadians Take
     on Health at Every Size," *Health at Every Size Journal* 19, no. 4 (2006):
     195–206.
116 Gail Bell, "'Go Ahead and Get Pregnant,' says BIG MOTHER," *Bolster*,
     February 1984, 7.
117 "List of Physicians," *Bolster*, March 1984, 8. Sharing the names of fat-
     friendly physicians appears to have been a common practice. Suzanne
     Bell and Doris Maranda also told me that they kept such information for
     their clients and friends. Suzanne Bell, follow-up interview with author,
     digital recording (New Westminster, BC, 16 August 2006); Maranda,
     interview with author.
118 Gail Bell, "Editorial: Educating an M.D.," *Bolster*, March 1984, 2. Note the
     researchers Bell is describing, Janet Polivy and Peter Herman, were mem-
     bers of the "Promoting Healthy Weights" expert group discussed earlier
     in the book.
119 "If You'd Lose Some Weight," *Bolster*, March 1984, 1.
120 "Weight Wobble Unsafe, Research Shows," *Bolster*, March 1984, 4.
121 Ibid., 6.
122 Campos, *The Obesity Myth*, 176.
123 Kassirer and Angell, "Losing weight – an Ill-Fated New Year's
     Resolution," 55.
124 Polivy and Herman, *Breaking the Diet Habit*, 97.
125 Bell, interview with author; Booth, follow-up interview with author;
     Donaldson, interview with author; Ellison, interview with
     author; Masterton, interview with author; McKay-Panos, interview
     with author; Partridge, interview with author; Siegler, interview with
     author.
126 Health Services and Promotion Branch, "Promoting Healthy Weights:
     A Discussion Paper" (Ottawa: Health and Welfare Canada, 1988), i.
127 Garner et al., "Cultural Expectations of Thinness in Women," 483–91.

128   Christa Costas-Bradstreet, "Spreading the Message through Community Mobilization, Education and Leadership," supplement, *Canadian Journal of Public Health* 95, no. S2 (May/June 2004): S25.

129   Health Services and Promotion Branch, "Promoting Healthy Weights," 1.

130   Ibid., 53.

131   Fraser and Greco, "Introduction," 18–19.

132   Health Services and Promotion Branch, "Promoting Healthy Weights," 5.

133   Georgina Feldberg, Molly Ladd-Taylor, and Kathryn McPherson, eds., *Women, Health, and Nation: Canada and the U.S. since 1945* (Montreal: McGill-Queen's University Press, 2001), 28.

134   Ciliska's supervisory committee included David Garner and Janet Polivy. Dr Ciliska went on to work in the School of Nursing at McMaster University and is now retired.

135   Ciliska, interview with author.

136   Andrea Siegler and Donna Ciliska, "Beyond Dieting," *Bulletin: National Eating Disorder Information Centre*, April 1991, 1. In the clinical study, participants were all female and at 120 per cent to 200 per cent of their "ideal" weight defined by Canadian Department of Health and Welfare tables. Ciliska accepted women of all weights in later groups run through the National Eating Disorder Information Centre; women of all sizes who were weight preoccupied were allowed to join. See Donna Ciliska, *Beyond Dieting: Psychoeducational Interventions for Chronically Obese Women: A Non-Dieting Approach* (New York: Brunner/Mazel Publishers, 1990), 45, 83.

137   Ciliska, *Beyond Dieting*, 47.

138   Ciliska, interview with author.

139   Ciliska used the medical term "obesity" in her publications, but she attempted to get participants to be more comfortable with the word "fat" during Beyond Dieting sessions.

140   Ciliska, interview with author; Siegler, interview with author.

141   Centre des femmes de Verdun, *L'obsession de la minceur: Un guide d'intervention* (Verdun: Centre des femmes de Verdun, 1991); Catrina Brown, *Getting Beyond Weight: Women Helping Women. A How To Manual about the Development and Operation of Self Help Groups for Women Preoccupied with Weight* (Winnipeg, MB: Women's Health Clinic, 1985); Diane Forrest, "Stop the Diet, We Want to Get Off! These Large Women Learn to Quit Worrying about Their Weight and Start Living Their Lives," *Canadian Living*, January 1993.

142   Ciliska, interview with author.

143   Ibid.

144   Ibid.

145   Mary Frances Ellison, follow-up interview with author, digital recording (Toronto, ON, 25 January 2006).

146   Ciliska, interview with author.

147 Ciliska, *Beyond Dieting*, 47; Ellison, follow-up interview with author.
148 Ciliska, *Beyond Dieting*, 47; Siegler, interview with author; Ciliska, interview with author.
149 Siegler, interview with author.
150 Ciliska, interview with author.
151 Landsberg's story indicates that employees of the National Eating Disorder Information Centre, including Carla Rice, were unhappy with the clinic's incorporation into the Toronto General Hospital's eating disorder clinic. Landsberg, "Another Clinic Swallowed by Power Hungry Establishment," G1; Georgina Feldberg, "Holism and History in Toronto's Women's Health Movements," in *The Politics of Healing: Histories of Alternative Medicine in Twentieth-Century North America*, ed. Robert D. Johnston (New York: Routledge, 2004), 185.
152 Smith, *Lesbian and Gay Rights in Canada*, 27.
153 Wine and Ristock, *Women and Social Change*, 10.
154 Cooper, *Fat Activism*, 54.
155 Ibid., 57.
156 Ciliska, *Beyond Dieting*, 63.
157 Roswitha Roese conducted a study of four Beyond Dieting participants in 1996. Of these, two were white women, aged twenty-nine and fifty-two, one was British-Indian, aged sixty-two, and the fourth was a thirty-two-year-old African Canadian woman. Roese did not think it was possible to make generalizations about ethnicity. Roswitha Roese, "Wanting to Fit: A Grounded Theory of Chronically Obese Women's Experiences of a Non-Dieting Treatment Program" (PhD diss., York University, 1996), 23.
158 Ibid., 280.
159 Ellison, follow-up interview with author.
160 Ciliska, interview with author.
161 Enke, *Finding the Movement*, 243.
162 Davis, *The Making of Our Bodies, Ourselves*, 125.

5 "Let Me Hear Your Body Talk": Aerobics for Fat Women Only

  1 Darcy C. Plymire, "Positive Addiction: Running and Human Potential in the 1970s," *Journal of Sport History* 31, no. 3 (2004): 302.
  2 Aerobics, dancercise, and jazzercise would vary in format. Dancercise and jazzercise tend to be more dance-based whereas aerobics is more callisthenic. I have chosen the word aerobics as an umbrella term to describe fitness classes set to music. For a more detailed explanation of the differences and evolution of different types of aerobic exercise see Beth Swanson, "A History of the Rise of Aerobic Dance

in the United States through 1980" (master's thesis, San Jose State University, 1996).

3 Wolf, *The Beauty Myth*, 77.

4 Amy Hribar, "Consuming Lifestyles: Transforming the Body and the Self in Postfeminist America" (PhD diss., University of Illinois at Urbana-Champaign, 2001), 37.

5 Susan Balcom, "Here's a No-Frills Workout for Those Who'll Never Be a Fonda," *Vancouver Sun*, 20 November 1986, E4.

6 Wolf, *The Beauty Myth*, 161–73.

7 Jennifer Ellison, "Our Most Charming Girls: Female Athletes in Canadian Advertisements, 1928 to 2002" (master's thesis, Carleton University, 2002), 106; Nancy Theberge, "A Content Analysis of Print Media Coverage of Gender, Women and Physical Activity," *Journal of Applied Sport Psychology* 3 (1991): 42; Helen Lenskyj, *Out of Bounds: Women, Sport and Sexuality* (Toronto: The Women's Press, 1986), 130.

8 Partridge, interview with author.

9 "Current Large as Life Projects," *Large as Life Newsletter*, August 1981.

10 Suzanne Bell, "Watch This! An Inside Vew," *Bolster*, June 1982, 7; Sal Thomson, "Fitness Circuit," *Bolster*, March 1983, 15–16; "New Classes to Start: Generous Jiggles," *Bolster*, January 1984, 15; "LaL in Motion," *Bolster*, September 1982, 10.

11 Calgary Board of Education, *Spring 1983 Program Calendar*, 11.

12 Donaldson, interview with author.

13 McKay-Panos, interview with author; Donaldson, interview with author.

14 Carol Peat, interview with author, digital recording (London, ON, 17 June 2006).

15 Levasseur, interview with author; White, interview with author.

16 Gillingham, interview with author.

17 Bell, interview with author; Kate Partridge, "Retiring President Tireless, Says LAL Founder," *Bolster*, May 1984, 3; Partridge, interview with author.

18 Suzanne Bell's Fitness and Fashion Enlarged,"Suzanne Bell's Fitness and Fashion Enlarged" (Pamphlet), September 1985, Personal Papers of Suzanne Bell; Suzanne Bell's Fitness and Fashion Enlarged, "News Update for 'Living Large'" (Newsletter), January 1985, Personal papers of Suzanne Bell.

19 Bell, interview with author.

20 Suzanne Bell's Fitness and Fashion Enlarged, "Largely Yours" (Newsletter), Fall 1985, Personal Papers of Suzanne Bell, 8.

21 Bell, interview with author.

22 Sandler, interview with author.

23 Selling one thousand videos was considered a bestseller in Canada in 1986. Sandler, interview with author.
24 Bell, interview with author.
25 Sandler, interview with author.
26 Aerobics for fat women in Canada were not limited to the examples discussed in this chapter. Shorter-term initiatives included Jackqueline Hope's "Big on Fitness" program for fat women at her store in downtown Toronto in the early 1990s. Brief references to initiatives such as an instructor-training program for large women in Vancouver and a physical activity club for overweight adults in Montreal also appeared in some sources but no further information was available. Jackqueline Hope, *Big, Bold and Beautiful* (Toronto: Macmillan Canada, 1996), 191.
27 Brad Clark, "The Corpulent '90s: A New Health Program Suggests It's All Right to Be 'Big,'" *Alberta Report*, 18 February 1991, 44.
28 Pauline Bartel, "Women at Large – Empathy Is Key to Helping 'Fluffy Ladies' Regain Esteem," *St Petersburg Times*, 5 April 1987, n.p.; Liz Reardon, "Heavyweight Instructors Direct Health Clubs for Big Women," *Omaha World-Herald*, 29 November 1987, E1.
29 Fiander, interview with author.
30 Maureen Downey, "'Women at Large' Helps Bodies and Self-Images," *Atlanta Constitution*, 13 October 1986, B1.
31 Ibid.; Bartel, "Women at Large," 6F.
32 *Radiance*, Summer/Fall 1986, 30; *Radiance*, Spring 1988, 48; *Radiance*, Fall 1988, 53; *Radiance*, Summer 1991, 48; *Radiance*, Fall 1992, 48. BBW is an acronym for Big Beautiful Woman. It is intended to signal a fat-positive attitude.
33 Pat Lyons and Debbie Burgard, *Great Shape: The First Exercise Guide for Large Women* (New York: Arbor House – William Morrow, 1988), 9.
34 Lyons and Burgard, *Great Shape*, 11, 9.
35 Ibid., 173–7.
36 Lenskyj, *Out of Bounds*, 129.
37 Jane Fonda, *Jane Fonda's Workout Book* (New York: Simon and Schuster, 1981), 45, 47.
38 Bordo, "Anorexia Nervosa: Psychopathology as the Crystallization of Culture," 90. See also Mona Lloyd, "Feminism, Aerobics and the Politics of the Body," *Body and Society* 2, no. 2 (June 1996).
39 Lenskyj, *Out of Bounds*, 129.
40 Helen Lenskyj, "Good Sports: Feminists Organizing on Sport Issues in the 1970s and 1980s," *Resources for Feminist Research* 20, no. 3/4 (1991): 130.
41 M. Ann Hall, *Feminism and Sporting Bodies* (Windsor, ON: Human Kinetics, 1996), 96–7.
42 Lenskyj, "Good Sports," 131–2, 134.

43 Canada Fitness Survey, *Changing Times: Women and Physical Activity* (Ottawa: Fitness and Amateur Sport Canada, 1984), 18.

44 Canada Fitness Survey, *Fitness and Lifestyle in Canada: A Report* (Ottawa: Fitness and Amateur Sport Canada, 1983), 18.

45 Canada Fitness Survey, *Changing Times*, 19.

46 Canada Fitness Survey, *Fitness and Lifestyle in Canada*, 29.

47 Paul Rutherford, *Endless Propaganda: The Advertising of Public Goods* (Toronto: University of Toronto Press, 2000), 73.

48 Michel Foucault, *Discipline and Punish: The Birth of the Prison*, trans. Alan Sheridan (1977; repr., New York: Vintage Books, 1995), 26.

49 Bartky, "Foucault, Femininity, and the Modernization of Patriarchal Power," 65.

50 Lloyd, "Feminism, Aerobics and the Politics of the Body," 91.

51 Foucault, *Discipline and Punish*, 201.

52 Nancy Fraser, *Unruly Practices: Power, Discourse, and Gender in Contemporary Social Theory* (Minneapolis: University of Minnesota Press, 1989), 23.

53 Nina Waaler Loland, "The Art of Concealment in a Culture of Display: Aerobicizing Women's and Men's Experience and Use of Their Own Bodies," *Sociology of Sport Journal* 17 (2000): 119.

54 Audrey MacNevin, "Exercising Options: Holistic Health and Technical Beauty in Gendered Accounts of Bodywork," *Sociological Quarterly* 44, no. 2 (2002): 277.

55 Hilary Radner, "Producing the Body: Jane Fonda and the New Public Feminine," in *Constructing the New Consumer Society*, ed. Hilary Radner et al. (New York: St Martin's Press, 1997), 130.

56 Joseph Maguire and Louise Mansfield, "'Nobody's Perfect': Women, Aerobics, and the Body Beautiful," *Sociology of Sport Journal* 15 (1998): 125.

57 Pirkko Markula, "Firm but Shapely, Fit but Sexy, Strong but Thin: The Postmodern Aerobicizing Female Bodies," *Sociology of Sport Journal* 12, no. 4 (1995): 434.

58 Pirkko Markula, "Technologies of the Self: Sport, Feminism, and Foucault," *Sociology of Sport Journal* 20, no. 2 (2003): 102.

59 Although aerobics, keep-fit classes, jazzercise, and similar programs had grown exponentially in the late 1970s, in Canada the industry was largely unregulated in the early 1980s. It was not necessary for a person to obtain certification to teach a class, but workshops teaching people how to lead fitness classes were available through organizations like the YMCA/YWCA. By the mid-1980s organizations like the British Columbia Parks and Recreation Association (BCRPA) governed and mandated certification at the provincial level. Later, instructors for Suzanne Bell and Jody Sandler were trained through BCRPA.

60 YWCA Fitness Leadership Course, Personal Notes of Kate Partridge, 1981. Personal Papers of Kate Partridge.
61 Ibid. Emphasis in original.
62 Dal Santo, interview with author.
63 Bell, interview with author.
64 Donaldson, interview with author.
65 Ibid.
66 YWCA Fitness Leadership Course, Personal Notes of Kate Partridge. Emphasis in original.
67 The ideal numbers given for men and women were different because women's bodies naturally carry more body fat. Personal Notes of Kate Partridge.
68 In 2006 I took the revised YMCA Fitness Leadership course at Toronto's West End YMCA. I did so because I wanted to understand if messaging about weight had changed in the course and also to see what it might feel like to participate in a fitness leadership course. In the 2006 course, ideal body fat percentages were given verbally but were not central to the training. For women the ceiling for acceptable body fat was given at 30 per cent and for men 24 per cent. A section on "Healthy Lifestyles" in the *Basic Theory Manual* further noted, "although excess body fat is considered ... [a] risk factor, existing evidence suggest[s] ... that the relationship is co-dependent with such factors as hypertension, diabetes, and cigarette smoking."[69] By the 2000s the YMCA was taking a more holistic and less weight-centred approach to physical fitness.
69 Dal Santo, interview with author.
70 Bell, interview with author.
71 Ibid.; Dal Santo, interview with author; Partridge, interview with author.
72 Peat, interview with author.
73 Laue, interview with author.
74 Walker, interview with author.
75 Suzanne Bell, "Fitness Circuit," *Bolster*, May 1983, 23.
76 Radner, "Producing the Body: Jane Fonda and the New Public Feminine," 116.
77 Suzanne Bell, "Fitness anyone?," *Bolster*, May 1982, 14.
78 Bell, interview with author.
79 Suzanne Bell, "Before and After," *Bolster*, September 1982, 7–8.
80 White, interview with author.
81 Laue, interview with author.
82 Sandler, interview with author.
83 Bell, interview with author; Nada Vuksic, interview with author, digital recording (Vancouver, BC, 14 August 2006).
84 Bell, "Fitness Circuit," 7–8.

85 Levasseur, interview with author.
86 Bell, interview with author; Gillingham, interview with author; Peat, interview with author; Sandler, interview with author; Vuksic, interview with author; White, interview with author.
87 King, interview with author.
88 Peat, interview with author.
89 Sandler, interview with author.
90 "Interview of Kate Partridge and Joan Dal Santo by Stan Peters and Ann Mitchell," *CBC Radio Noon* (15 September 1981). Tape recording, Personal Papers of Kate Partridge.
91 Vuksic, interview with author.
92 Dana Schuster and Lisa Tealer, "Exorcising the Exercise Myth: Creating Women of Substance," in *The Fat Studies Reader*, ed. Esther Rothblum and Sandra Solovay (New York: New York University Press).
93 Bell, follow-up interview with author.
94 Bell, "Fitness Anyone?" 14.
95 King, interview with author.
96 Suzanne Bell, "Feeling Great: Fitness Anyone?" *Bolster*, April 1982, 11.
97 Walker, interview with author.
98 Booth, interview with author. Emphasis added.
99 Suzanne Bell, "Fat and Fit: Classes for Women," *Kinesis* (May 1984): n.p.
100 Berry, "'Naturally the Choice Is up to You'," 11.
101 Ingrid Laue, "Editor's Sphere," *Bolster*, February 1982, 1.
102 Ibid.
103 Mary Nemeth, "Body Obsession," *Maclean's*, 2 May 1994, 44–9.
104 King, interview with author.
105 Shari Stone-Mediatore as cited in Davis, *The Making of Our Bodies, Ourselves*, 133.
106 Nancy Theberge, "Sport and Women's Empowerment," *Women's Studies International Forum* 10, no. 4 (1987): 389.
107 Adam Lent, *British Social Movements since 1945: Sex, Colour, Peace, and Power* (New York: Palgrave, 2001), 189.
108 Ibid., 191.
109 Sandler, interview with author.
110 Gillingham, interview with author.
111 Cusack, interview with author.
112 Levasseur, interview with author.
113 Suzanne Bell, "Clothesline," *Bolster*, February 1983, 6.
114 Kelley, "Talent + Skill x Action = Suzanne Bell," 6.
115 Bell, interview with author.
116 Sal Thomson, "Fitness Circuit, *Bolster*, March 1983, 16.
117 Bell, interview with author.

118 Suzanne Bell's Fitness and Fashion Enlarged, "Largely Yours" (Newsletter), Fall 1985, Personal Papers of Suzanne Bell, 9.

119 Dal Santo, interview with author.

120 Walker, interview with author.

121 Margaret MacNeill, "Ideology, Media and Images of Active Women," in *Women, Sport and Culture*, ed. Susan Birrell and Cheryl Cole (Champaign, IL: Human Kinetics, 1994), 278.

122 Bordo, "Anorexia Nervosa," 88.

123 Sandler, interview with author.

124 Jody Sandler, "In Grand Form Low Impact Aerobics with Jody Sandler (video)," (Vancouver 1986), cover.

125 Balcom, "Here's a No-Frills Workout for Those Who'll Never Be a Fonda," E4; Gail Johnston, "Women on the Move," *Radiance*, Summer 1990, 44. Note that the author of this last article, Gail Johnston, went on to develop the *Curves* fitness franchise that is currently popular in the US and Canada.

126 Sandler, interview with author.

127 Three participants made unsolicited references to Fonda during their interviews. The "not Jane Fonda" reference also came out in a few press stories. See Balcom, "Here's a No-Frills Workout for Those Who'll Never Be a Fonda"; Canadian Press, "Fitness Goes over in a Big Way: Heavy Women Can Still Be Fit, Vancouver Instructor Preaches," *Toronto Star*, 24 February 1986; Alicia Priest, "No Small Feat for Full-Figured: Fears Can Finally Be Overcome," *Vancouver Sun*, 8 November 1988; King, interview with author; Sandler, interview with author; Vuksic, interview with author.

6 Bodies in Fashion: Buying and Selling Plus-Size Clothing

1 Letter from Cindy Proskow, Edmonton, to Jenny Ellison, Toronto, August 2006.

2 Canadian Press, "Here's Hope for Big Brides," *Toronto Star*, 30 January 1992, F2.

3 Joanne Entwistle, "Fashion and the Fleshy Body: Dress as Embodied Practice," *Fashion Theory* 4, no. 3 (2000): 341; Lauren Downing, "Fashionably Fatshionable: A Consideration of the Fashion Practices of Self-Proclaimed Fat Women" (master's thesis, Parsons New School of Art and Design, 2012), 82.

4 See for example Herbert Blumer, "Fashion: From Class Differentiation to Collective Selection," *Sociological Quarterly* 10, no. 3 (1969).

5 Entwistle, "Fashion and the Fleshy Body," 338.

6 Fred Davis, *Fashion, Culture and Identity* (Chicago: University of Chicago Press, 1992), 25.

7 Entwistle, "Fashion and the Fleshy Body," 334, 338.

8 Jennifer Craik, *The Face of Fashion: Cultural Studies in Fashion* (New York: Routledge, 1994), 2.

9 Jane Nicholas, *The Modern Girl: Feminine Modernities, The Body, and Commodities in the 1920s* (Toronto: University of Toronto Press, 2015), 9.

10 T. Eaton Co, "Fall–Winter Catalogue," 1920, 109.

11 T. Eaton Co, "Fall–Winter Catalogue," 1904–5, 27, 146.

12 Ibid., 146.

13 T. Eaton Co, "Fall–Winter Catalogue," 1884–5, 11.

14 T. Eaton Co, "Fall–Winter Catalogue," 1914–5, 29.

15 Ibid., 50. Dresses are the subject of discussion.

16 Ibid., 53. A black sateen petticoat is being described in this case.

17 Ibid., 98. Nemo corsets this time.

18 T. Eaton Co, "Fall–Winter Catalogue," 1920, 58, 68, 166.

19 T. Eaton Co, "Spring–Summer Catalogue," 1940, 77.

20 T. Eaton Co, "Fall–Winter Catalogue," 1945–6, 155.

21 T. Eaton Co, "Fall–Winter Catalogue," 1960–1, 45.

22 T. Eaton Co, "Spring–Summer Catalogue," 1970, 129.

23 T. Eaton Co, "Spring–Summer Catalogue," 1976, 115.

24 Angela Durante and Jenny Ellison, "The Body and Dress," in *The Encyclopedia of Fashion and Dress*, ed. Phyllis Tortora, vol. 3, *The United States and Canada*, (Oxford: Berg, 2010), 180.

25 T. Eaton Co, "Spring–Summer Catalogue," 116.

26 T. Eaton Co, "Spring–Summer Catalogue," 1956, 76.

27 This observation is made more difficult by inconsistent and overlapping sizing systems, that is, pants and bust sizes were measured in inches and dresses came in sizes ten through twenty-four and sweaters in small, medium, and large. Nonetheless, there was a clear shift towards offering "half-sizes" for larger women in the 1950s.

28 n.a., "Stout Women," *Time*, 4 June 1928, accessed 31 May 2012, http://www.time.com/time/magazine/article/0,9171,731870,00.html.

29 Lane Bryant, *The Style Book of Slenderizing Fashions* (New York: Lane Bryant, 1932).

30 n.a., "Stout Women."

31 n.a., "For the Pregnant and Plump," *Time*, 10 February 1947, accessed 31 May 2012, http://www.time.com/time/magazine/article/0,9171,854601,00.html.

32 Isadore Barmash, "Purchase of Lane Bryant Set," *New York Times*, 8 April 1982, D6.

33 Sol Armel, interview with author, digital recording (Toronto, ON, 18 May 2006).

34 Ibid.

35 Terry Poulton, "Plump Profits: By Dominating the Market in Oversized Women's Wear, Penningtons Is Living – Literally – off the Fat of the Land," *Canadian Business*, June 1978, 57.
36 Armel, interview with author.
37 Frances Phillips, "At Penningtons, It's Coming up Mostly Roses, Thank You," *Financial Post*, 12 June 1982, 1.
38 Poulton, "Plump Profits Penningtons," 57.
39 Phillips, "At Penningtons, It's Coming up Mostly Roses, Thank You," 1.
40 Ibid., 2.
41 Canadian Press, "Penningtons Gets New Life," *Calgary Herald*, 14 January 1995, D5.
42 Poulton, "Plump Profits Penningtons," 55.
43 In the early 1980s Poulton went on a very public diet, losing 60 pounds in six months and appearing on the cover of *Chatelaine*. Poulton later gave up dieting and published a book about her experiences and the dangers of dieting. See Terry Poulton, *No Fat Chicks: How Big Business Profits by Making Women Hate Their Bodies – and How to Fight Back* (Toronto: Birch Lane Press, 1998); "Chatelaine's 6-Month Slimdown Plan, Part One," *Chatelaine*, January 1982, 40–2, 96–100; "Fat Like Me," *Chatelaine*, September 1985, 87–8, 105–7.
44 Poulton, "Plump Profits Penningtons," 57.
45 Ibid., 54.
46 Margaret Burka, interview with author, digital recording (Toronto, ON, 14 February 2006).
47 Spring, interview with author.
48 Ellison, interview with author.
49 Bergeron, interview with author.
50 Kate Partridge, "Dear Friends," *Bolster*, September 1982, 3.
51 White, interview with author.
52 Max Konigsberg, *Max and Shirmax: More Than a Love Affair* (Montreal: Shirley K Holdings, 2006), 87.
53 Antels, "Big Is Beautiful at Antels," *Toronto Star*, 3 September 1981, B2.
54 Ingrid Laue, "Clothesline," *Bolster*, January 1982, 6; Ingrid Laue, "Clothesline: One Step Ahead," *Bolster*, May 1982, 7.
55 Mary Peacock, "The Fashion Industry Courts 'the Big Woman'," *Ms*, June 1980, 83–4; Jean Fraser, "Sizing up a New Market; Retailers Catering to Larger Women – at Last," *Edmonton Journal*, 30 August 1994, C2; Karen Schwartz, "Larger Women Finally Get Gift of Fashion Freedom," *Vancouver Sun*, 7 December 1989, C4; Rebecca Howard, "Designers Target Large Women,"*Ottawa Citizen*, 12 November 1992, H2.
56 Renee Doruyter, "A Plus for Large-Sized People: Easy Wear and East Care Hallmarks of New Stores," *Province*, 22 August 1991, 53.

57 n.a., "Report on Business Index: Company News," *Globe and Mail*, 9 November 1995, B1; Michael Prentice, "Giant Zellers Store out to Prove Bigger is Better; Gatineau Becomes Battlefield for Retail Giants," *Ottawa Citizen*, 11 November 1995, E15; Shirley Won, "Low Prices Bring High Profits at Zellers; The Jewel in the Hudson's Bay Crown," *Gazette*, 4 February 1991, B8.

58 Marie Tison, "Reitmans Closes Two Divisions," *Calgary Herald*, 18 June 1999, E12.

59 Partridge, interview with author.

60 Spring, interview with author.

61 Masterton, interview with author; Kate Partridge and Lynn Warnock, "Program for May 5, 1984: Largely Fashion: A Fashion Survival Workshop for Large Women," 5 May 1984. Personal Collection of the Author.

62 White, interview with author.

63 Burka, interview with author; Walker, interview with author.

64 Jaffe as cited in Downing, "Fashionably Fatshionable," 56.

65 Mindlin, interview with author.

66 White, interview with author.

67 Lynn Burzese, interview with author, digital recording (Toronto, ON, 11 April 2006); Savage, interview with author; White, interview with author.

68 Bell, interview with author; Bergeron, interview with author; Cusack, interview with author; Walker, interview with author.

69 Burka, interview with author.

70 Masterton, interview with author.

71 Bergeron, interview with author.

72 Gillingham, interview with author.

73 King, interview with author.

74 Savage, interview with author.

75 Brumberg, *The Body Project*.

76 Konigsberg, *Max and Shirmax*, 86–7.

77 Masterton, interview with author.

78 Mindlin, interview with author.

79 Ibid.

80 McKay-Panos, interview with author.

81 Bell, interview with author.

82 Donaldson, interview with author.

83 Spring, "Let's Go Shopping!," 9.

84 *Canada WYDE*, "CW Marketplace," *Canada WYDE*, Summer 1996, 12; *Canada WYDE*, "Marketplace," *Canada WYDE*, Fall/Winter 1997, 2; *Canada WYDE*, "Shopping, Shopping, Shopping!" *Canada WYDE*, Fall 1996, 13; Large as Life Calgary, "Large Size Fashions Resource List," *Large*

as Life Newsletter, March 1983, 10; Large as Life Clothing Committee, "Clothesline," *Bolster*, June 1982, 9–10.

85 King, interview with author.

86 Donaldson, interview with author.

87 Palmer, *Couture & Commerce: The Transatlantic Fashion Trade in the 1950s*, 4.

88 Ibid., 220.

89 Davis, *Fashion, Culture and Identity*, 164.

90 Linda Welters, "The Natural Look: American Style in the 1970s," *Fashion Theory* 12, no. 4 (2008): 495.

91 Ross, "How Lavender Jane Loved Women: Re-Figuring Identity-Based Life/Stylism in 1970s Lesbian Feminism," 111.

92 Charland and Turcotte, interview with author.

93 Valerie Steele, "Anti-Fashion: The 1970s," *Fashion Theory* 1, no. 3 (1997): 280.

94 Davis, *Fashion, Culture and Identity*, 161, 164.

95 Ibid., 175.

96 Mary Dahonick, interview with author, digital recording (Toronto, ON, 13 February 2006).

97 Ellison, interview with author.

98 Ingrid Laue, "Clothesline," *Bolster*, January 1982, 8.

99 Lori Wilson, "Menswear: Big and Colourful," *Bolster*, March 1984, 12.

100 Pretty Porky and Pissed Off, "Queen Sized Revolt," 22–3. Emphasis in original.

101 LeBesco, *Revolting Bodies*, 68.

102 Ibid., 70–2.

103 Downing, "Fashionably Fatshionable," 17.

104 n.a., "Fashion," *Bolster*, October 1981, 6.

105 Gail Bell, "Outward Appearances," *Bolster*, December 1981, 7.

106 Booth booked a few models around Vancouver in the mid-1980s. She eventually shut down her operation because it was not as profitable as she had hoped. Booth also felt some ambivalence about whether it was fair to allow women to think they could model because there was not enough demand in Vancouver. Booth, follow-up interview with author.

107 "Fabulous Fall Fashions for Big Beautiful Women," *Bolster*, September 1982, 12.

108 Dal Santo, interview with author.

109 Colls, "Big Girls Having Fun," 18.

110 Entwistle, "Fashion and the Fleshy Body: Dress as Embodied Practice," 327, 337.

111 Laue, interview with author; Dal Santo, interview with author; Partridge, interview with author.

112 Bell, "Outward Appearances," 8.

113   Walker, interview with author.

114   Ibid.

115   Dal Santo, interview with author.

116   Ibid.

117   Burka, interview with author; Sieben-Kuhn, interview with author.

118   Cindy Proskow, *Big & Beautiful Fashions Show*, c. 1980.

119   Jean-Francois Lyotard, *The Postmodern Condition: A Report on Knowledge*, trans. Geoff Bennington and Brian Massumi (1979; repr., Minneapolis: University of Minnesota Press, 2002), 46. Lyotard argues that performativity governs "truth" in a postmodern society. The more proof you produce, the more right you are.

120   Downing, "Fashionably Fatshionable," 17.

121   Kate Partridge and Lynn Warnock, "Largely Fashion: A Fashion Survival Workshop for Large Women (pamphlet)," (Vancouver: Large as Life Action Group, 5 May 1984). Personal collection of the author.

122   Partridge and Warnock, "Program for May 5, 1984: Largely Fashion: A Fashion Survival Workshop for Large Women."

123   Mary Peacock, "The Comfortable Shoe Guide," *Ms* (1982): 10; Trucia Kushner, "Finding a Personal Style," *Ms* 2, no. 8 (1974): 45; Laurie Stone, "Personal Style: Browsing in Boys' Wear," *Ms* 9 (1981): 14; Linda Ellerbee, "Personal Style: Someday My Look Will Come," *Ms* 15, no. 5 (1986): 36; Julianne Malveaux, "Suitably Attired," *Ms* 16 (1988): 38–9.

124   Partridge and Warnock, "Program for May 5, 1984: Largely Fashion: A Fashion Survival Workshop for Large Women." Emphasis in original.

125   Ibid.

126   Carol Pierce, "Clothesline: Ample Jeans," *Bolster*, May 1982, 9.

127   "Advertisement for Second Time Around," *Bolster*, October 1981, 5.

128   "Advertisement for Of Grand Design by Jan Mindlin," *Bolster*, December 1981, 16.

129   "Advertisement for Alex's Mistress," *Bolster*, May 1982, 10.

130   "Advertisement for Southlands Ladies Wear," *Bolster*, December 1982, 9.

131   "Advertisement for Jaegal's Fashions," *Bolster*, May 1983, 5. Many of these ads appeared more than once. With the exception of Jan Mindlin, I was not able to track any of these retailers.

132   "Advertisement for S.O.F.I. 'Omar the Tentmaker'," *Bolster*, March 1983, 7.

133   Letter from Indrid Laue, North Vancouver, to Jenny Ellison, Toronto, 30 June 2007.

134   Valerie Steele, ed., *Encyclopedia of Clothing and Fashion* (New York: Thomson Gale, 2005), xvi.

135   I did not interview any retailers from east of Toronto, despite attempts to contact stores in these parts of Canada. One of my criteria was that the stores had some longevity – I was looking for retailers who had opened in the

1980s and had survived changes in the retail landscape. This was an indicator that a retailer had built a successful formula. Stores that came and went within a span of a few years were difficult to track down and did not have as significant an impact on a community as the stores that were open for a long period of time. They may have existed, but my search through listings of plus-size retailers did not yield any results. This is a topic for further inquiry, pointing to regional economic and population differences in Canada.

136   Kathy Peiss, *Hope in a Jar: The Making of American Beauty Culture* (New York: Metropolitan Books, 1998), 78.
137   Mindlin, interview with author.
138   Burzese, interview with author.
139   Lynne Schneider, interview with author, digital recording (Winnipeg, MB, 13 July 2006).
140   Sieben-Kuhn, interview with author.
141   Bell, interview with author; Suzanne Bell's Fashions, *Suzanne Bell's Fashions by Mail Fall and Winter Catalogue*, vol. Fall/Winter 1994/1995 (Vancouver: Suzanne Bell's Fashions, 1994).
142   Greg Burns, "Clothier Caters to Forgotten Women," *Chicago Sun-Times*, 30 March 1986, 2; Donna Steph Hansard, "Fashioning a Niche in Retailing: Large-Size-Apparel Chain Finding Sizable Demand," *Dallas Morning News*, 30 November 1986, 1H.
143   Schneider, interview with author.
144   Burka, interview with author.
145   Ibid., Bell, interview with author.
146   Sieben-Kuhn, interview with author.
147   Schneider, interview with author.
148   Mindlin, interview with author.
149   Cindy Proskow, interview with author, digital recording (Edmonton, AB, 25 July 2006).
150   Burka, interview with author.
151   Burzese, interview with author; Ellison, interview with author; White, interview with author.
152   Bell, interview with author.
153   Ibid.
154   Suzanne Bell's Fashions, *Suzanne Bell's Fashions by Mail Fall and Winter Catalogue*, Fall/Winter 1994/1995. This chart is a reproduction of one that appeared in inserts to Suzanne Bell's mail-order catalogues.
155   Bell, interview with author.
156   Marilyn Goneau, "SOFI Brings Fashion to a Large-Sized Market Niche," *Small Business Magazine*, c.1983, 8–9, SOFI press clippings file. A program called Sault Enterprising Women held a seminar on LEAP in 1979, which Burzese attended. Burzese secured $52,000 to develop a business plan.

She then received two subsequent LEAP grants, $250,000 in 1981 and $203,000 in 1982–3.

157 Beverly Bowen, "SOFI for Large Sizes," *Globe and Mail*, 12 October 1982, F2.

158 Canadian Press, "Designer Creates Clothes for Larger-Sized Women," *Gazette*, 23 November 1982. SOFI agents eventually began to travel to Toronto, Montreal, and Chicago to sell their clothes at wholesaling shows. The company suffered what Burzese considered a premature death, when the bank foreclosed on the company. Despite promising sales to independent retailers in Canada and the United States in 1983–4, the company was cash poor. Complications regarding the original government funding of the company made it impossible to privatize SOFI. Debbie Shuchat went on to design her own line, which was available through Proskow's Big & Beautiful in Edmonton.

159 Colls, "Big Girls Having Fun," 18.

160 Bell, interview with author; Laue, interview with author.

161 Proskow, interview with author.

162 Bell, interview with author.

163 Proskow, interview with author.

164 Sieben-Kuhn, interview with author.

165 Ellison, follow-up interview with author.

166 White, interview with author.

167 Ibid.

168 Helena Spring, "A New Beginning for the Size Acceptance Movement in Canada," *Canada WYDE*, Spring 1996, 1–2.

169 Burka, interview with author.

170 Proskow, interview with author.

171 Schneider, interview with author.

172 Of the retailers I interviewed, Suzanne Bell's Fashions Vancouver, Big & Beautiful Edmonton, Full Bloom Winnipeg, and Full Figure Fashions of Calgary were or are located outside of common fashion districts. They were in more remote sections of the city, away from other retailers of any kind.

173 Schneider, interview with author.

174 Downing, "Fashionably Fatshionable," 60.

175 Burka, interview with author.

176 Armel, interview with author.

177 Sieben-Kuhn, interview with author.

178 Burka, interview with author.

179 Proskow, interview with author.

180 Schneider, interview with author.

181 Craik, *The Face of Fashion*, 44.

182 Alison Lurie, *The Language of Clothes* (Toronto: Random House, 1981), 210.

183 Ibid., 225.

184 Judith P. Butler, "Performative Acts and Gender Constitution: An Essay in Phenomenology and Feminist Theory" in *Feminist Theory Reader: Local and Global Perspectives*, ed. C. McCann and S.K. Kim (New York: Routledge, 2003), 415.
185 Judith P. Butler, *Gender Trouble* (New York: Routledge, 1999), 181.
186 Butler, *Bodies that Matter*, 2.
187 Scott, *Fresh Lipstick: Redressing Fashion and Feminism*, 1; Elizabeth Wilson, "Fashion and the Postmodern Body," in *Chic Thrills: A Fashion Reader*, ed. Elizabeth Wilson and Juliet Ash (Berkeley: University of California Press 1993), 9.
188 Wilson, "Fashion and the Postmodern Body," 10.
189 Wilson, "Fashion and the Postmodern Body," 10; Craik, *The Face of Fashion*; Davis, *Fashion, Culture and Identity*.
190 Ingrid Laue, "Forum: Go for Quality," *Bolster*, May 1983.
191 Masterton, interview with author.
192 Davis, *Fashion, Culture and* Identity, 25.

Conclusion: When We Rise the Earth Will Shake

1 Nicholas, *The Modern Girl*; Andrée Lévesque, *Making and Breaking the Rules: Women in Quebec, 1919–1939*, trans. Yvonne M. Klein (Toronto: McLelland and Stewart, 1989).
2 Cooper 2016, 144; Murray 2005.
3 Butler, *Bodies That Matter*, 21.
4 After being cancelled in 2001, ParticipACTION was relaunched, and refocused on Canada's "inactivity and obesity crisis" in 2007. Canadian federal government bodies have also undertaken at least two extended studies on the matter. Both studies outline rising rates of obesity; estimated economic costs of obesity; and outlined individual, local, and public health strategies to reduce and prevent obesity. Since 2006, public funds have also been dedicated to founding a professional network and conferences of the Canadian Obesity Network (CON) that claims a membership of thirteen thousand people. In addition to national funding, numerous local and provincial projects have launched to combat obesity. See National Post, "Ottawa Revives ParticipACTION Campaign to Promote Fitness," *National Post*, 17 February 2007, A10; Participaction, "For Immediate Release: ParticipACTION Launches National Movement to Move," press release, 15 October 2007, http://files.participaction.com/pressreleases/en/participactionnr.pdf; Public Health Agency of Canada and Canadian Institute for Health Information, "Obesity in Canada: A Joint Report from the Public Health

Agency of Canada and the Canadian Institute for Health Information," (Ottawa 2011); Standing Senate Committee on Social Affairs, Science and Technology, Report, *Obesity in Canada: A Whole-of-Society Approach for a Healthier Canada*; Obesity Canada, accessed 4 October 2019, http://www.obesitynetwork.ca/pro-home. See for example Natalie Beausoleil and Pamela Ward, "Fat Panic in Canadian Public Health Policy: Obesity as Different and Unhealthy," *Radical Psychology*, 8, no. 1 (2010). Accessed 10 November 2015.

5 Paradis, "'Obesity' as Process," 64.

6 Gard, "Hearing Noises and Noticing Silence: A Short History of Canadian Bodyweight Statistics."

7 In 1988 an "Expert Group Convened by Health Promotion Directorate, Health Services and Promotion Branch" on weight released a report, the purpose of which was to "establish appropriate, realistic weights which relate to positive body image." Included in this report was a BMI nomogram that looks quite different from the 2003 guidelines currently in use by Health Canada. The 1988 table includes zones (A through D) that correspond with different BMI ranges. Rather than having firm lines and divisions, weight ranges are indicated by an arrow. Zone A, classified as a BMI under 20, "may be associated with health problems for some people," Zone B, BMI 20–25 represents a "Good weight for most people" and Zone C "may lead to health problems in some people" and Zone D indicates an "increasing risk of developing health problems." The 2003 table's numbers are lower and also indicate firmer dividing lines between the weight categories. The language has also shifted to a more normative and definitive division. Gone is the relativism of the 1988 chart, replaced with the categories of "Underweight," "Normal Weight," "Overweight," and "Obese" classes I through III. Health Canada, *Canadian Guidelines for Healthy Weights: Report of an Expert Group Convened by Health Promotion Directorate, Health Services and Promotion Branch*: 5.

8 Michael Gard, "Truth, Belief and the Cultural Politics of Obesity Scholarship and Public Health Policy," *Critical Public Health* 21, no. 1 (2011): 37.

Appendix A: Research Methods

1 Deborah Lupton, *Fat* (New York: Routledge, 2013), 88.

2 Smith, *The Everyday World*, 18.

3 Marjorie L. Devault, "Talking and Listening from Women's Standpoint: Feminist Strategies for Interviewing and Analysis," *Social Problems* 37, no. 1 (February 1990): 104.

4 Judith Stacey, "Can There Be a Feminist Ethnography?," in *Women's Words: The Feminist Practice of Oral History*, ed. Sherna Berger Gluck and Daphne Patai (New York: Routledge, 1991), 113.

5 Manjit Bola, "Questions of Legitimacy? The Fit between Researcher and Researched," *Feminism and Psychology* 5, no. 2 (1995): 290–303.

6 Studies from the 1990s show that black and Hispanic women in the United States are more likely to be "obese" than Caucasian women, suggesting that body weight has overlapping ethnic and class dimensions. Others argue that black people are more accepting of thickness and women and so the problem of "overweight" is culturally white. Another group argues that weight is an issue for African Americans and the idea that it is culturally acceptable to be a fat black woman is a myth. Michael Fumento, *The Fat of the Land: The Obesity Epidemic and How Overweight Americans Can Help Themselves* (New York: Penguin, 1997), 104; Mitchell and Mitchell, *Livin' Large*, 3; Avner Offer, "Body Weight and Self-Control in the US and Britain since the 1950s," *The Society for the Social History of Medicine* 14, no. 1 (2001); Retha Powers, "Fat Is a Black Woman's Issue," 75; Tamara Beauboeuf-Lafontant, "Strong and Large Black Women? Exploring Relationships between Deviant Womanhood and Weight," *Gender & Society* 17, no. 1 (February 2003): 111–21.

Bibliography

Primary Sources

Archival Sources

THE ARQUIVES (FORMERLY THE CANADIAN GAY AND LESBIAN ARCHIVES),
TORONTO, ONTARIO.
Christine Donald Papers, CLGA 2006-090/1 Shelf 20.1.2.

CANADIAN WOMEN'S MOVEMENT ARCHIVES, OTTAWA, ONTARIO
Bolster: Large as Life newsletter, 1981–3.
CWMA X10-1 Box 39, *Hersize newsletters*.
CWMA X10-1 Box 72, *Bulletin: National Eating Disorder Information Centre.*
Healthsharing newsletter, 1979–93.

LE CENTRE DE DOCUMENTATION SUR L'ÉDUCATION DES ADULTES ET LA
CONDITION FÉMININE (CDÉACF), MONTREAL, QUEBEC
Amazones d'hier, lesbiennes d'aujourd'hui, vol. 5, no 3.
Amazones d'hier, lesbiennes d'aujourd'hui, no. 23.

JUNE L. MAZER LESBIAN ARCHIVES, LOS ANGELES, CALIFORNIA
Judy Freespirit Papers, 1971–93, LSC.1956

LESBIAN HERSTORY ARCHIVES, BROOKLYN, NEW YORK
Fat Liberation subject files.
Michigan Womyn's Music Festival, SP Coll 2005–17.

LIBRARY AND ARCHIVES CANADA, OTTAWA, ONTARIO
Canada WYDE newsletter, 1990 to 1996, PER.REG.1996.578.
Hersize: A Weight Prejudice Action Group (newsletter), vol. 1, no. 1, J-115-3

Initiative: The Self-Help Newsletter, Canadian Council on Social Development, 1984–92, A-23-6.

NELLIE LANGFORD ROWELL LIBRARY, YORK UNIVERSITY, TORONTO, CANADA
Radiance, 1985–2000.

YORK UNIVERSITY ARCHIVES, TORONTO, CANADA
T. Eaton Co. *Fall–Winter and Spring–Summer catalogues*, 1884–1976.

SCHLESINGER LIBRARY, RADCLIFFE INSTITUTE FOR ADVANCED STUDY, HARVARD UNIVERSITY, BOSTON, MASSACHUSETTS
Judith Stein Fonds 2005-MIS8.

SIMON FRASER UNIVERSITY ARCHIVES, BURNABY, BRITISH COLUMBIA
Simon Fraser University Women's Centre Fonds, newsletter, 1976–82 (F-40-5-8-0-4).

WINNIPEG WOMEN'S HEALTH CLINIC LIBRARY, WINNIPEG, MANITOBA
Bentley, Caryl B. "Meeting Lisa." *Inciter,* 1980.
Brown, Catrina. *Getting beyond Weight: Women Helping Women, a How-To Manual about the Development and Operation of Self Help Groups for Women Preoccupied with Weight*, n.d.
Fat Lip Readers Theatre (video). *Nothing to Lose*, 1989.
L'obsession de la minceur: Un guide d'intervention, Centre des femmes de Verdun, 1991.
The Womanly Times: Women's Health Clinic newsletter, 1985.

Personal and Private Collections

ANONYMOUS DONOR
Toronto General Hospital Political Group Records.

SUZANNE BELL
Scrapbook.
Suzanne Bell's *Coming Attractions*.
Suzanne Bell's Fashion Catalogue.
Images from Suzanne Bell's Fitness and Fashion.

LYNN BURSEZE
SOFI press Clippings File.

CALGARY STATUS OF WOMEN ACTION COMMITTEE, CALGARY, ALBERTA.
Fat Issues file.

LE CENTRE D'AIDES TECHNIQUES (CDAT), MONTREAL, QUEBEC
Aide aux personnes obèses handicapées du Québec press clippings file.
Lettres patentes for APOHQ

MARY FRANCES ELLISON
Videotape of "Midday [Toronto]," CBC Television, 2 January 1990.

WILLIAM J. FABREY
NAAFA Convention Speech, 1980.
Personal Communication with Llewellyn Louderback, 1968.
What is NAAFA pamphlet, 1969.

SANDRA FRIEDMAN
Maranda-Friedman workshop flyers.

DORIS MARANDA
Maranda-Friedman press clippings file.

KATE PARTRIDGE
"A Redefinition of Treatment Goals for Obesity." Paper presented at the
    Canadian Psychological Association Section on Women and Psychology,
    Montreal 1982.
Audio recording of interview with Kate Partridge and Joan Dal Santo by Stan
    Peters and Ann Mitchell, "CBC Radio Noon [Vancouver]," CBC Radio,
    15 September 1981.
Bolster, September 1983 to November 1984.
Large as Life Calgary newsletters, 1982–84.
Notes for "Largely Fashion: A Fashion Survival Workshop for Large Women,"
    1984.
"obesity: facts & fiction." Vancouver: Large as Life Association, 1984.
YWCA Fitness Leadership course notes, 1981.

CINDY PROSKOW
Photographs from "Big & Beautiful," Edmonton, c. 1979–90.
Video of Big & Beautiful fashion show, Edmonton, Alberta, c. 1981.

JODY SANDLER
In Grand Form press clippings file.
In Grand Form fitness (video), 1986.

HELENA SPRING
"Foxy Fables and Facts about Dieting" (pamphlet), NEDIC, 1996.

ELLEN TALLMAN
Cold Mountain Health Retreat course guide.
Cold Mountain Journal

LOUISE TURCOTTE
Amazones d'hier lesbiennes d'aujourd'hui, vol. 2, no. 4.
Amazones d'hier lesbiennes d'aujourd'hui, vol. 3, no. 2–3.
Amazones d'hier lesbiennes d'aujourd'hui, vol. 3, no. 4.
Amazones d'hier lesbiennes d'aujourd'hui, vol. 4, no. 1.
Amazones d'hier lesbiennes d'aujourd'hui, vol. 4, no. 3.
Amazones d'hier lesbiennes d'aujourd'hui, no. 21.

PERSONAL COMMUNICATIONS
William J. Fabrey, re: NAAFA USA.
Cindy Proskow, re: Big & Beautiful, Edmonton, Alberta.
Lynda Gardiner, re: Your Perfect Weight workshops, Calgary, Alberta.
Barry Gang, The College of Psychologists of Ontario, re: David Garner.
Ingrid Laue, re: Large as Life Vancouver.

PERSONAL COLLECTION OF THE AUTHOR
Amazones d'hier lesbiennes d'aujourd'hui, vol. 1, no 1.
Calgary Board of Education. *Spring 1983 Program Calendar.*
Hersize records.
"YMCA Fitness Leader's Basic Theory Manual." Toronto: YMCA Canada, 1999.

Interviews

Armel, Sol. Interview with author, digital recording. Toronto, Ontario, 18 May
    2006.
Atkins, Terryl. Interview with author, digital recording. Kamloops, British
    Columbia, 12 August 2006.
Beauchamp, André. Interview with author, digitial recording. Montreal,
    Quebec, 25 May 2006.
Bell, Suzanne. Interview with author, digital recording. New Westminster,
    British Columbia, 4 October 2005.
– Follow-up interview, digital recording. New Westminster, British Columbia,
    16 August 2006.
Bergeron, Lise. Interview with author, digital recording. Montreal, Quebec,
    23 May 2006.
Booth, Evelyn. Interview with author, digital recording. North Vancouver,
    British Columbia, 11 October 2005.

– Follow-up interview with author, digital recording. Vancouver, British Columbia, 12 August 2006.

Boschman, Lorna R. Interview with author, digital recording. 30 April 2012.

Bulcock, Pat [Donaldson *aka* Nokomis]. Interview with author, digital recording. Empress, Alberta, 25 July 2006.

Burka, Margaret. Interview with author, digital recording. Toronto, Ontario, 14 February 2006.

Burzese, Lynn. Interview with author, digital recording. Toronto, Ontario, 11 April 2006.

Carter, Jessica. Interview with author, digital recording. Toronto, Ontario, 16 January 2006.

Charland, Michèle, and Louise Turcotte. Interview with author, digital recording. Montreal, Québec, 22 October 2006.

Ciliska, Donna. Interview with author, digital recording. Hamilton, Ontario, 11 January 2006.

Cusack, Joyce. Interview with author, digital recording. Calgary, Alberta, 21 July 2006.

Dahonick, Mary. Interview with author, digital recording. Toronto, Ontario, 13 February 2006.

Dal Santo, Joan [O'Brien]. Interview with author, digital recording. Sechelt, British Columbia, 7 October 2005.

Dykewomon, Elana. Interview with author, digital recording. San Francisco, California, 22 March 2008.

Ellison, Mary Frances. Interview with author, digital recording. Toronto, Ontario, 15 December 2005.

– Follow-up interview with author, digital recording. Toronto, Ontario, 25 January 2006.

Fiander, Runa. Interview with author, digital recording. Victoria, British Columbia, 2 August 2006.

Friedman, Sandra. Interview with author, digital recording. Sechelt, British Columbia, 7 October 2005.

Gillingham, Ruth. Interview with author, digital recording. Prince Albert, Saskatchewan, 27 July 2006.

Grace, Dr. David Michael Interview with author, digital recording. London, Ontario, 10 April 2006.

Grauer, Lynne. Interview with author, digital recording. Burnaby, British Columbia, 8 August 2006.

Henley, Kaca. Interview with author, digital recording. Lindsay, Ontario, 8 March 2006.

King, Sarah. Interview with author, digital recording. North Vancouver, British Columbia, 12 October 2005.

Laue, Ingrid. Interview with author, digital recording. North Vancouver, British Columbia, 3 October 2005.

Levasseur, Julie. Interview with author, digital recording. Winnipeg, Manitoba, 14 July 2006.

Maranda, Doris. Interview with author, digital recording. Vancouver, British Columbia, 14 August 2006.

Masterton, Susan. Interview with author, digital recording. North Vancouver, British Columbia, 11 October 2005.

McKay-Panos, Linda. Interview with author, digital recording. Calgary, Alberta, 18 July 2006.

Mindlin, Jan. Interview with author, digital recording. Burnaby, British Columbia, 20 August 2006.

Norman, Trudy. Interview with author, digital recording. Victoria, British Columbia, 3 August 2006.

Partridge, Kate. Interview with author, digital recording. Crediton, Ontario, 20 September 2005.

– Follow-up Interview with author, digital recording. Exeter, Ontario, 16 April 2006.

Peat, Carol. Interview with author, digital recording. London, Ontario, 17 June 2006.

Proskow, Cindy. Interview with author, digital recording. Edmonton, Alberta, 25 July 2006.

Raino, Lynda. Interview with author, digital recording. Victoria, British Columbia, 10 October 2005.

Rankin, Pauline. Interview with author, digital recording. Vancouver, British Columbia, 21 August 2005.

Sandler, Jody. Interview with author, digital recording. North Vancouver, British Columbia, 5 October 2005.

Savage, Claudia. Interview with author, digital recording. Burnaby, British Columbia, 17 August 2006.

Schneider, Lynne. Interview with author, digital recording. Winnipeg, Manitoba, 13 July 2006.

Scriver, Amanda. Interview with author, digital recording. Toronto, Ontario, 22 May 2015.

Sieben-Kuhn, Monica. Interview with author, digital recording. Calgary, Alberta, 20 July 2006.

Siegler, Andria. Interview with author, digital recording. Toronto, Ontario, 7 June 2006.

Smith, Lois. Interview with author, digital recording. New Westminster, British Columbia, 9 August 2006.

Spring, Helena. Interview with author, digital recording. Toronto, Ontario, 5 January 2006.

Stein, Judith. Interview with author, digital recording. Cambridge, Massachusetts, 14 April 2012.

Tallman, Ellen. Interview with author, digital recording. Vancouver, British Columbia, 12 October 2005.

Thaw, Laura. Interview with author, digital recording. Surrey, British Columbia, 6 October 2005.

Vail, Diann. Interview with author, digital recording. London, Ontario 13 April 2006.

Vuksic, Nada. Interview with author, digital recording. Vancouver, British Columbia, 14 August 2006.

Walker, Janet. Interview with author, digital recording. White Rock, British Columbia, 6 October 2005.

White, Susan. Interview with author, digital recording. Winnipeg, Manitoba, 11 July 2006.

Zatylny, Anne. Interview with author, digital recording. Toronto, Ontario, 20 June 2006.

Other Primary Sources

"'Activités-soleil,' une initiée de l'aide aux obèses handicapées: De jeunes obèses de 10 a 15 ans apprennent a vivre sainement." *Journal de Montréal*, 29 July–4 August 1979, 18.

Antels. "Big Is Beautiful at Antels." *Toronto Star*, 3 September 1981, B2.

Associated Press. "Big Girls: U.K. Housewife Campaigns for Fashion in Outsized Clothes." *Globe and Mail*, 11 November 1966, 13.

Balcom, Susan. "Here's a No-Frills Workout for Those Who'll Never Be a Fonda." *Vancouver Sun*, 20 November 1986, E4.

Barmash, Isadore. "Purchase of Lane Bryant Set." *New York Times*, 8 April 1982, D6.

Bartel, Pauline. "Women at Large – Empathy Is Key to Helping 'Fluffy Ladies' Regain Esteem." *St Petersburg Times*, 5 April 1987, 6F.

Bastien, Mark. "Fat People Fight Back." *Toronto Star*, 27 October 1990, H2.

Bédard, Marie-Louise. "Gilles Leblanc: Vous, les bourreaux des obèses." *La semaine: Le magazine de l'actualité*, 22 October 1983, 36–7.

Bell, Suzanne. "Fat and Fit: Classes for Women." *Kinesis*, May 1984, n.p.

Berthault, Madelaine. "Des insultes pour les obèses." *La Presse*, 23 July 1979, A3.

Bot, Ellen. "Hope for Full Figured Model." *Toronto Star*, 24 July 1986, H5.

Bowen, Beverly. "SOFI for Large Sizes." *Globe and Mail*, 12 October 1982, F2.

Bragg, Rebecca. "Fat, Fashionable Woman Shares Tips on Beauty." *Toronto Star*, 5 October 1989, L3.

Burns, Greg. "Clothier Caters to Forgotten Women." *Chicago Sun-Times*, 30 March 1986, 2.

Canada Fitness Survey. *Fitness and Lifestyle in Canada: A Report*. Ottawa: Fitness and Amateur Sport Canada, 1983.

Canada Fitness Survey. *Changing Times: Women and Physical Activity*. Ottawa: Fitness and Amateur Sport Canada, 1984.

Canadian Council on Nutrition, The. "A Dietary Standard for Canada" *Canadian Bulletin on Nutrition* 6, no. 1 (1963): 1–77.

Canadian Press. "444-Pound Man Loses 16 Pounds on Hunger Strike." *Globe and Mail*, 18 January 1978, 14.

– "Designer Creates Clothes for Larger-Sized Women." *Gazette*, 23 November 1982, D8.

– "Fitness Goes over in a Big Way: Heavy Women Can Still Be Fit, Vancouver Instructor Preaches." *Toronto Star*, 24 February 1986, D7.

– "Here's Hope for Big Brides." *Toronto Star*, 30 January 1992, F2.

– "Participaction Seeks New CEO to Re-Launch Federal Fitness Program." *CBC.ca*. 13 December 2006. http://www.cbc.ca/news/health/story /2006/12/13/participaction.html.

– "Penningtons Gets New Life." *Calgary Herald*, 14 January 1995, D5.

Ciliska, Donna. *Beyond Dieting: Psychoeducational Interventions for Chronically Obese Women: A Non-Dieting Approach*. New York: Brunner/Mazel Publishers, 1990.

Clark, Brad. "The Corpulent '90s: A New Health Program Suggests It's All Right to Be 'Big.'" *Alberta Report*, 18 February 1991, 44.

Combahee River Collective. "A Black Feminist Statement." In *Feminist Theory Reader: Local and Global Perspectives*, edited by Carole McCann and Seung-Kyung Kim, 164–71. New York: Routledge, 2003. First published 1977.

Cooper, Charlotte. "A Queer and Trans Fat Activist Timeline: Queering Fat Activist Nationality and Cultural Imperialism." *Fat Studies* 1 (2012): 61–74. https://doi.org/10.1080/21604851.2012.627503.

– "Queering Fat Activism: Burger Queen." Obesity Timebomb (blog). 9 April 2011. Accessed 23 January 2013. http://obesitytimebomb.blogspot. ca/2011/04/queering-fat-activism-burger-queen.html.

"Curves Have Their Day in Park; 500 at a 'Fat-in' Call for Obesity." *New York Times*, 5 June 1967, 54.

Dancel, François. *Obesity, or Excessive Corpulence: The Various Causes and the Rational Means of Cure*. Translated by Michael Barrett. Toronto: W.C. Chewett, King Street East, 1864. Available from the Canadian Institute for Historical Microreproduction.

de Beauvoir, Simone. "The Second Sex: Introduction." In *Feminist Theory Reader: Local and Global Perspectives*, edited by Carole McCann and Seung-Kyung Kim, 32–40. New York: Routledge, 2003.

Donald, Christine. *The Fat Woman Measures Up*. Charlottetown, PEI: Ragweed Press, 1986.

Downey, Maureen. "Fat People's Advocacy Group Battles Attitudes." *Atlanta Constitution*, 8 September 1987, D1.

– "'Women at Large' Helps Bodies and Self-Images." *Atlanta Constitution*, 13 October 1986, B1.

Ellerbee, Linda. "Personal Style: Someday My Look Will Come." *Ms* 15, no. 5 (1986): 36.

Fat Underground, The. "More Women Are on Diets Than in Jail." *Sister*, November 1974.

Fonda, Jane. *Jane Fonda's Workout Book*. New York: Simon and Schuster, 1981.

Forrest, Diane. "Stop the Diet, We Want to Get Off! These Large Women Learn to Quit Worrying about Their Weight and Start Living Their Lives." *Canadian Living*, January 1993, 48–52.

"For the Pregnant and Plump." *Time*, 10 February 1947.

Friscolanti, Michael. "Flyer Celebrates 'Significant Victory for Obese People.'" *National Post*, 13 December 2001, A2.

Fulford, Robert. "The Second Revolt of 'Modern' Women." *Maclean's*, 25 July 1954, 7–9, 42–4.

"Gilles Leblanc remplace la marche par le sit-in." *Le devoir*, 25 juillet 1979.

Hampton, Edna. "Diet Success Story." *Globe and Mail*, 23 April 1969, 11.

Hannah, Sharon Bas. "Naomi Cohen Choked on the Culture." *Sister*, September 1974, 1.

Hansard, Donna Steph. "Fashioning a Niche in Retailing: Large-Size-Apparel Chain Finding Sizable Demand." *Dallas Morning News*, 30 November 1986, 1H.

Health Canada. BMI Nomogram. Accessed 12 December 2011. http://www.hc-sc.gc.ca/fn-an/nutrition/weights-poids/guide-ld-adult/bmi_chart_java-graph_imc_java-eng.php.

Health Services and Promotion Branch. *Canadian Guidelines for Healthy Weights: Report of an Expert Group Convened by Health Promotion Directorate, Health Services and Promotion Branch*. Ottawa: Health and Welfare Canada, 1988.

Health Services and Promotion Branch. *Promoting Healthy Weights: A Discussion Paper*. Ottawa: Health and Welfare Canada, 1988.

Hobbs, Anna. "Big Can Be Beautiful: Solving Fashion Problems When You're Size 16 and Up." *Canadian Living*, August 1982, 84–90.

Hope, Jackqueline. *Big, Bold and Beautiful*. Toronto: Macmillan Canada, 1996.

Horton, Pene. "Big Is Beautiful." *Woman to Woman*, May 1987, 27.

Hower, Mary. "From Indoor Exercise to Outdoor Fitness: This Canadian Aerobics Enthusiast Brings Large Women a Grand Form." *Radiance*, Winter 1991, 8–11.

Jill Andrew and the Body Confidence Canada Awards. "#SizeismSUCKS!
  Help Make Size & Appearance-Based Discrimination Illegal in Ontario."
  Change.org. Accessed 27 December 2019. https://www.change.org/p
  /sizeismsucks-you-can-help-make-size-appearance-based-discrimination
  -illegal-in-ontario-bodyconfidence.
Johnston, Gail. "Women on the Move." *Radiance*, Summer 1990, 44–5.
Kelley, Caffyn. "Talent + Skill X Action = Suzanne Bell." *Radiance*, Winter 1992,
  6–7, 13.
Klemesrud, Judy. "There Are a Lot of People Willing to Believe That Fat Is
  Beautiful." *New York Times*, 18 August 1970, 38.
Konigsberg, Max. *Max and Shirmax: More Than a Love Affair*. Montreal: Shirley
  K Holdings, 2006.
Lane Bryant. *The Style Book of Slenderizing Fashions*. New York: Lane Bryant,
  1932.
Le collectif LG5. "Something to Think About." *Furie lesbienne/Lesbian Fury*,
  vol. 3, no. 2 (Summer–Fall 1986): 28.
Louderback, Llewellyn. *Fat Power: Whatever You Weigh Is Right*. New York:
  Hawthorn Books, 1970.
– "More People Should Be Fat." *Saturday Evening Post* 240, no. 22
  (4 November 1967): 10–12.
Lyons, Pat, and Debbie Burgard. *Great Shape: The First Exercise Guide for Large
  Women*. New York: Arbor House – William Morrow, 1988.
Manitoba Action Committee on the Status of Women. "Fat Is a Feminist
  Issue." *Action: MACSW*, December 1981, 29.
Marie-Michèle. "Une torche sert à éclairer; une 'grosse torche' à insulter
  ou c'est dans la tête qu'on est grosse! Hommage à LG5." *Treize* III, no. 1:
  20 (September 1986).
McKay, Jeff. *Fat Chance*. National Film Board of Canada, 1994. https://
  www.nfb.ca/film/fat_chance/.
McLaren, Leah. "Porky Pride: Fat Lot of Good That Does." *Globe and Mail*, 27
  January 2001, R3.
MediaWatch, Canadian Coalition Against Media Pornography, and National
  Action Committee on the Status of Women. *Adjusting the Image: Women
  and Canadian Advertising (Report of the National Conference on Canadian
  Broadcasting Policy)*. Ottawa: Government of Canada Department of
  Communications, 20–2 March 1987.
Millman, Marcia. *Such a Pretty Face*. New York: WW Norton, 1980.
Mitchell, Allyson. "Fat Craft." Accessed 26 June 2017. http://www
  .allysonmitchell.com/project.html?project=fat-craft.
Orbach, Susie. *Fat Is a Feminist Issue: A Self-Help Guide for Compulsive
  Overeaters*. New York: Berkley Books, 1979. First published 1978.

– *Fat Is a Feminist Issue II: A Program to Conquer Compulsive Eating*. New York: Berkley Books, 1984. First published 1982.

Phillips, Frances. "At Penningtons, It's Coming up Mostly Roses, Thank You." *Financial Post*, 12 June 1982, 1–2.

Potvin, Rose, and Samantha Sanderson. *Adjusting the Image: Women and Canadian Advertising, Report of the National Conference on Canadian Broadcasting Policy*. Ottawa: MediaWatch, Canadian Coalition Against Media Pornography, National Action Committee on the Status of Women, 20–2, March 1987.

Pretty Porky and Pissed Off. "Queen Sized Revolt." *Fireweed* 67 (1999): 22–3.

Rabkin, Brenda. "The Big Body Beautiful." *Maclean's*, 15 March 1982, 50.

Reardon, Liz. "Heavyweight Instructors Direct Health Clubs for Big Women." *Omaha World-Herald*, 29 November 1987, E1.

Report of the Standing Senate Committee on Social Affairs, Science and Technology. *Obesity in Canada: A Whole-of-Society Approach for a Healthier Canada*. Ottawa: Senate of Canada, 2016.

Rockett, Eve. "Five Days on a Fat Farm." *Chatelaine*, May 1980, 42, 136, 138, 140, 142, 146, 148.

Schoenfielder, Lisa, and Barb Wieser, eds. *Shadow on a Tightrope: Writings by Women on Fat Oppression*. Iowa City: Aunt Lute Publishing Company, 1983.

Schwartz, Karen. "Larger Women Finally Get Gift of Fashion Freedom." *Vancouver Sun*, 7 December 1989, C4.

Starky, Sheena. *The Obesity Epidemic in Canada*. Ottawa: Library of Parliament, Economics Division, 15 July 2005.

"Stout Women." *Time*, 4 June 1928.

Walker, Joan. "Soft-Drink Basting for Apples Part of Weight Watchers' Diet." *Globe and Mail*, 7 March 1968, W5.

"We Are Organizing a CR Group." *Calgary Women's Newspaper*, July/August 1980, 6.

Wilson, Jane. "Fat Underground Throws Weight into Obesity War." *Los Angeles Times*, 8 January 1976, 8.

Worth, Liz. "A Big, Fat Revolution; The Fat Femme Mafia Are Performance Artists, Cabaret Dancers and the Latest in a Budding Local History of Activists for Plus-Sized Women, Writes Liz Worth." *Toronto Star*, 7 December 2006, D4.

Young, Vinne. *It's Fun to Be Fat!* New York: A.A. Wyn, 1953.

Secondary Sources

Abel, Emily K., Joanne Leslie, and Antoinette K. Yancey. "Obesity at the Crossroads: Feminist and Public Health Perspectives." *Signs: Journal of Women in Culture and Society* 31, no. 2 (Winter 2006): 425–43. https://doi.org/10.1086/491682.

Adams, Mary Louise. "Youth, Corruptibility, and English-Canadian Postwar Campaigns against Indecency, 1948–1955." *Journal of the History of Sexuality* 6, no. 1 (1995): 89–117.

Adelson, Naomi. *Being Alive Well: Health and the Politics of Cree Well-Being.* Toronto: University of Toronto Press, 2000.

Agnew, Vijay. *Women's Health, Women's Rights: Perspectives on Global Health Issues Form the 9th International Women's Health Meeting.* Toronto: Centre for Feminist Research, York University, 2003.

Ahmad, Marina Wolf. "Dispute, Distract, or Dance Your Ass Off: Strategies of Size-Diverse Dancers for Creating and Performing in a Fat-Phobic World." Paper presented at the Popular Culture Association, Fat Studies, Boston, MA, May 2007.

Alcoff, Linda. *Visible Identities: Race, Gender and the Self.* New York: Oxford University Press, 2006.

Anderson, Jenn. "Whose Voice Counts? A Critical Examination of Discourses Surrounding the Body Mass Index." *The Fat Studies Journal* 1, no. 2 (2012): 195–207. https://doi.org/10.1080/21604851.2012.656500.

Aphramor, Lucy, Emma Rich, and Lee Monaghan. *Debating Obesity: Critical Perspectives.* London: Palgrave Macmillan, 2010.

Arnup, Katherine. *Education for Motherhood: Advice for Mothers in Twentieth-Century Canada.* Toronto: University of Toronto Press, 1994.

Ascena Retail Group Ltd. "Lane Bryant." Accessed 20 February 2013. http://www.ascenaretail.com/lanebryant.jsp.

Attwood, Feona. "Pornography and Objectification: Re-Reading 'the Picture That Divided Britain.'" *Feminist Media Studies* 4, no. 1 (2004): 7–19. https://doi.org/10.1080/14680770410001674617.

Backhouse, Constance. *Colour-Coded: A Legal History of Racism in Canada, 1900–1950.* Toronto: University of Toronto Press, 1999.

Backhouse, Constance, and David H. Flaherty. "Introduction." In *Challenging Times: The Women's Movement in Canada and the United States,* edited by Constance Backhouse and David H. Flaherty, 3–21. Montreal: McGill-Queen's University Press, 1992.

Bacon, Linda. *Health at Every Size: The Surprising Truth about Your Weight.* Carlsbad, CA: Gurze Books, 2008.

Bailey, M.E. "Foucauldian Feminism: Contesting Bodies, Sexuality and Identity." In *Up against Foucault: Explorations of Some Tensions between Foucault and Feminism,* edited by Caroline Ramazanoglu, 99–122. London: Routledge, 1993.

Baillargeon, Denyse. *Un Québec en mal d'enfants. La médicalisation de la maternité, 1910–1970.* Montreal: Éditions du remue-ménage, 2004.

Banner, Lois. *American Beauty.* Chicago: University of Chicago Press, 1983.

Barrett, Michèle, and Anne Phillips, eds. *Destabilizing Theory: Contemporary Feminist Debates*. Cambridge: Polity Press, 1992.

Bartky, Sandra Lee. "Foucault, Femininity, and the Modernization of Patriarchal Power." In *Feminism and Foucault: Reflections on Resistance*, edited by Irene Diamond and Lee Quinby, 61–86. Boston: Northeastern University Press, 1988.

Beaubeouf-Lafontant, Tamara. "Strong and Large Black Women? Exploring Relationships between Deviant Womanhood and Weight." *Gender & Society* 17, no. 1 (February 2003): 111–21. https://doi.org/10.1177/0891243202238981.

Béland, Daniel, and André Lecouts. "Nationalisme et protection sociale: Une approche comparative." *Canadian Public Policy* 30, no. 3 (2004): 319–31. https://doi.org/10.2307/3552305.

Bernell, Bonnie. *Bountiful Women: Large Women's Secrets for Living the Life They Desire*. Tulsa, OK: Council Oak Books, 2000.

Bernstein, Mary. "Identities and Politics: Toward a Historical Understanding of the Lesbian and Gay Movement." *Social Science History* 26, no. 3 (2002): 531–81. https://doi.org/10.1215/01455532-26-3-531.

Blumer, Herbert. "Fashion: From Class Differentiation to Collective Selection." *Sociological Quarterly* 10, no. 3 (1969): 275–91. https://doi.org/10.1111/j.1533-8525.1969.tb01292.x.

Bola, Manjit. "Questions of Legitimacy? The Fit between Researcher and Researched." *Feminism & Psychology* 5, no. 2 (May 1995): 290–303. https://doi.org/10.1177/0959353595052024.

Bordo, Susan. "Anorexia Nervosa: Psychopathology as the Crystallization of Culture." In *Feminism & Foucault: Reflections on Resistance*, edited by Irene Diamond and Lee Quinby, 87–117. Boston: Northeastern University Press, 1988.

Boris, Eileen. "Desirable Dress: Rosies, Sky Girls, and the Politics of Appearance." *International Labor and Working-Class History* 69, no. 1 (2006): 132–42. https://doi.org/10.1017/S014754790600007X.

Boscoe, Madeline, Gwynne Basen, Ghislaine Alleyne, Barbara Bourriere-LaCroix, and Susan White. "The Women's Health Movement: Looking Back and Moving Forward" In *Canadian Woman Studies: An Introductory Reader*, edited by Andrea Medovarski and Brenda Cranney, 503–13. Toronto: Inanna Publications 2006.

Boston Women's Health Book Collective. *The New Our Bodies Ourselves: A Book by and for Women*. New York: Touchstone, 1992.

Bouchard, Gerard. "La sexualité comme pratique et rapport social chez les couples paysans du Saguenay (1860–1930)." *Revue d'histoire de l'Amerique francaise* 54, no. 2 (2000): 183–217. https://doi.org/10.7202/005337ar.

Boutelier, Mary, and Lucinda SanGiovanni. "Politics, Public Policy & Title IX." In *Women, Sport and Culture*, edited by Susan Birrell. Champaign, IL: Human Kinetics, 1994.

Bovey, Shelley. *Being Fat Is Not a Sin*. Boston: Pandora, 1989.

Bradley, Patricia. *Mass Media and the Shaping of American Feminism, 1963–1975*. Jackson: University Press of Mississippi, 2003.

Brady, Jennifer, and Jacqui Gingras. "'Celebrating Unruly Experiences': Queering Health at Every Size as a Response to the Politics of Postponement." In *Obesity in Canada: Critical Perspectives*, edited by Jenny Ellison, Deborah McPhail, and Wendy Mitchinson, 399–418. Toronto: University of Toronto Press, 2016.

Braziel, Jana Evans, and Kathleen LeBesco. *Bodies out of Bounds: Fatness and Transgression*. Berkeley: University of California Press, 2001.

Brown, Catrina, and Karin Jasper, eds. *Consuming Passions: Feminist Approaches to Weight Preoccupation and Eating Disorders*. Toronto: Second Story Press, 1993.

Brownlie, Robin Jarvis. *A Fatherly Eye: Indian Agents, Government Power, and Aboriginal Resistance in Ontario, 1918–1939*. Don Mills, ON: Oxford University Press, 2003.

Bruhn, John G. "An Epidemiological Study of Myocardial Infarctions in an Italian-American Community: A Preliminary Sociological Study." *Journal of Chronic Diseases* 18, no. 4 (1965): 353–65. https://doi.org/10.1016/0021-9681(65)90039-1.

Brumberg, Joan Jacobs. *The Body Project: An Intimate History of American Girls*. New York: Random House, 1997.

– *Fasting Girls: The History of Anorexia Nervosa*. New York: Penguin, 1989.

Budgeon, Shelley. "Identity as an Embodied Event." *Body and Society* 9, no. 1 (2003): 35–55. https://doi.org/10.1177/1357034X03009001045.

Bunch, Charlotte. "Lesbians in Revolt." In *Feminist Theory Reader: Local and Global Perspectives*, edited by Carole McCann and Seung-Kyung Kim, 83–7. New York: Routledge, 2003.

Burgard, Deb. "What Is 'Health at Every Size'?" In *The Fat Studies Reader*, edited by Sandra Solovay and Esther Rothblum, 42–53. New York: New York University Press, 2009.

Butler, Judith P. *Bodies That Matter: On the Discursive Limits of "Sex."* New York: Routledge, 1993.

– *Gender Trouble*. New York: Routledge, 1999.

Cade, Janet, and Shaun O'Connell. "Management of Weight Problems and Obesity: Knowledge, Attitudes and Current Practice of General Practitioners." *British Journal of General Practice* 41 (1991): 147–50.

Cahn, Susan K. "Sports Talk: Oral History and Its Uses, Problems, and Possibilities for Sport History." *The Journal of American History* 81, no. 2 (September 1994): 594–609. https://doi.org/10.2307/2081175.

Campos, Paul. *The Obesity Myth: Why America's Obsession with Weight Is Hazardous to Your Health*. New York: Gotham Books, 2004.

Canning, Kathleen. *Gender History in Practice: Historical Perspectives on Bodies, Class and Citizenship*. Ithaca, NY: Cornell University Press, 2006.

– "The Body as Method? Reflections on the Place of the Body in Gender History." In *Gender and History: Retrospect and Prospect*, edited by Leonore Davidoff, Keith McCLelland, and Eleni Varikas, 81–96. Oxford: Blackwell, 1999.

Carter, Sarah. "In Sharp Relief: Representations of Aboriginal Women in the Colonial Imagination." In *Capturing Women: The Manipulation of Cultural Imagery in Canada's Prairie West*, 158–93. Montreal: McGill-Queen's University Press, 1997.

Charming Shoppes Inc. *2005 Annual Review*. Bensalem, PA, 2005.

Chenier, Elise. "Rethinking Class in Lesbian Bar Culture: Living 'The Gay Life' in Toronto, 1955–1965." In *Rethinking Canada: The Promise of Women's History*, edited by Adele Perry and Mona Gleason, 301–22. Toronto: Oxford University Press, 2006.

Chernin, Kim. *The Obsession: Reflections on the Tyranny of Slenderness*. New York: Harper and Row Perennial Library, 1981.

Chivers, Sally. "Barrier by Barrier: The Canadian Disability Movement and the Fight for Equal Rights." In *Group Politics and Social Movements in Canada*, edited by Miriam Smith, 307–27. Toronto: University of Toronto Press, 2008.

Churchill, David S. "Personal Ad Politics: Race, Sexuality and Power at *The Body Politic*." *Left History* 8, no. 2 (2003): 114–34. https://doi.org/10.25071/1913-9632.5514.

Code, Lorraine. "How Do We Know? Questions of Method in Feminist Practice." In *Changing Methods: Feminist Transforming Practice*, edited by Sandra Burt and Lorraine Code, 13–44. Peterborough, ON: Broadview Press, 1995.

– *What Can She Know: Feminist Theory and the Construction of Knowledge*. Ithaca, NY: Cornell University Press, 1991.

Cole, Cheryl L. "Addiction, Exercise, and Cyborgs: Technologies of Deviant Bodies." In *Sport and Postmodern Times*, edited by Geneviève Rail, 261–76. Albany: SUNY Press, 1998.

Colls, Rachel. "Big Girls Having Fun: Reflections on a 'Fat Accepting Space.'" *Somatechnics* 2, no. 1 (2012): 18–37. https://doi.org/10.3366/soma.2012.0036.

Consentino, Frank, and Maxwell Howell. *A History of Physical Education in Canada*. Toronto: General Publishing Company Limited, 1971.

Cooper, Charlotte. *Fat Activism: A Radical Social Movement*. Bristol, UK: Hammer ON Press, 2016.

– *Fat and Proud*. London: Women's Press, 1998.

- "Fat Studies: Mapping the Field." *Sociology Compass* 4, no. 12 (2010): 1020–34. https://doi.org/10.1111/j.1751-9020.2010.00336.x.

Costas-Bradstreet, Christa. "Spreading the Message through Community Mobilization, Education and Leadership." Supplement, *Canadian Journal of Public Health* 95, no. S2 (May/June 2004): S25–9.

Counihan, Carole M. "Food Rules in the United States: Individualism, Control and Hierarchy." *Anthropological Quarterly* 65, no. 2 (April 1992): 55–66. https://doi.org/10.2307/3318134.

Craig, Maxine Leeds. *Ain't I a Beauty Queen: Black Women, Beauty, and the Politics of Race*. New York: Oxford University Press, 2002.

Craik, Jennifer. *The Face of Fashion: Cultural Studies in Fashion*. New York: Routledge, 1994.

Creet, M. Julia. "A Test of Unity: Lesbian Visibility in the British Columbia Federation of Women." In *Lesbians in Canada*, edited by Sharon Dale Stone, 183–97. Toronto: Between the Lines, 1990.

Curtis, Bruce. *The Politics of Population: State Formation, Statistics, and the Census of Canada, 1840–1875*. Toronto: University of Toronto Press, 2001.

Davies, Megan J. "Mapping 'Region' In Canadian Medical History: The Case of British Columbia." *Canadian Bulletin of Medical History* 17, no.1 (2000): 73–92. https://doi.org/10.3138/cbmh.17.1.73.

Davis, Fred. *Fashion, Culture and Identity*. Chicago: University of Chicago Press, 1992.

Davis, Kathy. *The Making of Our Bodies, Ourselves: How Feminism Travels across Borders*. Durham, NC: Duke University Press, 2007.

- "Feminist Body/Politics as World Traveler: Translating *Our Bodies, Ourselves*." *European Journal of Women's Studies* 9, no. 3 (2002): 223–47. https://doi.org/10.1177/1350506802009003373.

- "Remaking the She-Devil: A Critical Look at Feminist Approaches to Beauty." *Hypatia: A Journal of Feminist Philosophy* 6, no. 2 (Summer 1991): 21–43. https://doi.org/10.1111/j.1527-2001.1991.tb01391.x.

Davis, Lennard J. "Crips Strike Back: The Rise of Disability Studies." *American Literary History* 11, no. 3 (Autumn 1999): 500–12. https://doi.org/10.1093/alh/11.3.500.

- "Visualising the Disabled Body." In *The Body: A Reader*, edited by Miriam Fraser and Monica Greco, 166–81. New York: Routledge, 2005.

Deem, Rosemary. "Unleisured Lives; Sport in the Context of Women's Leisure." *Women's Studies International Forum* 10, no. 4 (1987): 423–32. https://doi.org/10.1016/0277-5395(87)90059-8.

Demczuk, Irène, and Frank W. Remiggi, eds. *Sortir de l'ombre: Histoires des communautés lesbienne et gaie de Montréal*. Montreal, QC: VLB Éditeur, 1998.

Demerson, Velma. *Incorrigible*. Waterloo, ON: Wilfred Laurier University Press, 2004.

Denesse, Kimberly M. *The Fat Girl Chronicles: A Handbook for Fat Chicks*. Lincoln, NE: iUniverse, 2006.

Devault, Marjorie L. "Talking and Listening from Women's Standpoint: Feminist Strategies for Interviewing and Analysis." *Social Problems* 37, no. 1 (February 1990): 96–116. https://doi.org/10.2307/800797.

Diamond, Nicky "Thin Is the Feminist Issue." In *The Body: A Reader*, edited by Miriam Fraser and Monica Greco, 115–16. New York: Routledge, 2005. First published 1985.

Doruyter, Renee. "A Plus for Large-Sized People: Easy Wear and Easy Care Hallmarks of New Stores." *Province*, 22 August 1991, 53.

Downing, Lauren. "Fashionably Fatshionable: A Consideration of the Fashion Practices of Self-Proclaimed Fat Women." Master's thesis, Parsons School of Art and Design, 2012.

Dunphy, Cathy. "Breaking an Obsession with Food." *Toronto Star*, 2 November 1985, L1.

Durante, Angela, and Jenny Ellison. "The Body and Dress." In *The Encyclopedia of Fashion and Dress, Volume 3: The United States and Canada*, edited by Phyllis Tortora, 171–82. Oxford: Berg, 2010.

"Eating Disorder Expert Faces Sex Charges." *Edmonton Journal*, 12 December 2003, A10.

Echols, Alice. *Daring to Be Bad: Radical Feminism in America, 1967–1975*. Minneapolis: University of Minnesota Press, 1989.

Ehrhardt, Julia. "You-Unlimited!: The Fat-Positive(?) Message of 1950s 'Plumps' Consultant Vinne Young." Paper presented at the Popular Culture Association (Fat Studies), San Francisco, CA, May 2008.

Ellison, Jenny, Deborah McPhail, and Wendy Mitchinson, eds. *Obesity in Canada: Critical Perspectives*. Toronto: University of Toronto Press, 2016.

Ellison, Jennifer. "Our Most Charming Girls: Female Athletes in Canadian Advertisements, 1928 to 2002." Master's thesis, Carleton University, 2002.

Ellison, Jenny. "From 'F.U.' to Be Yourself: Fat Activisms in Canada." In *Obesity in Canada: Historical and Critical Perspectives*, edited by Jenny Ellison, Deborah McPhail, and Wendy Mitchinson, 293–319. Toronto: University of Toronto Press, 2016.

– "Large as Life: Self-Acceptance and the Fat Body in Canada, 1977–2000." PhD diss., York University, 2010.

– "Not Jane Fonda: Aerobics for Fat Women Only." In *The Fat Studies Reader*, edited by Sondra Solovay and Esther Rothblum, 312–19. New York: New York University Press, 2009.

– "'Stop Postponing Your Life until You Lose Weight and Start Living Now': Vancouver's Large as Life Action Group, 1979–1985." *Journal of the Canadian Historical Association* 18, no. 1 (2007): 241–65. https://doi.org/10.7202/018261ar.

Enke, A. Finn. *Finding the Movement: Sexuality, Contested Space, and Feminist Activism*. Durham, NC: Duke University Press, 2007.

Entwistle, Joanne. "Fashion and the Fleshy Body: Dress as Embodied Practice." *Fashion Theory* 4, no. 3 (2000): 323–48. https://doi.org/10.2752/136270400778995471.

Erdman, Cheri K. *Nothing to Lose: A Guide to Sane Living in a Larger Body*. San Francisco: HarperCollins, 1995.

Faludi, Susan. *Backlash: The Undeclared War against American Women*. Toronto: Doubleday, 1991.

Farrell, Amy Erdman. *Fat Shame: Stigma and the Fat Body in American Culture*. New York: New York University Press, 2011.

Fat Girl Food Squad. "About." Accessed 4 October 2019. https://fatgirlfoodsquad.wordpress.com/about/

Feldberg, Georgina. "Holism and History in Toronto's Women's Health Movements." In *The Politics of Healing: Histories of Alternative Medicine in Twentieth-Century North America*, edited by Robert D. Johnston, 181–94. New York: Routledge, 2004.

Feldberg, Georgina, Molly Ladd-Taylor, and Kathryn McPherson, eds. *Women, Health, and Nation: Canada and the U.S. since 1945*. Montreal: McGill-Queen's University Press, 2001.

Fishman, Sara Golda Bracha. "Life in the Fat Underground." *Radiance*, Winter 1998, 32–5, 50.

Foucault, Michel. *Discipline and Punish: The Birth of the Prison*. Translated by Alan Sheridan. New York: Vintage Books, 1995. First published 1977.

Francis, Daniel. *The Imaginary Indian: The Image of the Indian in Canadian Culture*. Vancouver: Arsenal Pulp Press, 1992.

Fraser, Jean. "Sizing up a New Market; Retailers Catering to Larger Women – at Last." *Edmonton Journal*, 30 August 1994, C2.

Fraser, Laura. *Losing It: America's Obsession with Weight and the Industry That Feeds on It*. New York: Dutton Books, 1997.

Fraser, Miriam, and Monica Greco. *The Body: A Reader*. New York: Routledge, 2005.

Fraser, Nancy. *Unruly Practices: Power, Discourse, and Gender in Contemporary Social Theory*. Minneapolis: University of Minnesota Press, 1989.

Frater, Lara. *Fat Chicks Rule: How to Survive in a Thin-Centric World*. Brooklyn, NY: IG Publishing, 2005.

Freedman, Estelle B. *No Turning Back: The History of Feminism and the Future of Women*. New York: Ballantine, 2002.

Freeman, Barbara. *The Satellite Sex: The Media and Women's Issues in English Canada, 1966–1971*. Waterloo, ON: Wilfred Laurier University Press, 2001.

– "'A Public Sense of Ourselves': Communication and Community-Building in Canada's Lesbianews/Lnews, 1989–1998." *Westminster Papers* 8, no. 3 (December 2011): 143–67. https://doi.org/10.16997/wpcc.138.

Freund, Peter. "Bodies, Disability and Spaces." In *The Body: A Reader*, edited by Miriam Fraser and Monica Greco, 182–6. New York: Routledge, 2005.

Friedan, Betty. *The Feminine Mystique*. New York: Dell, 1963.

Friedman, Sandra. *Body Thieves: Help Girls Reclaim Their Natural Bodies and Become Physically Active*. Vancouver: Salal Books, 2002.

– *When Girls Feel Fat: Helping Girls through Adolescence*. Toronto: HarperCollins, 1997.

Friefeld, Franceen, and Claire Friefeld. *Fill Up, Not Out: A Healthy Approach to Weight Control for Life*. Ottawa: Creative Bound, 2004.

– *The Healthy Weigh: Learn How to Eat, Not How to Diet*. Ottawa: Creative Bound, 1993.

Fumento, Michael. *The Fat of the Land: The Obesity Epidemic and How Overweight Americans Can Help Themselves*. New York: Penguin, 1997.

Gaesser, Glenn A. *Big Fat Lies: The Truth about Your Weight and Your Health*. New York: Fawcett-Columbine, 1996.

Gamble, Sarah, ed. *The Routledge Companion to Feminism and Postfeminism*. London: Routledge, 1998.

Gard, Michael. "Hearing Noises and Noticing Silences: Towards a Critical Engagement with Body Weight Statistics." In *Obesity in Canada: Critical Perspectives*, edited by Jenny Ellison, Deborah McPhail, and Wendy Mitchinson, 31–55. Toronto: University of Toronto Press, 2016.

– "Truth, Belief and the Cultural Politics of Obesity Scholarship and Public Health Policy." *Critical Public Health* 21, no. 1 (2011): 37–48. https://doi.org/10.1080/09581596.2010.529421.

– "Friends, Enemies and the Cultural Politics of Critical Obesity Research." In *Biopolitics and the 'Obesity Epidemic': Governing Bodies*, edited by Jane Wright and Valerie Harwood, 31–44. New York: Routledge, 2009.

Garland-Thomson, Rosemarie, ed. *Freakery: Cultural Spectacles of the Extraordinary Body*. New York: New York University Press, 1996.

Garner, David, P. Garfinkel, D. Schwartz, and M. Thompson. "Cultural Expectations of Thinness in Women." *Psychological Reports* 47, no. 2 (October 1980): 483–91. https://doi.org/10.2466/pr0.1980.47.2.483.

Gelfand Malka, Susan. *Daring to Care: American Nursing and Second-Wave Feminism*. Chicago: University of Illinois Press, 2007.

Gilman, Sander L. "Fat as Disability: The Case of the Jews." *Literature and Medicine* 23, no. 1 (Spring 2004): 46–60. https://doi.org/10.1353/lm.2004.0003.

– *Fat Boys: A Slim Book*. Lincoln: University of Nebraska Press, 2004.

Gimlin, Debra L. *Body Work: Beauty and Self-Image in American Culture*. Berkeley: University of California Press, 2002.

Gingras, Jacqui. "Throwing Their Weight Around: Canadians Take on Health at Every Size." *Health at Every Size Journal* 19, no. 4 (2006): 195–206.

Gleason, Mona. *Normalizing the Ideal: Psychology, Schooling, and the Family in Postwar Canada*. Toronto: University of Toronto Press, 1999.

Goodman, Charisse M. *The Invisible Woman: Confronting Weight Prejudice in America*. Carlsbad, CA: Gurze Books, 1995.

Griswold, Robert. "The 'Flabby American,' the Body and the Cold War." In *Shared Experiences: Men, Women and the History of Gender*, edited by Laura McCall and Donald Yacovone, 323–48. New York: New York University Press, 1998.

Groneman, Carol. "Nymphomania: The Historical Construction of Female Sexuality." In *Deviant Bodies: Critical Perspectives on Difference in Science and Popular Culture*, edited by Jennifer Terry and Jacqueline Urla, 219–49. Indianapolis: Indiana University Press, 1995.

Hall, M. Ann. *Feminism and Sporting Bodies*. Windsor, ON: Human Kinetics, 1996.

– *The Girl and the Game: A History of Women's Sports in Canada*. Toronto: Broadview Press, 2002.

Harding, Kate, and Marianne Kirby. *Lessons from the Fat-O-Sphere: Quit Dieting and Declare a Truce with Your Body*. New York: Penguin Group/Perigee Book, 2009.

Hartman, Crystal. *Fat Is Beautiful*. Portland, OR: Microcosm Publishing, 2007.

Heaman, E.A. "Rights Talk and the Liberal Order Framework." In *Liberalism and Hegemony: Debating the Canadian Liberal Revolution*, edited by Jean-François Constant and Michel Ducharme, 147–75. Toronto: University of Toronto Press, 2009.

Henderson, Stuart. *Making the Scene: Yorkville and Hip Toronto in the 1960s*. Toronto: University of Toronto Press, 2011.

Herndon, April. "Disparate but Disabled: Fat Embodiment and Disability Studies." *National Women's Studies Association Journal* 14, no. 3 (Fall 2002): 120–37. https://doi.org/10.2979/NWS.2002.14.3.120.

Heyes, Cressida. "Identity Politics." In *The Stanford Encyclopedia of Philosophy* (Fall 2018 edition), ed. Edward N. Zalta. Accessed 4 October 2019. https://plato.stanford.edu/archives/fall2018/entries/identity-politics/

Higginbotham, Anastasia. "Nomy Lamm, Ms. Women of the Year: For Inspiring a New Generation of Feminists to Fight Back against Fat Oppression." *Ms*, January/February 1997, 60–3.

Hollows, Joanne. *Feminism, Femininity and Popular Culture*. Manchester, UK: Manchester University Press, 2000.

Howard, Rebecca. "Designers Target Large Women." *Ottawa Citizen*, 12 November 1992, H2.

Howell, Colin D. *Blood, Sweat, and Cheers: Sport and the Making of Modern Canada*. Toronto: University of Toronto Press, 2001.

Hribar, Amy. "Consuming Lifestyles: Transforming the Body and the Self in Postfeminist America." PhD diss., University of Illinois at Urbana-Champaign, 2001.

Iacovetta, Franca, and Valerie J. Korinek. "Jell-O Salads, One Stop Shopping and Maria the Homemaker: The Gender Politics of Food." In *Sisters or Strangers? Immigrant, Ethnic and Racialized Women in Canadian History*, edited by Marlene Epp, Franca Iacovetta, and Frances Swyripa, 190–230. Toronto: University of Toronto Press, 2004.

Ignatieff, Michael. *The Rights Revolution*. Toronto: House of Anansi, 2000.

Jackson, John J. *Mr. 5BX Canadian Fitness Pioneer: A Biography of William A.R. Orban*. Victoria, BC: Sono Nis Press, 1982.

Jaffe, Karen. "Forming Fat Identities." PhD diss., Rutger's University, 2008.

Jasper, Karin. "Hersize: A Weight-Prejudice Action Group." In *Consuming Passions: Feminist Approaches to Weight Preoccupation and Eating Disorders*, edited by Catrina Brown and Karin Jasper, 421–8. Toronto: Second Story Press, 1993.

Jeffrey, C. A., and S. Kitto. "Struggling to Care: Nurses' Perceptions of Caring for Obese Patients in an Australian Bariatric Ward." *Health Sociology Review* 15, no. 1 (2006): 71–83. https://doi.org/10.5172/hesr.2006.15.1.71.

Joanisse, Leanne, and Anthony Synnott. "Fighting Back: Reactions and Resistance to the Stigma of Obesity." In *Interpreting Weight: The Social Management of Fatness and Thinness*, edited by Jeffery Sobal and Donna Maurer, 49–70. New York: Aldine de Gruyter, 1999.

Johnston, Josée, and Judith Taylor. "Feminist Consumerism and Fat Activists: A Comparative Study of Grassroots Activism and the Dove Real Beauty Campaign." *Signs: Journal of Women in Culture and Society* 33, no. 4 (2008): 941–66. https://doi.org/10.1086/528849.

Kassirer, Jerome P., and Marcia Angell. "Losing Weight – an Ill-Fated New Year's Resolution." *New England Journal of Medicine* 338, no. 1 (1 January 1998): 52–5. https://doi.org/10.1056/NEJM199801013380109.

Kilbourne, Jean. *Deadly Persuasion*. New York: The Free Press, 1999.

Kipnis, Laura. *Bound and Gagged: Pornography and the Politics of Fantasy in America*. Durham, NC: Duke University Press, 1999.

Kirkland, Anna. *Fat Rights: Dilemmas of Difference and Personhood*. New York: New York University Press, 2008.

– "Representations of Fatness and Personhood: Pro-Advocacy and the Limits of the Law." *Representations* 82, no. 1 (Spring 2003): 24–51. https://doi.org/10.1525/rep.2003.82.1.24.

Klein, Richard. *Eat Fat*. New York: Pantheon Books, 1996.

Kline, Wendy. "'Please Include This in Your Book': Readers Respond to *Our Bodies, Ourselves*." *Bulletin of Medical History* 79 (2005): 81–110. https://doi.org/10.1353/bhm.2005.0030.

Knight, P.G. "Naming the Problem: Feminism and the Figuration of Conspiracy." *Cultural Studies* 11, no. 1 (1997): 40–63. https://doi.org/10.1080/09502389700490031.

Korinek, Valerie J. *Roughing It in the Suburbs: Reading Chatelaine Magazine in the Fifties and Sixties*. Toronto: University of Toronto Press, 2000.

Kulick, Don, and Anne Meneley, eds. *Fat: The Anthropology of an Obsession*. New York: Penguin Group, 2005.

Kuppers, Petra. "Fatties on Stage: Feminist Performances." In *Bodies out of Bounds: Fatness and Transgression*, edited by Jana Evans Braziel and Kathleen LeBesco, 277–91. Berkeley: University of California Press, 2001.

Kushner, Trucia. "Finding a Personal Style." *Ms* 2, no. 8 (1974): 45.

LeBesco, Kathleen. *Revolting Bodies: The Struggle to Redefine Fat Identity*. Amherst: University of Massachusetts Press, 2004.

Lenskyj, Helen. "Good Sports: Feminists Organizing on Sport Issues in the 1970s and 1980s." *Resources for Feminist Research* 20, no. 2/4 (1991): 130–5.

– *Out of Bounds: Women, Sport and Sexuality*. Toronto: The Women's Press, 1986.

Lent, Adam. *British Social Movements since 1945: Sex, Colour, Peace, and Power*. New York: Palgrave, 2001.

Lévesque, Andrée. *Making and Breaking the Rules: Women in Québec, 1919–1939*. Translated by Yvonne M. Klein. Toronto: McLelland and Stewart, 1989.

Levy-Navarro, Elena. "Fattening Queer History: Where Does Fat History Go from Here?" In *The Fat Studies Reader*, edited by Sandra Solovay and Esther Rothblum, 15–22. New York: New York University Press, 2009.

Lippincott, Catherine. *Well-Rounded: 8 Simple Steps for Changing Your Life ... Not Your Size*. New York: Simon and Schuster, 1997.

Lloyd, Mona. "Feminism, Aerobics and the Politics of the Body." *Body and Society* 2, no. 2 (June 1996): 79–98. https://doi.org/10.1177/1357034X96002002005.

Loland, Nina Waaler. "The Art of Concealment in a Culture of Display: Aerobicizing Women's and Men's Experience and Use of Their Own Bodies." *Sociology of Sport Journal* 17, no. 2 (2000): 111–29. https://doi.org/10.1123/ssj.17.2.111.

Lupton, Deborah. *Fat*. New York: Routledge, 2013.

Lurie, Alison. *The Language of Clothes*. Toronto: Random House, 1981.

Lyons, Pat. "Prescription for Harm: Diet Insutry Influence, Public Health Policy, and the 'Obesity Epidemic.'" In *The Fat Studies Reader*, edited by Sandra Solovay and Esther Rothblum, 75–87. New York: New York University Press, 2009.

Lyotard, Jean-Francois. *The Postmodern Condition: A Report on Knowledge*. Translated by Geoff Bennington and Brian Massumi. Minneapolis: University of Minnesota Press, 2002. First published 1979.

MacInnis, Beth. "Fat Oppression." In *Consuming Passions: Feminist Approaches to Weight Preoccupation and Eating Disorders*, edited by Catrina Brown and Karin Jasper, 69–79. Toronto: Second Story Press, 1993.

MacNeill, Margaret. "Ideology, Media and Images of Active Women." In *Women, Sport and Culture*, edited by Susan Birrell and Cheryl Cole, 273–87. Champaign, IL: Human Kinetics, 1994.

MacNevin, Audrey. "Exercising Options: Holistic Health and Technical Beauty in Gendered Accounts of Bodywork." *Sociological Quarterly* 44, no. 2 (2002): 271–89. https://doi.org/10.1111/j.1533-8525.2003.tb00558.x.

Maguire, Joseph, and Louise Mansfield. "'Nobody's Perfect': Women, Aerobics, and the Body Beautiful." *Sociology of Sport Journal* 15, no. 2 (1998): 109–37. https://doi.org/10.1123/ssj.15.2.109.

Malveaux, Julianne. "Suitably Attired." *Ms* 16 (1988): 38–9.

Manfred, Erica. "Fat, Flash – and Fashionable." *Ms*, March 1984, 100–3.

Maor, Maya. "The Body That Does Not Diminish Itself: Fat Acceptance in Israel's Lesbian Queer Communities." *Journal of Lesbian Studies* 16, no. 2 (2012): 177–98. https://doi.org/10.1080/10894160.2011.597660.

Markula, Pirkko. "Firm but Shapely, Fit but Sexy, Strong but Thin: The Postmodern Aerobicizing Female Bodies." *Sociology of Sport Journal* 12, no. 4 (1995): 424–53.

– "Technologies of the Self: Sport, Feminism, and Foucault." *Sociology of Sport Journal* 20, no. 2 (2003): 87–107. https://doi.org/10.1123/ssj.20.2.87.

Maynard, Steven. "Through a Hole in the Lavatory Wall: Homosexual Subcultures, Police Surveillance, and the Dialectics of Discovery, Toronto, 1890–1930." *Journal of the History of Sexuality* 5, no. 2 (1994): 207–42.

Martin, Luther H., Huck Gutman, and Patrick H. Hutton, eds. *Technologies of the Self: A Seminar with Michel Foucault*. Amherst: University of Massachusetts Press, 1988.

McCann, Carole, and Seung-Kyung Kim, eds. *Feminist Theory Reader: Local and Global Perspectives*. New York: Routledge, 2003.

McDermott, Lisa. "A Critical Interrogation of Contemporary Discourses of Physical (In)Activity amongst Canadian Children: Back to the Future." *Journal of Canadian Studies* 42, no. 2 (Spring 2008): 5–42. https://doi.org/10.3138/jcs.43.5.

McGorman, Selma. *This Ad Offends Me! How to Write Letters of Complaint with Regard to the Objectionable Portrayal of Women in Advertising*. Windsor, ON: Selma McGorman, c. 1989.

McKay, Ian. "The Liberal Order Framework: A Prospectus for a Reconnaissance of Canadian History." *Canadian Historical Review* 81, no. 4 (2000): 617–45. https://doi.org/10.3138/chr.81.4.616.

McKinnon, Julie. "Sylvania Psychologist Cedes License in Sex Charge, Female Patient Complained." *Toledo Blade*, 22 October 2008, accessed 20 May 2009.

http://toledoblade.com/apps/pbcs.dll/article?AID=/20081022/NEWS02
/810220368.

McPhail, Deborah. "Canada Weighs In: Gender, Race, and the Making of
'Obesity,' 1945–1970." PhD diss., York University, 2009.

– "Indigenous People's Clinical Encounters with Obesity: A Conversation
with Barry Lavallee." In *Obesity in Canada: Critical Perspectives*, edited by
Jenny Ellison, Deborah McPhail, and Wendy Mitchinson, 175–84. Toronto:
University of Toronto Press, 2016.

– "What to Do with the 'Tubby Hubby'? 'Obesity,' the Crisis of Masculinity,
and the Nuclear Family in Early Cold War Canada." *Antipode* 41, no. 5
(2009): 1021–50. https://doi.org/10.1111/j.1467-8330.2009.00708.x.

McRoberts, Kenneth. *Québec: Social Change and Political Crisis*. 3rd ed. Toronto:
McLelland and Stewart, 1988.

MediaWatch. *Tracing the Roots of Mediawatch*. Toronto: Mediawatch, 1993.

Merrill, E. L. "Women's Stories of Their Experiences as Overweight Patients."
PhD diss., Texas Woman's University, 2007.

Mills, Sean. *The Empire Within: Postcolonial Thought and Political Activism in
Sixties Montreal*. Kingston: McGill-Queens University Press, 2010.

Mitchell, Stacy Ann, and Teri D. Mitchell. *Livin' Large: African American Sisters
Confront Obesity*. Roscoe, IL: Hilton Publishing Company, 2004.

Mitchinson, Wendy. *Fighting Fat: Canada, 1920–1980*. Toronto: University of
Toronto Press, 2018.

– *The Nature of Their Bodies: Women and Their Doctors in Victorian Canada*.
Toronto: University of Toronto Press, 1991.

Monaghan, Lee F. "Discussion Piece: A Critical Take on the Obesity Debate."
Social Theory and Health 3, no. 4 (2005): 302–14. https://doi.org/10.1057/
palgrave.sth.8700058

Mosby, Ian. "Administering Colonial Science: Nutrition Research and Human
Biomedical Experimentation in Aboriginal Communities and Residential
Schools, 1942–1952." *Histoire sociale/Social History* 46, no. 91 (May 2013):
145–72.

Mukherjee, Arun. "A House Divided: Women of Colour and American
Feminist Theory." In *Challenging Times: The Women's Movement in Canada and
the United States*, edited by Constance Backhouse and David H. Flaherty,
165–74. Montreal: McGill-Queens University Press, 1992.

Murphy, Michelle. "Immodest Witnessing: The Epistemology of Vaginal Self-
Examination in the U.S. Feminist Self-Help Movement." *Feminist Studies* 30,
no. 1 (Spring 2004): 115–47.

Murray, Samantha. "Doing Politics or Selling Out? Living the Fat Body."
Women's Studies: An Inter-Disciplinary Journal 34, no. 3–4 (2005): 265–77.
https://doi.org/10.1080/00497870590964165.

Nemeth, Mary. "Body Obsession." *Maclean's*, 2 May 1994, 44–9.

– "Who's Afraid of Naomi Wolf." *Maclean's*, 6 December 1993, 70–2.

Nicholas, Jane. *The Modern Girl: Feminine Modernities, the Body, and Commodities in the 1920s*. Toronto: University of Toronto Press, 2015.

Nidetch, Jean. *The Story of Weight Watchers*. Winnipeg: Signet, 1970.

Offer, Avner. "Body Weight and Self-Control in the U.S. and Britain since the 1950s." *Society for the Social History of Medicine* 14, no. 1 (April 2001): 79–106. https://doi.org/10.1093/shm/14.1.79.

Orbach, Susie. *Bodies*. New York: Picador, 2009.

O'Reily, Jane. "Click! The Housewife's Moment of Truth." *Ms*, Spring 2002 (1972): 5–8.

Owram, Douglas. *Born at the Right Time: A History of the Baby Boom Generation*. Toronto: University of Toronto Press, 1996.

Padwal, Raj S., Nicholas M. Pajewski, David B. Allison, and Arya M. Sharma. "Using the Edmonton Obesity Staging System to Predict Mortality in a Population-Representative Cohort of People with Overweight and Obesity." *Canadian Medical Association Journal* 183, no. 14 (4 October 2011): E1059–66. https://doi.org/10.1503/cmaj.110387.

Palmer, Alexandra. *Couture & Commerce: The Transatlantic Fashion Trade in the 1950s*. Vancouver: UBC Press, 2001.

Paquette, Carmen. "Personal Reflections on Lesbian Organizing in Ottawa." In *Lesbians in Canada*, edited by Sharon Dale Stone, 221–9. Toronto: Between the Lines, 1990.

Paradis, Elise. "'Obesity' as Process: The Medicalization of Fatness by Canadian Researchers, 1971–2010." In *Obesity in Canada: Critical Perspectives*, edited by Jenny Ellison, Deborah McPhail, and Wendy Mitchinson, 56–88. Toronto: University of Toronto Press, 2016.

ParticipACTION. "Feeling Great! ParticipACTION Takes a New Look at Health and Your Weight." *Maclean's*, 20 March 1989, insert.

Peacock, Mary. "The Comfortable Shoe Guide." *Ms* (1982): 10.

– "Personal Style: The Fashion Industry Courts 'the Big Woman.'" *Ms* 8, no. 12 (1980): 83–90.

Peel, Elizabeth. "Effeminate 'Fudge Nudgers' and Tomboyish 'Lettuce Lickers': Language and the Construction of Sexualities in Diversity Training." *Psychology of Women Section Review* 7, no. 2 (Autumn 2005): 24–36.

Peiss, Kathy. *Hope in a Jar: The Making of American Beauty Culture*. New York: Metropolitan Books, 1998.

Perls, Frederick, Ralph Hefferline, and Paul Goodman. *Gestalt Therapy: Excitement and Growth in the Human Personality*. New York: Dell Publishing Company, 1951.

Perreault, Isabelle. "Morale catholique et genre féminin: La sexualité dissertée dans les manuels de sexualité maritale au Québec, 1930–1960." *Revue d'histoire de l'Amerique francaise* 57, no. 4 (Summer 1999): 93–119. https://doi.org/10.7202/009642ar.

Pertman, Shea. "Being a Fat Woman in North America: A Theoretical Perspective on Fat Liberation." Master's thesis, Simon Fraser University, 1999.

Pett, L.B., and G.F. Ogilvie. "The Report on Canadian Average Weights, Heights and Skinfolds." *Canadian Bulletin on Nutrition* 5, no. 1 (1957): 1–81.

Plymire, Darcy C. "Positive Addiction: Running and Human Potential in the 1970s." *Journal of Sport History* 31, no. 3 (2004): 297–315.

Polivy, Janet, and C. Peter Herman. *Breaking the Diet Habit*. New York: Basic Books, 1983.

Pollack, Griselda. "What's Wrong with Images of Women?" In *Looking On*, edited by Rosemary Betterton, 40–9. London: Pandora, 1987.

Poudrier, Jennifer. "The Geneticization of Aboriginal Diabetes and Obesity." In *Obesity in Canada: Critical Perspectives*, edited by Jenny Ellison, Deborah McPhail, and Wendy Mitchinson, 89–121. Toronto: University of Toronto Press, 2016.

Poudrier, Jennifer, and Janice Kennedy. "Embodiment and the Meaning of the 'Healthy Body': An Exploration of Aboriginal Women's Perspectives of Healthy Body Weight and Body Image." *Journal of Aboriginal Health* 4, no. 1 (2007): 15–24.

Poulton, Terry. "Chatelaine's 6-Month Slimdown Plan, Part One." *Chatelaine*, January 1982, 40–2, 96–100.

– "Fat Like Me." *Chatelaine*, September 1985, 87–8, 105–7.

– *No Fat Chicks: How Big Business Profits by Making Women Hate Their Bodies – and How to Fight Back*. Toronto: Birch Lane Press, 1998.

– "Plump Profits: By Dominating the Market in Oversized Women's Wear, Penningtons Is Living – Literally – Off the Fat of the Land." *Canadian Business*, June 1978, 51–7, 90–2.

Powers, Retha. "Fat Is a Black Woman's Issue." *Essence*, October 1989, 75, 78, 134, 136.

Prentice, Michael. "Giant Zellers Store out to Prove Bigger Is Better; Gatineau Becomes Battlefield for Retail Giants." *Ottawa Citizen*, 11 November 1995, E15.

Priest, Alicia. "No Small Feat for Full-Figured: Fears Can Finally Be Overcome." *Vancouver Sun*, 8 November 1988, C1.

Probyn, Elspeth. "The Body Which Is Not One: Speaking the Embodied Self." *Hypatia* 6, no. 3 (1991): 111–23. https://doi.org/10.1111/j.1527-2001.1991.tb00258.x.

Puhl, Rebecca M., and Chelsea A. Heuer. "The Stigma of Obesity: A Review and Update." *Obesity* 17, no. 5 (2009): 941–64. https://doi.org/10.1038/oby.2008.636.

Radner, Hilary. "Producing the Body: Jane Fonda and the New Public Feminine." In *Constructing the New Consumer Society*, edited by Hilary

Radner, Pekka Sulkunen, John Holmwood, and Gerhard Schulze, 108–33. New York: St Martin's Press, 1997.

Ramsey, Danielle. "Second Wave Feminism." In *Feminism and Postfeminism*, edited by Sarah Gamble, 168–78. London: Routledge, 1998.

Raphael, Dennis. "Social Justice Is Good for Our Hearts: Why Societal Factors – Not Lifestyles – Are Major Causes of Heart Disease in Canada and Elsewhere." 1–102. Toronto: Centre for Social Justice, 2002. http://www.socialjustice.org/uploads/pubs/SocialJusticeisGoodforOurHearts.pdf.

Remington, Robert. "Labelling Obese People Disabled an Insult: Group." *National Post*, 26 September 2001, A14.

"Report on Business Index: Company News." *Globe and Mail*, 9 November 1995, B1.

Rice, Carla. "Flesh of Hope and the Slimness of Despair." *Rites: For Lesbian and Gay Liberation* 5, no. 2 (1988): 15.

– "Becoming the Fat Girl: Emergence of an Unfit Identity." *Women's Studies International Forum* 30, no. 2 (2007): 158–72. https://doi.org/10.1016/j.wsif.2007.01.001.

Rich, Emma, and John Evans. "'Fat Ethics' – the Obesity Discourse and Body Politics." *Social Theory and Health* 3, no. 4 (2005): 341–58. https://doi.org/10.1057/palgrave.sth.8700057.

Richards, Norah. "An Evaluation of the Weight Preoccupation Group Program at the Winnipeg Women's Health Clinic." Master's thesis, Carleton University, 1996.

Riga, Andy. "Reitmans Bags Rival Shirmax: Shirmax Founder Agrees to Sell 174-Store Firm for $85.4 Million." *Gazette*, 11 April 2002, C1.

Rimke, Heidi Marie. "Governing Citizens through Self-Help Literature." *Cultural Studies* 14, no. 1 (2000): 61–78. https://doi.org/10.1080/095023800334986.

Roberge, Huguette. "Santé et bien-être." *La Presse*, 4 July 1988, A13.

Robnett, Belinda. "African American Women in the Civil Rights Movement: Spontaneity and Emotion in Social Movement Theory." In *No Middle Ground: Women and Radical Protest*, edited by Kathleen M. Blee, 65–95. New York: New York University Press, 1998.

Roese, Roswitha. "Wanting to Fit: A Grounded Theory of Chronically Obese Women's Experiences of a Non-Dieting Treatment Program." PhD diss., York University, 1996.

Rooks, Noliwe. *Hair Raising: Beauty, Culture, and African American Women*. New Brunswick, NJ: Rutgers University Press, 1996.

Rose, Nikolas. *Governing the Soul: The Shaping of the Private Self*. London: Routledge, 1989.

Ross, Becki L. *The House That Jill Built: A Lesbian Nation in Formation*. Toronto: University of Toronto Press, 1995.

- "The House That Jill Built: Lesbian Feminist Organizing in Toronto, 1976–1980." *Feminist Review* 35 (Summer 1990): 75–91. https://doi.org/10.1057/fr.1990.30.
- "How Lavender Jane Loved Women: Re-Figuring Identity-Based Life/Stylism in 1970s Lesbian Feminism." *Journal of Canadian Studies* 30, no. 4 (Winter 1995–6): 110–28. https://doi.org/10.3138/jcs.30.4.110.
Rothblum, Esther. "'I'll Die for the Revolution but Don't Ask Me Not to Diet': Feminism and the Continuing Stigmatization of Obesity." In *Feminist Perspectives on Eating Disorders*, edited by Patricia Fallon, Melanie Katzman, and Susan Wooley, 53–76. New York: Guilford Press, 1994.
- "The Stigma of Women's Weight: Social and Economic Realities." *Feminism and Psychology* 2, no. 1 (1992): 61–73. https://doi.org/10.1177/0959353592021005.
- "Women and Weight: Fad and Fiction." *The Journal of Psychology* 124, no. 1 (1989): 5–24. https://doi.org/10.1080/00223980.1990.10543202.
Russo, Mary. "Female Grotesques: Carnival and Theory." In *Feminist Studies Critical Studies*, edited by Teresa de Laurentis, 213–29. Bloomington: Indiana University Press, 1986.
Rutherford, Paul. *Endless Propaganda: The Advertising of Public Goods*. Toronto: University of Toronto Press, 2000.
- *A World Made Sexy: Freud to Madonna*. Toronto: University of Toronto Press, 2007.
Ruzek, Sheryl Burt. *The Women's Health Movement: Feminist Alternatives to Medical Control*. New York: Praeger, 1978.
Sangster, Joan. *Girl Trouble: Female Delinquency in English Canada*. Toronto: Between the Lines, 2002.
- "Invoking Experience as Evidence." *Canadian Historical Review* 92, no. 1 (2011): 135–61. https://doi.org/10.3138/chr.92.1.135.
Savage, Jan. "Participant Observation: Standing in the Shoes of Others." *Qualitative Health Research* 10, no. 3 (2000): 324–9. https://doi.org/10.1177/104973200129118471.
Schuster, Dana, and Lisa Tealer. "Exorcising the Exercise Myth: Creating Women of Substance." In *The Fat Studies Reader*, edited by Esther Rothblum and Sandra Solovay, 320–4. New York: New York University Press.
Schwartz, Hillel. *Never Satisfied: A Cultural History of Diets, Fantasies and Fat*. New York: Anchor Books, 1986.
Scott, Joan Wallach. "The Evidence of Experience." *Critical Inquiry* 17, no. 4 (Summer 1991): 773–97. https://doi.org/10.1086/448612.
Scott, Linda M. *Fresh Lipstick: Redressing Fashion and Feminism*. New York: Palgrave MacMillan 2005.
Sedgwick, Eve Kosofsky. *Epistemology of the Closet*. Berkeley: University of California Press, 1990.

Seid, Roberta Pollack. *Never Too Thin: Why Women Are at War with Their Bodies*. New York: Prentice Hall Press, 1989.

Seifrit Weigley, Emma. "Average? Ideal? Desirable? A Brief Overview of Height-Weight Tables in the United States." *Journal of the American Diabetic Association* 84, no. 4 (April 1984): 417–23.

Shanker, Wendy. *The Fat Girl's Guide to Life*. New York: Bloomsbury, 2004.

Smith, Dorothy. *The Everyday World as Problematic: A Feminist Sociology*. New York: Open University Press, 1987.

– "Femininity as Discourse." In *Becoming Feminine: The Politics of Popular Culture*, edited by Leslie Roman and Linda Christian-Smith, 37–59. London: The Falmer Press, 1988.

Smith, Miriam Catherine. *Lesbian and Gay Rights in Canada: Social Movements and Equality-Seeking, 1971–1995*. Toronto, ON: University of Toronto Press, 1999.

Solovay, Sandra, and Esther Rothblum, eds. *The Fat Studies Reader*. New York: New York University Press, 2009.

Squire, Susan. "Is the Binge-Purge Cycle Catching? A New Outbreak of Eating Disorders." *Ms*, October 1983, 41–5.

Stacey, Judith. "Can There Be a Feminist Ethnography?" In *Women's Words: The Feminist Practice of Oral History*, edited by Sherna Berger Gluck and Daphne Patai, 111–19. New York: Routledge, 1991.

Stearns, Peter N. *Fat History: Bodies and Beauty in the Modern West*. New York: New York University Press, 1997.

Steele, Valerie. "Anti-Fashion: The 1970s." *Fashion Theory* 1, no. 3 (1997): 279–96. https://doi.org/10.2752/136270497779640134.

–, ed. *Encyclopedia of Clothing and Fashion*. New York: Thomson Gale, 2005.

Steinem, Gloria. *Revolution from Within: A Book of Self-Esteem*. Toronto: Little, Brown, 1992.

Stephen, Jennifer Anne. *Pick One Intelligent Girl: Employability, Domesticity, and the Gendering of Canada's Welfare State, 1939–1947*. Toronto: University of Toronto Press, 2007.

Stinson, Kandi. *Women and Dieting Culture: Inside a Commercial Weight Loss Group*. New Brunswick, NJ: Rutgers University Press, 2001.

Stone, Donald. "The Human Potential Movement." *Society*, May/June 1978, 66–8.

Stunkard, Albert, and Mavis McLaren-Hume. "The Results of Treatment for Obesity: A Review of the Literature and Report of a Series." *Archives of Internal Medicine* 103, no. 1 (1959): 79–85. https://doi.org/10.1001/archinte.1959.00270010085011.

Sui, Xuemei, Micheal J. LaMonte, James N. Laditka, James W. Hardin, Nancy Chase, Steven P. Hooker, and Steven N. Blair. "Cardiorespoiratory Fitness and Adiposity as Mortality Predictors in Older Adults." *Journal of the American Medical Association* 298, no. 21 (2007): 2507–16. https://doi.org/10.1001/jama.298.21.2507

Swanson, Beth. "A History of the Rise of Aerobic Dance in the United States through 1980." Master's thesis, San Jose State University, 1996.

Sweet, Lois. "Group Fights Our Obsession with Thinness." *Toronto Star*, 24 February 1988, D1.

Tait, Kathy. "For the Big at Heart." *Province* [BC], 16 December 1986, 31.

Theberge, Nancy. "A Content Analysis of Print Media Coverage of Gender, Women and Physical Activity." *Journal of Applied Sport Psychology* 3 (1991): 36–48. https://doi.org/10.1080/10413209108406433.

– "Sport and Women's Empowerment." *Women's Studies International Forum* 10, no. 4 (1987): 387–93. https://doi.org/10.1016/0277-5395(87)90056-2.

Tison, Marie. "Reitmans Closes Two Divisions." *Calgary Herald*, 18 June 1999, E12.

Trimble, Linda. "Coming Soon to a Station near You?: The CRTC Policy on Sex-Role Stereotyping." *Canadian Public Policy* 16, no. 3 (September 1990): 326–38. https://doi.org/10.2307/3551086.

Turcotte, Louise. "Itinéraire d'un courant politique: Le lesbianism radical au Québec." In *Sortir de l'ombre: Histoires des communautés lesbienne et gaie de Montréal*, edited by Irène Demczuk and Frank W. Remiggi, 362–98. Montreal, QC: VLB Éditeur, 1998.

– "Queer Theory: Transgression or Regression?" In *Canadian Woman Studies: An Introductory Reader*, edited by Nuzhat Amin, 53–9. Toronto: Inanna, 1999.

Tyler, Tracey. "Psychologist Fired in Metro Scandal Now Forced to Leave Job in Michigan." *Toronto Star*, 9 February 1989, A29.

Vacek, Lauren. "Perspective: Sensitivity Training for Nurses Caring for Morbidly Obese Patients." *Bariatric Nursing and Surgical Patient Care* 2, no. 4 (2008): 251–3. https://doi.org/10.1089/bar.2007.9953.

Valverde, Mariana. *The Age of Light, Soap and Water: Moral Reform in English Canada, 1885–1925*. Toronto: McLelland and Stewart, 1991.

Vanhala, Lisa. "Disability Rights Activists in the Supreme Court of Canada: Legal Mobilization Theory and Accommodating Social Movements." *Canadian Journal of Political Science* 42, no. 4 (2009): 981–1002. https://doi.org/10.1017/S0008423909990709.

Vickers, Jill. "The Intellectual Origins of the Women's Movement in Canada." In *Challenging Times: The Women's Movement in Canada and the United States*, edited by Constance Backhouse and David H. Flaherty, 39–60. Montreal: McGill-Queen's University Press, 1992.

Walden, Keith. "The Road to Fat City: An Interpretation of the Development of Weight Consciousness in Western Society." *Historical Reflections/reflexions historiques* 12, no. 3 (1985): 331–73.

Walker, Barrington, ed. *The History of Immigration and Racism in Canada.* Toronto: Canadian Scholars' Press 2008.

Wann, Marilyn. *Fat!So?: Because You Don't Have to Apologize for Your Size.* Berkeley, California: Ten Speed Press, 1998.

Warsh, Cheryl Krasnick. *Prescribed Norms: Women and Health in Canada and the United States since 1800.* Toronto: University of Toronto Press, 2010.

Welters, Linda. "The Natural Look: American Style in the 1970s." *Fashion Theory* 12, no. 4 (2008): 489–510. https://doi.org/10.2752/175174108X346959.

Wilson, Elizabeth. "Fashion and the Postmodern Body." In *Chic Thrills: A Fashion Reader,* edited by Elizabeth Wilson and Juliet Ash, 3–15. Berkeley: University of California Press 1993.

Wine, Jeri Dawn, and Janice Ristock, eds. *Women and Social Change: Feminist Activism in Canada.* Toronto: James Lorimer, 1991.

Wolf, Naomi. *The Beauty Myth.* Toronto: Random House, 1990.

Wooley, Susan C., and Orland W. Wooley. "Obesity and Women I: A Closer Look at the Facts." *Women's Studies International Quarterly* 2, no. 1 (1979): 69–79. https://doi.org/10.1016/S0148-0685(79)93074-4.

Won, Shirley. "Low Prices Bring High Profits at Zellers; The Jewel in the Hudson's Bay Crown." *Gazette,* 4 February 1991, B8.

Wright, Jane. "Female Nurses' Perceptions of Acceptable Female Body Size: An Exploratory Study." *Journal of Clinical Nursing* 7, no. 4 (1998): 307–15. https://doi.org/10.1046/j.1365-2702.1998.00150.x.

Zelko, Frank. "Making Greenpeace: The Development of Direct Action Environmentalism in British Columbia." *BC Studies,* no. 142–3 (2004): 197–239.

Index

Page numbers in italics refer to figures and tables.

www.ingramcontent.com/pod-product-compliance
Lightning Source LLC
Chambersburg PA
CBHW030239030426
42336CB00009B/161